Tools and Tips for Using ELT Materials

A GUIDE FOR TEACHERS

Ruth Epstein *and* Mary Ormiston

Ann Arbor
University of Michigan Press

Published in the United States of America
The University of Michigan Press
Manufactured in the United States of America

∞ Printed on acid-free paper

2010   2009   2008   2007   4   3   2   1

ISBN-10: 0-472-03203-8
ISBN-13: 978-0-472-03203-7

Dedication and Acknowledgments

This book is dedicated to all those who made its publication possible.

We would like to thank the following people and organizations who helped make the production of this book possible: our editor, Kelly Sippell of University of Michigan Press; the many authors and experts who offered ideas related to materials for teaching English in their writings or personal communications; the following past and present University of Saskatchewan staff: Myra Zubot, the instructional designer for the first version of the course notes on which this book is based; Grace Milashenko, who allowed us to develop our course notes into a book manuscript; Perry Millar, for her editing skills and for encouraging us to submit the book for publication; the instructors who taught the course on which this book is based. The student teachers in the University of Saskatchewan's Certificate in Teaching English as a Second Language provided invaluable feedback on the course and, by extension, on this book. Appreciation is also extended to the many English language learners in our classes who, by readily trying out our materials over many years, helped us to develop our skills and knowledge related to English language teaching materials. Finally, warm thanks to our families for their patience and support throughout the writing and editing process.

Grateful acknowledgment is made to the following publisher for permission to reprint previously published material.

Cambridge University Press for excerpt from *Functions of American English* by L. Jones and C. von Baeyer. © Cambridge University Press 1983. Reprinted with the permission of Cambridge University Press.

Every effort has been made to contact the copyright holders for permission to reprint borrowed material. We regret any oversights that may have occurred and will rectify them in future printings of the book.

CONTENTS

ABOUT THIS BOOK

The origins of this book extend to more than a decade ago when Mary Ormiston was asked to develop a course on English language teaching materials for a new certificate program in teaching English as a Second Language at the University of Saskatchewan. Unfortunately, no one textbook could be found that provided enough information on materials selection and development to form the backbone of the course. So, after many months of research and writing, substantial course notes were completed. Several years later, as time came to revise the course, Mary searched again for a materials textbook that included both theory and practice. Although more and better books addressing materials development had been published, still nothing was comprehensive enough for an undergraduate course on materials selection and development. Undaunted, and with increased experience in teaching and materials development, including publishing a resource book of materials for the Language Instruction for Newcomers to Canada program (The ESL Tool Box), Mary further developed and updated the course material.

As part of a teacher training program, a course on ELT materials allows future teachers to refine their beliefs about language learning and teaching and provides them with tools and knowledge to make their teaching more interesting and effective. Learning about different types of materials—written, visual, auditory, computer-based—also helps teachers in training to learn to accommodate their students' individual learning styles and preferences. A solid background in materials selection, development, and use, along with TESL theory and methodology, facilitates the transition from theory to effective classroom practice for students in certificate and master's programs.

Students and instructors always rated the course highly. Many who had completed the course remembered how practical the content was and how immediately useful it was to them in their subsequent teaching positions. They also discovered that choosing, adapting, and developing effective materials was creative, enjoyable, and rewarding. Ruth Epstein, then Academic Coordinator of the Certificate Program in Teaching English as a Second Language (CERTESL) at the University of Saskatchewan and instructional designer for the second version of the course, felt that the material in the course would be of benefit to other teacher preparation programs and to English language teachers in general. Her research confirmed that a book on language teaching materials would indeed be welcomed. And so we began to update and edit the material into book form.

The contents of *Tools and Tips for Using ELT Materials: A Guide for Teachers* will help you, the teacher, come closer to the ideal of addressing your students' needs within a given teaching context regardless of whether or not you have an assigned textbook, by providing you with the theory and practice of materials selection, development, and adaptation for language teaching. With the vast number of published materials and resources that have increasingly become available, it is more and more challenging for language teachers and program administrators to decide which are the most effective, appropriate, and flexible for their students and for their programs. When the published materials do not work adequately for you, you will undoubtedly find yourself supplementing them with other published resources, adapting existing materials, and even developing new ones to meet your specific needs. Added to this mix is the variety of technology available (from print to digital technology) for presenting published and teacher-made materials. This book provides you with background to make sound, informed decisions about how to choose or adapt published materials or develop your own, and how to make the best use of materials that will enhance teaching and learning.

One chapter is available on the University of Michigan Press's website at *www.press.umich.edu/esl/tm/toolstips/*, Drills, Dialogues, and Role Plays.

CHAPTER 1

Basic Considerations in Materials Design and Evaluation

A MATERIALS SELECTION DILEMMA

Imagine this scenario: You have just started your first teaching job in an EFL school in a non–English speaking country. The school is reputable but short on teaching materials for your intermediate adolescent students. You have a rather old-fashioned grammatically based, locally written textbook. Your materials budget is small. Your dilemma is deciding which materials to select that will appropriately supplement the textbook.

- Should you buy some audiovisual material? Before leaving North America should you record a few episodes from a TV series, from documentaries, or the news? Should you make an audio recording from a radio newscast, from human interest programs such as *Oprah*, or tape yourself talking to friends?
- What reading enrichment materials should you choose? Should you buy tabloid newspapers such as *The National Enquirer, Young Teen* magazines, *National Geographic*, or perhaps a set of adapted readers for ESL?
- Which books should you select? Should you take a book of games and role plays or a book focusing on speaking or listening or writing? How will you know which books are best, and once you have decided, how can you order them?
- Judging from the size of the materials budget, you will have to produce some of your own materials. While you have confidence in your knowledge of teaching English, how will you be able to transfer that knowledge to the production of suitable materials?

In general, materials facilitate and support the teaching-learning process as well as student needs and program goals. However, only through careful selection and adaptation can you ensure that the materials you use match your particular students and program as well as your teaching style. We begin this book by providing you with some general information and guidelines for selecting, evaluating, and developing materials for English language teaching. The chapters that follow will provide you with detailed information for specific types of materials.

This chapter contains:

- definition of materials, resources, technology, and media
- discussion about authentic materials and their importance
- discussion about the role and advantages of published materials, teacher-produced materials, and student-produced materials
- discussion of teaching thematically
- guidance on applying the principles of the communicative approach to materials selection, development, and adaptation
- use of theme units and appropriate materials to accompany them
- guidance on locating published materials and reviews of published materials for English language teaching

Some Challenging Questions

Before you begin, answer these questions:

- What is the main purpose of teaching materials? How can you ensure that your objectives match your materials and that your materials do not determine what you teach?
- What are the differences between materials, resources, and technology?
- Is it preferable to use published materials or teacher-produced and student-produced materials?
- Is it preferable to use published authentic materials for language teaching?
- Is it possible and desirable to integrate teaching the four skills? If so, under what circumstances? What materials and approaches will help achieve skills integration?
- How can you apply the principles of the communicative approach to materials selection, development, and adaptation? Is it always appropriate to use materials that address a communicative approach?
- Where can you find published materials and reviews of published materials for English language teaching?

Materials, Resources, Technology, and Medium: Some Definitions

Let's start by defining the confusing and overlapping terminology related to materials. First, **a teaching material** is a tangible item that you can use to facilitate teaching and learning. Examples of materials include textbooks; handouts and worksheets; written text such as stories, songs, and poems; audiovisual materials on DVD, CD, or tape; and computer software. Materials differ from **resources,** which are what you use to help you develop or adapt materials. Examples of resources are reference books on theory and books that provide you with ideas but are not suitable for presentation to students.

The terms *technology* and *medium* are also potentially confusing and play a role in materials selection, development, and adaptation. A **medium,** according to Tony Bates (1995, 29–31), is a way to represent knowledge. Bates lists the five most important media: face-to-face teaching, print and graphics, audio, television, and computing. A **technology,** on the other hand, is a way to *transmit* a medium. For example, audio or sound can be transmitted using the media of radio, CDs, audiocassettes, or computers. According to this definition, the term *technology* does not necessarily connote computers. Bates notes that the difference between *medium* and *technology* is becoming less distinct as the type of medium becomes more closely associated with how it is delivered.

Authentic Materials

One challenge you will encounter as you select, adapt, and develop materials is how much to use authentic materials (for example, real newscasts or newspaper articles) versus materials simplified for language teaching. The issue is particularly relevant to reading and listening texts. In spite of the ongoing debate among language teaching professionals, there is still no agreement about best practice in this regard.

Julian Edge (1993) acknowledges the controversy but points out these compelling reasons for using authentic materials:

- Authentic materials represent the actual goal of language learning, including the difficulties that learning materials avoid. All learners must have practice in meeting these real challenges. Even at early stages, students should learn how to respond to language that they do not fully understand.
- Authentic materials bring the means of learning and the purpose of learning close together, and this establishes a direct link with the world outside the classroom (47).

When we discuss language teaching textbooks in Chapter 2, you will find that recent textbooks usually incorporate authentic readings and authentic listening texts. You need to decide what is best for your students, your program, and your teaching context. At higher levels and with adults, authentic materials are usually the most appropriate. For example, if you are teaching English for Academic Purposes (EAP), it is worthwhile providing students at higher levels with real audiovisual recordings of lectures and textbook readings in their academic discipline. Similarly, if you are teaching English in the Workplace (EWP), it is probably most appropriate to teach the actual instructions for using a piece of equipment rather than teaching adaptations. Although you may use the adapted instructions at lower-proficiency levels, eventually, for safety purposes, the actual instructions should be taught. If you are teaching children or young adolescents, it may be desirable to adapt material, regardless of language proficiency. For example, in teaching young adults a theme unit on world political systems, you would likely need to simplify the vocabulary to a degree that they could understand it at a similar level to their English-speaking peers.

Selecting Published Materials

Often you will be assigned published teaching materials such as textbooks, audio-tapes, computer software, and so on. You may decide the best way to meet your students' needs is to personalize and extend textbook exercises. However, some teaching situations, like those described here, may be better suited to not using a specific textbook:

- Elementary school EFL classes that use children's games, songs, and stories may form the basis of materials and activities, particularly in the early years.
- Language Experience Approach (LEA) and Whole Language (Gunderson 1991; Curtain and Dahlberg 2004), Community Language Learning (Larsen-Freeman 2000) and process writing all provide compelling reasons for using student-generated materials to increase personalization of materials, motivation, and student investment.
- In content-based classes in an English language K–12 system, content-area textbooks for mainstream students, not ESL textbooks, are usually used, along with teacher-developed or teacher-adapted material that provide support for ESL students.
- In advanced classes, the no-textbook option may be preferable. For example, the University of Saskatchewan once had a group of Chinese agronomists enrolled whose goal was to learn about local agriculture while improving their English. Activities such as visits to various farm operations and agri-business became the basis of language instruction, rather than a textbook.

The main disadvantage of published materials is their inability to address your local context and the individual goals and specific needs of your students and your program. Should you decide that these aspects are missing from the assigned published materials, you will become involved in materials adaptation and development. The information we provide in this book will help you personalize, localize, and supplement published materials.

On another note, publishers' catalogues, Books Received and Book Reviews sections of language teaching journals, your colleagues' book collections, and the resources shelves of teaching institutions will give you information on published materials. Keep in mind, however, that the reviews in professional journals and newsletters give you only one person's opinion of a book or material. Publishers' catalogues are available free-of-charge and can be found online. Appendix A contains a list of major ESL publishers. You can order desk copies and examination copies of books from publishers through your institution; check publishers' catalogues for their desk copy and examination copy policies. Of course, if you don't use published materials, you, or your students with your assistance, may need to make them.

Teacher-Made Materials

Your primary purpose in creating or adapting materials will be to compensate for deficiencies in published materials. These deficiencies are almost always related to the fact that textbook authors cannot anticipate your particular teaching context, your program goals, and your students' needs. Therefore, you will need to adapt existing published materials or develop new ones to fit your context and your individual students. For example, you can create a local map for a lesson on giving and following directions or use local stores for lessons on shopping by creating shopping lists or worksheets based on what you would find at a grocery store, followed by a field trip with the students to that store.

Student-Generated Materials

When adapting or developing your own materials, the more you can take advantage of students' experiences, intelligences, and creativities, the better! An effective way to do this is to have them produce their own materials. You will find many examples of student-generated material in this book. Here are a few examples to help you think about the benefits of student materials creation: ask students to make their own games, based on a textbook model, relating to their favorite sports, or ask students to make a school map for a lesson in giving and following directions, or ask students to design a questionnaire related to a textbook theme.

If you want to use the students themselves as materials as Edge (1993) suggests, note that "family relationships" is a common topic in many published textbooks, especially at lower levels. Often, there is a dialogue with one person asking another about his or her family and where family members reside. There may even be the opportunity to fill in a family tree, based on a text about a family. It is quite easy to personalize and localize this by having students bring family photos and introduce them, following the model in a textbook dialogue. You can also have students draw their own family trees and write a paragraph about them, similar to the one provided in a textbook. Of course, an effective, flexible textbook will allow for this bridge to the world of your students, but this is not always the case for all topics.

Because it is important to keep within program goals when creating or adapting materials, our discussion now moves to matching your materials to your syllabus.

Selecting Materials for Your Syllabus

A **syllabus** is a teaching plan identifying what topics to cover in a course of study. Syllabuses are usually designed according to language structures, functions, topics, or a combination of these. Chapter 2 will review syllabus types in more detail. Your choice of textbook and supplementary materials and activities should clearly further the teaching objectives that are ideally laid out in the syllabus.

To illustrate the link between syllabus content and material, let's look at the bingo game as a material and activity that can be adapted for many different topics, functions, grammar points and program types. In the example, the application is to the topic food and meals; the structure is the past tense.

Procedure for Bingo

Elicit nine or more vocabulary items from students on the chosen theme of food and meals. List the items on the board. Ask students to fill in nine of those vocabulary items anywhere they like on the bingo card, as illustrated.

	Breakfast	Lunch	Supper
Friday			
Saturday			sushi
Sunday	eggs		

Sample Script:

Teacher: Tamara, tell me about Sunday breakfast.

Tamara: I had eggs for breakfast on Sunday.

All students, including Tamara, who have eggs written in the Sunday breakfast square put an X through the square. The teacher asks different students to tell about information in specific squares, for example,

Teacher: Alexander, tell us about your Friday supper.

The game continues until one student has three squares in a straight or diagonal line with an X through them. The student calls out, "Bingo!" and the teacher checks the student's card.

Variations:

After a student has given information about a square, he or she then takes over the teacher role and asks another student for information. This example could work well in an immigrant settlement program or in a general communicative course in an EFL setting.

Here's another variation for the same theme, this time for an EAP class.

	I attended	I skipped	I wrote
Thursday	Sociology 101	Economics 110	a 5-page essay
Friday	Calculus 102		A Calculus exam

You could adapt this bingo game to future tense, or you could fill in other vocabulary, such as what you did on the weekend.

This book will provide you with many, many more ideas for choosing, developing, and adapting materials that match your syllabus and teaching context.

SELECTING MATERIALS FOR COMMUNICATIVE LANGUAGE TEACHING

In addition to matching materials to syllabus, it is important for teachers to consider how materials will match their pedagogical approach. Communicative Language Teaching (CLT) remains the most comprehensive and most used materials selection approach in North America; CLT views formal linguistic elements as necessary, but not sufficient, in learning to communicate. However, many aspects of CLT have incorporated the effective teaching aspects of other approaches, such as Audiolingualism and Community Language Learning.

Although CLT encompasses a wide range of material and activity types, don't rule out materials stemming from other teaching approaches. Avoid the "tyranny of the bandwagon" (Larsen-Freeman 1993); instead, always consider what is best for your students and your particular teaching situation. For example, if you are teaching in an EFL context or if English is not your first language, you may find yourself struggling with this issue as you choose and develop materials for your class:

> . . . it has been argued that a more grammatically-oriented syllabus is to be preferred in a context where English is a foreign language and where learners are unlikely to be [frequently] exposed to it. Again, some teachers whose mother tongue is not English claim to have little confidence when working with communicative materials . . . Does it always matter if the 'real world' is not being practised in the classroom? (McDonough and Shaw 1993, 35)

What is your opinion on this? This book describes a number of ways to select, adapt, and create materials communicatively.

Two additional general challenges exist in materials selection.

- selecting material for mainstreamed ESL students
- integrating the four skills—speaking, listening, reading, and writing—as well as helping students develop vocabulary and grammatical competency and learn about culture.

Teaching thematically is one way to address these challenges.

Selecting Materials to Support Topics or Themes

Topics or themes are common ways to organize teaching and learning. It is a strategy that articulates well within CLT and will affect the selection, development, and adaptation of language teaching materials. Teaching thematically has proven successful for ESL students in the regular school system. Marge Gianelli (1991) found that using thematic units allows teachers to balance language development and academic content simultaneously. It also allows skills integration along with the learning benefits gained in listening, speaking, reading, writing, vocabulary, and grammar development from the repetition of language and concepts.

If you are not assigned topics to teach by the school, the topics that you choose will depend on your students' ages, maturity levels, interests, needs, and language levels. Themes may vary from pollution, AIDS, interpersonal relationships, and travel, to food, weather, and animals. For example, a popular theme for young children in both EFL and ESL contexts is often animals; for adolescents, sports, music, and dating are appealing. Adults in EAP settings will be interested in topics such as campus life, study skills, and discipline-specific topics, while Workplace English and Business English students will be interested in themes and topics such as workplace culture, communication in the workplace, and technology at work. Immigrants will be interested in themes related to settling in a new country and caring for themselves and their families. Depending on their reasons for learning English, students in EFL settings may be motivated by topics such as North American culture and travel.

In many programs, themes or topics and objectives will already be established. For example, the second level Language Instruction for Newcomers to Canada, LINC 2 (or high-beginner and low-intermediate level), uses a commercial services theme that focuses on banking. You may find it helpful to visit an ESL or EFL program in your area and review syllabus documents for theme ideas and objectives that are appropriate and interesting for your teaching context. Such programs may have established theme units that are used repeatedly. You can also pursue the theme units available for language arts teaching.

You will often need to supplement or create materials to support your teaching of a theme or topic to ensure that it meets your students' specific goals and needs and your teaching context. For example, you may find the LINC 2 theme on banking is also appropriate for EFL professionals planning to work in a North American context. However, you may not have access to the realia used in the theme unit and will have to create your own. Or, you may find that aspects of an elementary school language arts theme unit on the environment are appropriate for your college-bound students. However, the activities that accompany the articles need to address ESL needs and be rephrased for a more mature student group.

In "Communicative Second Language Learning: A Thematic Integrated Approach," Jan Thompson (1982) suggests teachers start by choosing a topic of interest to students and then list functions, structures, and vocabulary that can be integrated into the topic. From there, teachers can develop activities and materials to provide meaningful practice of the functions and structures. The activities and materials should also attend to various skill areas (listening, speaking, reading, and writing) and to particular social contexts (relating to peers, the teacher, or a store clerk). Chapter 4 addresses key visuals, or visuals that teachers select, based on their effectiveness in teaching academic content. Part of the discussion on key visuals includes more detail about how to create theme units through thematic webbing and semantic mapping.

Relating materials to a theme or topic will come up in many chapters in this book, but what about some criteria for developing and evaluating materials for language teaching?

Criteria for Developing and Evaluating Materials

The appropriateness of CLT to students, program goals, and syllabus plays an important role in evaluating the suitability of the materials you select or adapt and developing supplementary materials appropriate for your class. Chapter 2 will consider the evaluation of textbook and non-textbook materials. Here are general evaluation criteria for materials:

- Language teaching materials should address language beyond the sentence level to provide context.
- In language teaching materials, language skills (listening, speaking, reading, writing, pronunciation, and grammar development) should be integrated wherever possible.
- Language teaching materials should prepare students for authentic encounters in English.
- Language teaching materials should offer a challenge to learners at different levels of English language proficiency.
- Language teaching materials should stimulate and develop student motivation through intrinsic, thematic, or topical interest and through associated techniques and activities.
- Language teaching materials should include accurate information that is appropriately sequenced and activities that address the stated objectives.
- Language teaching materials should encourage learners to express their own ideas; materials should tap into student experience, prior knowledge, intelligence, and creativity.
- Language teaching materials should be user friendly and include clear instructions for use by students and teacher.
- Language teaching materials for developing oral skills should focus on communication, fluency, and accuracy.
- Language teaching materials should be oriented to help students succeed since students at all proficiency levels must experience success to gain confidence.
- Language teaching materials should be flexible, allowing for adaptation to individual teaching contexts and students in those contexts.
- Language teaching materials should be inclusive and culturally sensitive; they should avoid stereotyping and cultural biases.
- Language teaching materials should be attractive in terms of layout and design.
- Students should find the materials beneficial. You can find this out by asking for feedback. Ask students how motivational and suitable they thought the materials were to their language learning. A sample feedback form is provided here.

Feedback Form

What I liked about this activity/material most is _____

_____

What I did not like about this activity/material is _____

_____

What you should continue doing is _____

_____

What you should not do anymore is _____

_____

In the following chapters, we highlight considerations in evaluating specific types of materials, such as pictures, textbooks, and realia. As you work through the chapters and experiment with materials in your classrooms, you will develop a sense of what criteria are most important to you in assessing materials. Keep in mind that materials review is an ongoing process. Teachers change, and so do student needs. Many of us lose enthusiasm if we don't continue to search for, adapt, and develop new materials.

CHAPTER 2

Textbooks

A TEACHER'S TALE

Once upon a time there was an enthusiastic and creative young ESL teacher. Teaching without the support of textbook or curriculum, she toiled from sun-up to sundown to prepare interesting classes for her group of 17 eager, appreciative students. From 7:30 to 8:30 AM, you could find her at the photocopy machine. From 8:30 to 2:30, she was in the classroom, sometimes dynamic, but sometimes exhausted from all the hours and energy of prep work. When she wasn't eating or exercising or grocery shopping, she was dreaming up innovative teaching ideas, flipping through resource book after resource book, cutting, pasting, drawing, writing, and organizing in preparation for her classes.

She did a great job, but she eventually burned out. Much of her stress was from trying to decide which activities to choose and how to fill five hours of class time five days weekly.

Then something happened that changed her life. She started working for an institution that provided her with a class set of textbooks. At first she thought it would stifle her creativity, but it didn't. On the contrary, she found it stimulating, and she discovered lots of new ideas for language presentation and practice. She also felt greater assurance that she was following a well–thought out progression in her teaching based on sound theory. She was more confident that what she was teaching was being adequately reviewed and recycled. "It's like a steady hand that helps me focus my teaching," she marveled.

She had been worried that her students might find regular use of the same book boring. Yet, much to her surprise, they too, enjoyed the textbook. They might have found it dull, but she supplemented it with other learning activities and adapted textbook activities to their lives and particular needs.

And do you know what else? She was more relaxed in her teaching and in her life in general. She started socializing with friends more and even found time to study a second language. All because she discovered textbooks.

This story is not too unlike the experiences many of us have had teaching with no prescribed textbooks. In such cases, we all know what happens! In other programs, teachers have the opportunity to teach using carefully selected textbooks, or teachers have had the responsibility to choose or suggest their own textbooks.

A textbook is often the most influential material you will use in the teaching-learning process. The information in this chapter will help you make well-informed decisions about choosing course textbooks. It will also make you aware of how to use and adapt your textbook to best serve student needs.

This chapter includes:

- discussion of the advantages and disadvantages of using textbooks
- discussion of the uses of textbooks in various teaching situations
- criteria for textbook assessment and selection
- guidance on how to identify the strengths and weaknesses of a textbook
- assessing teachers' guides and Web-based textbook supplements
- assessing vocabulary in textbooks
- suggestions for adapting textbook material
- implications of copyright in using and adapting textbooks

Some Challenging Questions

Before you begin, answer these questions:

- Did you use a textbook as a language learner? Did you enjoy using the textbook? What did you like or not like about using a textbook?
- Have you ever used course textbooks in your teaching? What were their strengths and limitations? How did they help or hinder your teaching? Did you adapt or supplement the textbook materials in any way?
- What do you look for when searching for a textbook for your students?

Textbooks as Language Teaching Materials

The Advantages and Disadvantages of Textbooks in Language Teaching

There is some controversy over the use of textbooks in language teaching; some are in favor of using them and others opposed to using them (Edge 1993). According to Edge, the key is to use textbooks appropriately to teach students rather than follow the textbooks uncritically.

Of course, some textbooks are better than others. The good ones should give efficient and effective language coverage, saving teachers' time, saving programs' money, and providing high-quality references that students want to use and refer to for linguistic support. The best textbooks tend to survive and live on in new editions and you will hear about them from colleagues and other teachers.

We have combined our own beliefs with those of Allwright (1990), Cunningsworth (1995), and O'Neill (1990) to outline the advantages and disadvantages of textbooks. The *advantages* of good textbooks are that they:

- provide a guide or framework as well as a rationale for language instruction by including a progression and manageable amounts of vocabulary and grammar instruction. This saves you time in doing this yourself and allows for efficient curriculum coverage.
- provide content that supports presentation, practice, and evaluation of linguistic elements, including sociocultural elements
- are based on sound pedagogy and language teaching and learning research
- act as resources that include sufficient flexibility to allow adaptation (e.g., in terms of presentation of activities) and supplementation
- provide content of general interest to learners
- include professionally produced layout, images, and presentation of linguistic elements (e.g., tables that clearly present grammatical information)
- include supplementary materials such as teacher manuals, student workbooks, answer keys, companion audio recordings (CDs or audiotapes), or companion websites

However, the *disadvantages* to using even good textbooks are that:

- Textbooks may control and limit teaching as well as learning.
- Teachers may rely too much on the textbook for all aspects of teaching, including their approach, procedures, syllabus, sequencing, content, evaluation, etc. That is, teachers may be less creative in their teaching, including materials development, and be less motivated to keep up with language teaching research and practice.
- Textbook coverage may become the center of teaching rather than the learners and their learning goals and needs, which is preferable.
- Textbooks do not address the needs of a particular group or individual student because textbook writers cannot write for every context and type of student.
- Textbooks may lack variety in teaching procedures required to maintain student interest and address different learning styles.
- Textbooks may impede spontaneity and taking advantage of teachable moments.

While some teachers, especially inexperienced ones, may adhere closely to the textbook and follow it lesson by lesson, most teachers in time will want to supplement a text to ensure they are meeting their students' needs and to ensure that they are developing professionally. If you have the choice, we suggest that you seek a balance in your use of textbooks and supplementary materials and always have a clear purpose for using all materials. The remainder of this chapter will provide you with the tools for textbook selection and adaptation.

The Uses of Textbooks in Language Teaching

Alan Cunningsworth (1995) notes that the role of textbooks is for use as resources that are intended to achieve the "aims and objectives that have already been set in terms of learner needs" (7). He stresses that because textbooks influence what is taught and how it is taught, they should be selected carefully and complement clearly articulated course objectives. He further notes that the teacher and the textbook can been seen as partners working together to address teacher aims and student goals and needs. As such, textbooks are resources to present written and spoken material; sources of communicative practice activities; and references for students on various aspects of language, especially grammar, vocabulary, and pronunciation.

Occasionally a textbook may seem to be a perfect fit for your context and your students such that you work through a textbook from beginning to end. These justifications seem reasonable. Although a good textbook can play a central and important role in the language class, having a dull text does not necessarily a dull class make. You should not see yourself as a technician who simply follows the textbook (Nunan and Lamb 1996). Your job is to capitalize on the strengths of the textbook in any of the ways previously listed. For example, if the book's only strengths are clear grammatical explanations and written exercises, perhaps you will use it only as a grammar reference or to assign homework. As a self-directed teacher, you can then supplement the text in other ways to best meet your students' needs.

Criteria for Textbook Selection

There are thousands of ESL/EFL textbooks now on the market; the majority are developed for adult learners, although choices for teaching children are expanding. Choosing "the best" textbook, if you are lucky enough to have a choice, can be overwhelming. Quality textbooks exist, but in an effort to compete and sell, some publishers may promote their book for a wide audience, even if it has been designed for a specialized audience. It is easy to overlook smaller publishers with less wide-ranging marketing strategies, even if their products are more relevant to your teaching context.

There is no definitive yardstick for measuring the value of a multiskills textbook. You will need to determine which criteria are essential for your particular teaching situation and which are merely desirable. If you are not permitted to choose your own textbook, the criteria discussed in this chapter will still be useful to you in evaluating the strengths and weaknesses of the text you are assigned and in supplementing it as needed.

Many of the criteria discussed in this chapter are relevant to English for Specific Purposes texts (for example, English for science and technology, business English, workplace English) and single-skill texts that focus on grammar, reading, speaking, listening, pronunciation, or writing. However, not all criteria will be relevant, so these types of specialized texts will be discussed later in this chapter. Also, there are additional considerations for textbooks for children, such as suitability of content related to student maturity, grade level, affordability, and durability (Curtain and Dalhberg 2004, 327–29).

Let's now look at the common textbook selection criteria: syllabus, methodology, presentation and practice of new language, personalization, grammar coverage, pronunciation, vocabulary coverage, coverage of the four skills, variety, grading, meaningful context, series, sexism and stereotyping, culture bias, self-directed learning, literacy level, and inclusion of supplementary materials.

Assessing the Syllabus in a Textbook

A *syllabus* (sometimes called a curriculum) is a teaching plan for a course of study, identifying topics to be covered. Most language teachers adhere to a syllabus. It may have been one that your school provided, or it may have been in the form of a textbook that you used. If you used a textbook, the contents of the book may have been your only syllabus or teaching guide.

Knowing about different kinds of EFL syllabi and the basis of each will make your teaching more communicative even within the limitations of an imposed syllabus. It will also help you understand the bases of the many textbooks and prepare you to adapt or supplement them.

As outlined in Table 2.1 on page 16, often there is a combination of syllabi, although usually one syllabus basis predominates. For example, a *grammatical syllabus* often includes vocabulary and may include themes. A *functional syllabus* often includes themes, grammar, and vocabulary. A *task-based syllabus* may also include themes and have sections on each of the skill areas (listening, speaking, reading, and writing) as well as grammar and vocabulary.

Table 2.1 Types of Syllabuses

Name of Syllabus	Basis of Syllabus	Sequencing /Organization of Topics	Examples of Topics in Sequence
Structural Syllabus	based on grammar and phonological structures	organized around grammar points; sequenced from easy to difficult structures, or from frequent to less frequently used structures	<u>Unit 1: Beginner Verb Tenses</u> • simple tenses • progressive tenses <u>Unit 2: Sentence Structures</u> • simple sentence • compound sentences
Situational Syllabus	based on the idea that language is found in situations or contexts (see examples)	sequenced according to student likelihood of encountering the situation (teaching of structures may be embedded within the situations)	• introductions • at the airport • in a taxi • in a restaurant • at a meeting • at a party (Note how these are all situations or contexts.)
Functional Syllabus	based on functions required to participate in society (see examples)	sequenced by sense of the usefulness of the functions, the most useful taught first (teaching of structures and/or situations may be embedded within the functions)	• greeting people • introducing a friend • buying a ticket • making an appointment • ordering at a restaurant • apologizing • persuading (Note how these differ from topics in the situational syllabus.)
Topical Syllabus	similar to situational syllabuses; based on topics or themes chosen as important to a particular student group (see examples)	sequenced according to students' likelihood of encountering the situation (grammar teaching may be embedded within the topics)	<u>From an Academic English text</u> • vocabulary building • reading for comprehension • applying what you read • communicating in class • essay writing
Skills-Based Syllabus	based on skills that students need in order to use the language (see examples)	sequenced by sense of the usefulness of the skill to be learned (teaching of structures and/or situations may be embedded within the functions)	<u>From a vocabulary text</u> • words in context • word analysis • prefixes and suffixes • roots • idioms and slang
Task-Based Syllabus	based on tasks or activities	sequenced by sense of the usefulness of the task to the students (teaching of structures and/or situations may be embedded within the functions)	<u>From a writing tasks book</u> • informal letters • writing instructions • describing people • describing past events • comparing and contrasting

If you have a course textbook, a good way to determine the basis of any dominant and secondary (or embedded) syllabus is to:

- examine the contents
- read the introduction and To the Teacher pages for an explanation of the syllabus basis
- look at a couple of sample lessons, chapters, or units to see if they really include more than one syllabus type

Being aware of which syllabus type dominates allows you to be consistent in presenting lessons to students and also tells you where you need to adapt.

Assessing Methodology in Textbooks

It is important to be aware of what textbook authors and publishers say about the text and about the methodology on which it is based. For example, *communicative* is a popular catchword, but you need to look beyond the introduction to see if the book truly is communicative. Before doing so, it may be helpful for you to review what is meant by *communicative*. Communicative Language Teaching includes four basic communicative competencies suggested by Canale and Swain (1980) and a fifth, functional competency (Pawlikowska-Smith 2002). These competencies are:

- **Grammatical competence**—addresses how well a person has learned and can apply the features and rules of vocabulary, pronunciation, and sentence formation—that is, how well does a person know and use the language?
- **Sociolinguistic competence**—addresses how well a person speaks and is understood in various social, cultural, and political contexts. This involves understanding and practicing register, which depends on factors such as status of interlocutors, the purpose of the interaction, and expectations of the interaction—that is, how socially acceptable is the person's use of the language in different social settings?
- **Discourse competence**—addresses how well a person can combine grammatical forms above the sentence level to form a meaning that is whole in different genres—that is, how well does one properly combine all the elements in order to speak or write the language?
- **Strategic competence**—addresses how well a person uses both verbal and non-verbal communication to compensate for lack of knowledge in the other competencies—that is, can the person find ways to communicate when lacking some knowledge of the language?
- **Functional competence**—addresses uses of language such as transmission of information, social interaction, negotiation, and persuasion and other tasks required for life and work (Holmes et al. 2001, 3)—that is, how well is the person able to use a variety of different linguistic forms to accomplish a task or address a problem?

You will need to evaluate whether a textbook helps your students to develop these aspects of communicative competence; you should not rely on the publisher's or author's claims. One indicator of a communicative textbook is that the activities promote interaction in situations resembling real-life situations. Again, if a required textbook does not adequately address the communicative competencies, you may need to develop supplementary activities.

Assessing Presentation and Practice of New Language in Textbooks

Some textbooks have wonderful practice activities but skip over presenting new language to the students. Yet, presentation is crucial for beginning language students.

Consider this example from a book for beginners:

> Students listen to a description of a criminal suspect while looking at mug shots of six suspects. From the description they hear, they must pick out the suspect from the six pictures. Following this activity, students draw their own picture of a criminal and write a paragraph describing the person they have drawn. This is a good practice activity, but nowhere in the book do we find presentation of structures and vocabulary useful in creating or understanding physical descriptions of people. Therefore, we recommend that rather than use this book as the course textbook, it might be better as a resource for further practice activities. Alternatively, you could write your own presentation information or find this information in another source. It is important that you choose books with a balance of presentation and practice activities.

Assessing Personalization in Textbooks

Something you should look for in controlled and freer practice in textbooks is the opportunity for personal investment, or activities that encourage your students to solve problems and to say and write about what they think, know, and feel. Personalization of language practice typically interests students and motivates them to produce more. They are more likely to elaborate when speaking or writing about themselves or their ideas because they are the experts on the subject. Personalization also makes the practice more meaningful to most students and thus aids in retention.

The following is an example from *The Art of Teaching Speaking* (Folse 2006) of a Liar activity. The teacher begins by making four statements about himself or herself—three of which are false. One is true. Students have to guess the one that is true.

1. My middle name is Scott.
2. I was born in New Orleans.
3. My parents met on a blind date.
4. I have three sisters.

Activities such as this one that succeed in generating personal sharing and discussion are usually those that people already have some knowledge of, some interest in, and some opinion on. They also don't require a lot of teacher preparation. We should caution you, though, that in some instances such activities can be difficult (e.g., beginning students in an EFL context with small active vocabularies and accustomed to rote learning). Be sure to prepare students before tackling these types of activities.

Assessing Grammar Coverage in Multiskills Textbooks

"Grammar is a major component of any general language course, whether it is acknowledged as such or disguised as something else" (Cunningsworth 1995, 32). Once you know the grammatical needs of your class, you may want to add pertinent specific grammar items to your multiskills or grammar textbook checklist. For example, how does it present the conditional, particularly in terms of its different meanings and uses? How does it teach article usage?

Note that you will not look for the same amount of attention to grammatical explanation and analysis in textbooks for children as you will in textbooks for adolescents and adults. In most contexts, you will want to select textbooks that have meaning-based rather than form-based grammar activities. Remember that communicative language teaching generally emphasizes meaning and use when teaching language, although adults also benefit from explanation of grammatical structures. When evaluating the grammar treatment in a textbook, consider these points (Cunningsworth, 55–56):

- Are items presented in small enough units to facilitate learning?
- How balanced is the treatment of meaning, form, and use? It is more acceptable for advanced levels and adults to have more explanations of the forms.
- Are items related to or contrasted to previously taught grammar?
- Are structures such as past tense and present perfect tense contrasted to each other?
- Are several relevant meanings for the structure taught although not necessarily together? For example, the present perfect can mean indefinite past, but it can also mean from a point in the past up to the present. You might teach these different meanings in different units. Similarly, use of *will* can mean a decision about the future made at the time of speaking, but it can also be used in predictions and in more formal language. Many structures are used with different meanings in different contexts.
- Are grammar items appropriate to the course goals, student proficiency levels, and curriculum? In particular, are the grammar presentation and practice tasks in keeping with the order in which grammar is presented in your syllabus?
- Are grammar topics and grammar practice activities appropriate to the teaching context? If you are teaching very young children in an EFL context, you would not need to teach passive voice for formal writing, so if that is included, you may want to consider whether or not the text in general is too advanced. Similarly, if you are teaching English for academic purposes to students approaching higher language proficiency levels, you would expect to see the passive voice in the text and lesser emphasis on more basic grammatical structures such as the simple past or present tenses.
- Is the presentation of the grammatical structure clear?

If some of these elements are missing, you may need to supplement the book. If some items are unsuitable for your students, for example, because of their ages, interests, or proficiency levels, you may need to make some adaptations.

Assessing Pronunciation Coverage in Textbooks

Pronunciation is an important part of oral communication. You can evaluate how pronunciation is treated in multiskills, speaking, or pronunciation textbooks by asking these questions:

- Are suprasegmental features such as stress, rhythm, and intonation increasingly emphasized beyond the beginner level?
- Is the presentation of grammar included where relevant as part of pronunciation?
- Are less controlled practice activities provided in addition to controlled practice?
- Is pronunciation recycled throughout?
- Is pronunciation practice provided in naturalistic and meaningful contexts?

As with grammar, you may need to make some adaptations or supplement your textbook to ensure that it addresses all of the above and meets your students' needs.

Assessing Vocabulary Coverage in Textbooks

Which is more important in assessing a textbook's merits—its treatment of grammar or its attention to vocabulary? A lot depends on where your students need the most practice and on your course objectives. However, in the past, many textbooks, particularly those for adults, emphasized grammar over lexicon. Michael Lewis and Keith Folse have urged us to rethink this and the scope of our vocabulary teaching. According to the lexical approach (Lewis 1993, 7), "language consists of chunks which, when combined, produce continuous coherent text." Lewis stresses the inclusion of these lexical categories in teaching and avoiding relegation of them to a marginal role after grammar:

- words that stand alone *(Hello! Exactly! carrots)*, which is the biggest category
- collocations, or words that occur together, often as fully fixed to relatively fixed combinations. Verb + noun partnerships are among the most useful to teach (e.g., *take the time to, do the dishes, commit a crime, take a seat)*
- completely fixed expressions such as *good night, how are you, I'd like to,* and *by the way,* as well as idioms. Analysis of real data, according to the lexical approach, indicates that a large proportion of what we say consists of "prefabricated multi-word" items (11), so although opportunities for original use of language are vital, equally so are opportunities to learn common fixed expressions.
- semi-fixed expressions, a large category that includes short and very long utterances. A sample short phrase, with substitutions, might be, *what a gorgeous/beautiful outfit/haircut/day.* A sample long one might be the opening for an academic paper: *In this paper I wish to discuss. . . . (7–11).*

Folse (2004) also suggests that teaching word lists is making a comeback and recommends that lists related to the curriculum and student-made lists support language learning.

Lewis emphasizes that chunks are bigger than adjective and preposition combinations such as *on time, tired of, interested in.* He asserts that "we store much of our mental lexicon in complete, fully-contextualized phrases" (9). In assessing the attention to vocabulary and lexicon, then, note whether the textbook consistently breaks language down into very small chunks and doesn't emphasize larger combinations of words for students to also learn.

In addition to presentation and practice of different kinds of single and multi-word chunks, these other textbook features are useful to examine in assessing vocabulary: a variety of listening and reading texts in order to expose learners to vocabulary in context; activities requiring dictionary use; and focus on high-frequency vocabulary such as the Academic Word List (AWL), rather than on any possible word or word combinations. In order to encourage learner autonomy in language and lexical development, look for activities that ask intermediate and advanced students to learn word roots and stems and that direct them to use context clues in figuring out the meanings of words and multi-word phrases. Folse (2004) notes that presenting target vocabulary in logical order is important. The way in which you organize lexical items may be determined by your curriculum, or you may select what you deem important vocabulary for your students' learning goals. For example, if you are teaching English to visiting agricultural specialists, you would want to target vocabulary in context that is relevant to agriculture and organize it in a logical way. This could mean presenting and practicing the most frequent and general terms and related words (e.g., seed, seedling, seeding; farm, farmer, farming) first and moving to more and more specialized terms as the course progresses.

Newer textbooks generally provide much better lexical focus than more traditional ones, but you will often still need to provide additional practice (Folse 2004). Examining textbooks based on the lexical approach can provide ideas for adapting other text material.

For example, *Conversation Lessons* (Martinez 1997), based on the lexical approach, contains humourous dialogues filled with common multi-word phrases. A dialogue on making decisions includes such phrases as, *I'm leaning toward, I could go either way, I have mixed feelings about* (12). Practice activities include jumbled phrases that students reorder, decision-making role plays in which students use phrases from the dialogue, and even memorization of the original dialogue. These kinds of practice activities—jumbled phrases, dialogue memorization, and role plays that encourage use of vocabulary from the original dialogue—could be adapted to dialogues in other texts.

Michael Lewis (1993, 28) suggests these activities with many textbook readings:

1. Ask learners to underline every noun that has a collocating verb in front of it.
2. Ask learners to call out the verb and noun partnerships that they find. The teacher will record the correct ones on a transparency.
3. Put students in small groups and ask them to use the collocations to recall and summarize the reading text.
4. Ask students to record the most useful collocations in their notebooks.

Coverage of the Four Skills

You can draw on what you've learned about teaching the four skills from your language teaching knowledge as well as from the information provided in this chapter. First, you should read the introductory pages of the book to see if the textbook emphasizes one skill over the others. For example, the introduction should tell you if the focus is on speaking and listening with less emphasis on reading and writing. The introductory pages should also indicate proficiency level (beginner, intermediate, advanced) and if the book has been designed for general English skills development or for English for specific purposes (English for academic purposes, workplace English, etc.). It is important to know this so that the textbook matches your curriculum, your context, and your students' goals and needs.

When examining a book for coverage of the four skills, remember to include coverage of culture, grammar, pronunciation, and vocabulary development. Development of these areas may be embedded within the four main skill areas. For example, vocabulary development may be found in development of reading, and pronunciation development may be located in the development of speaking. Cunningsworth (1995, 3–4) suggests that you ensure the skills are integrated and that topics and activities are relevant and interesting regardless of the skill area focus. He suggests that speaking activities such as dialogues prepare students for authentic interaction. He also suggests that you check to ensure there is a sufficient amount of level- and age-appropriate reading material as well as clearly recorded listening material that is realistic and with comprehension supports (e.g., questions and activities for students). Finally, Cunningsworth suggests that you check writing activities for suitability "in terms of guidance/control, degree of accuracy, organization of longer pieces of writing (e.g., paragraphing) and use of appropriate styles" (4).

Assessing Variety in Textbooks

Although some educators warn against the monotony of a predictable sequence of learning activities, many students feel secure with a certain routine and do not constantly need novelty to be engaged. This may be because language itself provides enough newness! There is nothing wrong with a textbook providing regular exercises and a predictable pattern that provides comfort for both you and your students. Students gain security in knowing how to proceed, and you spend less time teaching about activity procedures. A balance of routine and new exercises is ideal. Look for an appropriate amount of variety within each unit or section of a textbook in types of practice activities, in types of contexts or situations portrayed, in pacing, and in development of the four skills.

If you are required to use repetitive textbooks that include non-communicative drills, select those activities that are most relevant to your students' needs. These drills can be helpful for initial practice, particularly for lower levels. You can also make drills more communicative by recreating some as games or dialogues.

Assessing Grading in Textbooks

Cunningsworth (1995) includes sequencing, recycling, staging, and progressing in grading textbooks. Sequencing "is the order in which new items are taught, how the components fit with one another and how the range of language taught develops as learners progress through the course. Implicit in sequencing is the concept of progression. . . ." (59). When examining books based on a grammatical syllabus, you will note that texts on the market are quite similar in sequencing. This is because teacher experience and research has provided information on what to include and in what order—for example, what grammatical items are easiest and most common and should therefore be presented first. Similarly, you will note that in functionally based textbooks, similar types of functions are presented in similar order.

Also part of sequencing is the concept of recycling language—that is, helping students remember and become fluent by providing opportunities for them to practice a language point, such as a grammatical structure or a new word, several times in a variety of contexts.

Consider the amount of new information included in each section of a text and how fast it is to be covered. How quickly are new concepts introduced? True beginners and literacy students benefit from extensive practice of a small amount of new language, while intermediate and advanced students may be able to cope with a larger amount of new language content and fewer practice activities.

Finally, determine if the textbook has a cyclical or a linear progression. Books with a cyclical progression are more suitable for survey or overview courses because they progress from one language point to the next quite quickly, returning to each point later in the course in detail. Texts with a linear progression present each language point in detail before moving to the next. Sometimes this will also depend on whether the textbook focuses on speaking versus grammar, reading, or writing. When assessing for progression, consider your program goals and time frame.

Assessing Meaningful Context

Patricia Richard-Amato (1996) suggests that certain text or discourse types are "easier to reproduce, understand, and recall" because they are fully contextualized. They are motivating because they include the "conflict and the logical sequencing that is necessary to good storytelling and consistent with experience" (284). At the opposite extreme are textbook exercises or discourse that consist of disconnected lists of sentences. A textbook passage such as a dialogue may provide context in terms of time and place, but lack motivation, conflict, and logical sequence, as in the example that follows. Students remember grammatical and vocabulary features of a passage better if it is logical and interesting. This dialogue on the theme "visiting friends" is logical but not very motivational or intriguing. How might you improve it?

Scenario: Mary is visiting Ruth. Ruth picks Mary up on Tuesday evening at the bus station.

Ruth: Hi, Mary. I'm glad you could come.

Mary: Thank you, Ruth.

Ruth: How long can you stay?

Mary: My family wants me back home on Friday.

Ruth: I think there's only one bus a day so you'll have to leave on Thursday.

Mary: That's too bad, but I'll be back in two months.

Considering Textbooks Series

If students are moving through language proficiency levels with various teachers in a program, a carefully chosen textbook series can provide continuity and sequencing. In such a case, you should take extra care in choosing a series that will not become boring—at a minimum, it should have a wide variety of practice and language contexts. A number of teachers should also be able to work with it comfortably. The disadvantages of using a series across the institution are these: it may not meet the learning styles and needs of a wide range of learners, it may not match up with an institution's syllabus at every level, and students may feel there isn't enough variety.

Watching for -isms and Stereotyping in Textbooks

If you are stuck with using a textbook that engenders stereotypes or contains one of the "-isms"—sexism, racism, age-ism, or handicap-ism—use it as an opportunity to talk with your students about stereotypes. Newer textbooks are generally written with sensitivity, so this issue may not arise. If you have a choice, avoid textbooks that are unsatisfactory in these areas.

Watching for Language and Cultural Relevancy in Textbooks

In addition to the cultural relevance and usefulness of topics and situations, you should consider the English variety in the textbook. Is it North American, British, colloquial, formal? Is it suitable for your student population? Is it representative of what English speakers actually say?

It may be difficult to find a book with a high degree of appropriate cultural content that also satisfies your other criteria. You will need to decide what you need to do to supplement easily and to effectively adjust cultural content. For example, if you are teaching in North America, you may find a good British English textbook that is not culturally relevant. However, you may still want to choose it because of its solid grammatical progression, relevant functions and communicative practice, balance of controlled and less controlled practice activities, and activities addressing the skill areas. Given all the benefits of the textbook, it may not be too difficult for you to add appropriate, closer-to-home cultural content. For example, you may want to point out which expressions and language variations are most commonly used in your context in the same situations or change the setting and characters in some of the activities.

Cultural content can also refer to students' own cultural backgrounds. Grant (1995) notes that students say they prefer images, texts, and activities related to their countries and cultures because it makes them feel more "at home in a strange land" and as if their countries and cultures were important (113). We will give additional examples for supplementing cultural content, or localizing, later in this chapter in the section on adapting textbooks.

Assessing Self-Directed Learning in Textbooks

Current textbooks may include self-directed learner training. These are activities and ideas that enable students to discover and develop effective learning strategies. If you consider this important, look for this in textbooks: student self-assessment and progress checklists; grammar and vocabulary summaries; self-check questions with answer keys; study tips; strategies for how to approach a reading or writing activity; and advice on managing class notes.

Assessing Literacy Level in a Textbook

Many beginning texts rely heavily on students' literacy skills—students must be literate in their second language in order to carry out many of the controlled practice activities such as dialogue practice. If working with low-literacy level students, consider whether the oral and aural presentation and practice activities rely too heavily on students' abilities to read and write. Refer to your course curriculum to ensure appropriate level for intermediate and advanced students.

Inclusion of Supplementary Materials in Textbooks

You can often request examination copies of a book; some are under the publisher's 30-day examination policy. This opportunity will help you make the best possible textbook selection. Some textbooks include "extras" or ancillaries that may enhance your students' learning, such as student workbooks, CD-ROMs, audio or videotapes, computer software, companion websites, teacher's guides, answer keys, and testing materials or placement test packages.

Student workbooks are often a good investment because they provide additional review and the chance to work with the language in written form that is sometimes left out of the textbook (due to space constraints), or for classes that meet only once or twice weekly.

AUDIOVISUAL SUPPLEMENTS

Audio and visual inputs, provided on disk or tape, are widely available. Many publishers do not send out sample disks or tapes. Audio scripts are often provided in the teacher's manual or online, and you can use them to find out what's presented on the audio before purchasing or make your own recordings. The advantage of the audio material is exposure to voices other than your own, as well as offering students the possibility to work independently and to review audio input as many times as they need to. Be sure to listen to the disk or tape to determine sound quality and the kinds of voices used. Is it a fair representation of normal, spoken English (e.g., where reductions, idiomatic expressions, contractions, false starts, and redundancies occur)? Is the variety of English one that students are familiar with (e.g., American English for students studying in the United States)? In video material, are the images realistic?

Often your own voice is preferable to recorded sound, as long as there are not too many different roles in a dialogue. Don't underestimate the difficulty that learners face in listening to a voice that is unaccompanied by an image. Remember to facilitate the listening task with some pre-listening activities. The teacher's guide may contain ideas to help you do this. In EFL contexts the accompanying audio material can be particularly valuable because of exposure to native English speakers. More will be said about video material in Chapter 6.

COMPUTER SOFTWARE AND COMPANION WEBSITES

Computer software and companion websites are becoming common supplements to textbooks. When assessing the value of these supplements, check whether they offer more than workbook type (e.g., fill ins) exercises on screen. Even if that's all they do, you still may want to purchase the product if it is affordable and fits in well with your curriculum.

However, computer applications and companion websites ideally should offer you something more than a print-based workbook would. This is because these media have the capacity to bring language learning to life by integrating multimedia such as video clips of people interacting. Another strength is the inclusion of interactive elements that give students the opportunity to work independently or in small groups to check their work with immediate feedback, solve problems, and even improve pronunciation through voice recognition programs. For example, a series that our EAP program uses extensively, *Focus on Grammar*, includes audio CDs to present content (often accompanied by images in the textbook) to support the written text with voices that read the text and provide listening practice and audio responses to the written exercises and activities. Computer software will be discussed at greater length in Chapter 7.

TEACHER'S GUIDES AND ANSWER KEYS

The print-based teacher's guide or a companion website for teachers that accompany some textbooks may be worthwhile. Some provide a brief refresher course on the methodology or syllabus being used and include ideas for the presentation stage. Companion websites in particular can provide adaptations for a variety of teaching contexts, saving you the time required to do those adaptations yourself. Several guides that we have used provide optional, less-controlled practice activities, sometimes called extension activities. (Sometimes these are in the textbook.) Such extension activities can sometimes be more useful than those in the book.

Companion websites may include support and extension information and activities for students as well. These are becoming more and more popular.

Quizzes, test banks, and end-of-unit tests are also useful features of some teacher's manuals and supplementary websites. However, you may never find one that you like to use in its entirety, especially if you want to personalize written tests with students' names and familiar locations, making the questions more context-embedded and meaningful. Watch for fill-in-the-blank type tests that test knowledge about the language rather than performance. Take what you can from the teacher's guide or companion website, and leave the rest.

PLACEMENT TEST PACKAGES

Some textbook series include placement testing materials. Depending on the focus of the series, the placement tests may include oral interview questions, grammar, listening, vocabulary, and reading sections. The *Clear Grammar* series published by University of Michigan Press (Folse 2005), *Interchange Passages Placement Evaluation Package, 3rd Edition* (Lesley 2005), and the *New Interchange General English Series* published by Cambridge University Press (Richards, Hull, and Proctor 2002) are examples. Also, there are placement tests in the Instructor's Manual for *Interactions Mosaic Academic, 4th Edition*, published by McGraw Hill-Ryerson (Werner, Nelson, and Spaventa 2002). Components of series-specific placement tests are often useful in placing students in the appropriate level or textbook assignment even if you are not using the corresponding textbooks across all your program levels.

Some publishers also carry placement tests that are independent of any textbook series. If they test key areas of importance to your program, and in the appropriate range of levels, such tests can be useful components of student placement, regardless of your textbook choice. The *Comprehensive English Language Test for Learners of English* or CELT (Harris and Palmer 1986) and the *Nelson Quickcheck Placement Tests* (Fowler and Coe 1987) are two of these tests. You will read about computer- and Web-based tests in Chapter 6.

Assessing Specialized Types of Textbooks

ESP Textbooks

English for Specific Purposes (ESP) books and programs cover many fields, including medicine, tourism, business, science and technology, and academic preparation. Today, preparation for academic English is often called EAP, a subfield of ESP. The content will be different from that in general textbooks and the balance of skills may be different, but many of the selection guidelines you have read will be useful.

ESP textbooks can't address all of the subdisciplines of an academic subject (e.g., science contains subdisciplines such as life sciences, botany, or ecology), but sometimes students themselves can contribute some of the specifics. Working at a general discipline level is still valuable because of the common characteristics of disciplines. For example, scientific language has certain common features in terms of grammar (such as extensive use of passive voice), vocabulary, and discourse structure (Cunningsworth 1995, 133). If you are preparing students for university studies, textbooks that provide practice in listening to lectures and notetaking, writing essays, and seminar-style discussion will be useful, even if the subject matter is not always directly related to their discipline. Look for ESP books that focus on target skills and strategies as well as on appropriate content.

Skill-Based Texts

Textbooks focusing on one skill at one level, or sometimes two (listening and speaking together, reading and writing together), are quite common. They naturally are more detailed in the presentation and practice of the target skill(s) than are fully integrated four-skills textbooks. It is difficult to isolate one skill so look for some integration of other skills within these books. For example, writing or speaking about a reading helps students and teachers assess reading comprehension and reinforces learning.

Two skills-based books (also called integrated) have become popular in some intensive English for Academic Purposes (EAP) programs in which students are not beginners and may need to concentrate on reading, writing, and grammar competencies. In other programs, use of a single-skill text can supplement an area not dealt with in sufficient depth in the primary textbook. It can also provide extra practice in a particular skill area, allowing students who may not be at the same level in all four skills to improve in a problem area.

Be aware that using three or four different core textbooks can become a juggling act. Some programs accommodate this by dividing English programs into distinct courses—reading, writing, speaking, listening, grammar, and pronunciation, or some combination of these.

Adapting Textbooks

Most teachers adapt textbooks to address specific student needs, to make teaching more personal, to address program requirements, to overcome textbook limitations, and to fulfill one's own need to be a creative, responsive teacher. Part of becoming better at adapting materials is to look at the many ideas for activities that are in other textbooks. It is also useful to talk to your colleagues about their ideas. You don't always need to spend huge amounts of energy and time creating activities that already exist in published textbooks. Sometimes all you need to do is find an activity suitable to your objective and adapt it so that it is more local or more personal (Edge 1993). Keep an open mind, examining old and new books as well as those that are for different age groups and proficiency levels. You might just find the perfect adaptation in an unexpected place.

The teaching materials and associated activities discussed in this book will provide you with a wealth of ideas for textbook adaptations. As you read through this book, consider textbook adaptations that you are struggling with.

Examples of Textbook Adaptations

Following are two examples of textbook activity adaptations. Example 1 is adapted from *Discussion & Interaction in the Academic Community* by Madden and Rohlck (1997, 21–22). Example 2 is adapted from *Functions of American English* by Leo Jones and C. von Baeyer (1986, 50).

EXAMPLE 1

This worksheet has been adapted to a slightly lower proficiency level, made more gender neutral, and made applicable to English-speaking countries other than the United States.

Original Worksheet

Excuses and Messages

Read the following episodes and decide what you would do. Are there any differences between these situations in the United States and similar situations in your country?

1. You want to make an appointment with your advisor. You haven't been able to reach her by phone so you will try to e-mail her. Write the message to your advisor.

    Date:

    From:

    To:

    Subject:

2. You're late for an appointment with your advisor. When you arrive at her office you find that she is not there. What would you do?

    ____ just leave

    ____ try to find someone (i.e., a secretary or administrator) and try to explain to him/her why you are late

    ____ leave a note

    Write a note to your advisor.

3. You missed a class because you couldn't get the assignment completed on time. What would you do?

    ____ go to the next class with the assignment and say nothing

    ____ go to the next class and explain why the assignment was late

    ____ e-mail the instructor and explain

    Write an e-mail message explaining your absence and the late assignment.

    Date:

    From:

    To:

    Subject:

4. You go to your professor's office during his regular office hours, and he is not there. You have something important to find out about your assignment. What would you do?

    ____ find a secretary and see if you can find out when he will be in his office

    ____ leave your number with a note in his mailbox

    ____ phone his home

    Write a note including your phone number for the professor. What kind of information do you include?

Adaptation

Excuses and Messages

What you would do in each problem below. What is different in your country?

1. You want to see your advisor. Your advisor does not answer the phone, so you send an e-mail. Write the message to your advisor below.

   Date:

   From:

   To:

   Subject:

2. You are late for a meeting with your advisor. Your advisor is not in the office when you get there. What would you do?

   ____ leave

   ____ tell a secretary why you are late

   ____ leave a note

   Write a note to your advisor.

3. You did not finish your assignment so you did not go to class. What would you do?

   ____ Go to the next class. Hand in the assignment. Do not say anything.

   ____ Go to the next class. Tell the instructor why the assignment is late.

   ____ Tell the instructor why the assignment is late in an e-mail message.

   Write an e-mail message to tell the instructor why the assignment is late and why you did not go to class.

   Date:

   From:

   To:

   Subject:

4. You go to your professor's office during office hours. Your professor is not there. You want to know about your assignment. What would you do?

   ____ ask a secretary when the professor will be back

   ____ leave your phone number and a note in the professor's mailbox

   ____ phone your professor's home

   Write a note to your professor. Give your professor your phone number. What information do you include?

EXAMPLE 2

This second example is a presentation and exercise on giving step-by-step instructions. We have provided two adaptations. The first has been adapted to a intermediate level of four Japanese technicians hired to oversee installation of specialized equipment for four new automotive factories in an English-speaking country. The second adaptation is for a class of 24 low-intermediate 15- to 16-year-old adolescents who are studying English in an EFL setting.

Original Presentation and Exercise

9.6 Presentation: step-by-step instructions

There is not much difference between telling someone how something works and instructing them how to do it themselves. More detail is needed and more repetition, too. When giving instructions, we often link the steps together like this:

First of all you...

The first thing you have to do is...

After you've done that, you...

The next thing you do is...

Oh, and then don't forget to...

Make sure you remember to...

Oh, and be careful not to...

The amount of detail and repetition usually depends on whom you are talking to and how much they know already.

Decide with your teacher how you would continue after using the expressions above.

9.7 Exercise

Pick one of the items you described in 9.5. Explain to your teacher how to use it. However, your teacher is going to pretend to be less mechanical than he or she usually is. Your teacher is also going to play a number of different roles: an old lady, a child, a know-it-all, your boss.

Adaptation 1 for Japanese Supervisors

9.6 Presentation: step-by-step instructions

Now you need to learn how to tell your employees how to install the computers they need in the factory. Here are some phrases to help you connect instructions together:

First you. . .

Second, you. . .

Next, you. . .

Remember to. . .

Be careful to. . .

Be careful not to. . .

Finally, you. . .

If you are speaking to a new employee, you may need to repeat the instructions more times, or give more details.

Now we will practise using these expressions.

9.7 Exercise

Pick one of the pieces of equipment we identified in 9.5. Explain to your partner how to install it. Your partner should pretend to be a new factory worker (teacher may wish to model this with a student).

Adaptation 2 for EFL Adolescents

9.6 Presentation: step-by-step instructions

Yesterday we saw a DVD on driving. Today you will tell your partner how to parallel park. Your partner will understand your instructions better if you link the instructions. You can use the words below to help you do this:

First you. . .

Second, you. . .

Next, you. . .

Remember to. . .

Be careful to. . .

Be careful not to. . .

Finally, you. . .

If your partner does not know much about driving, you may need to repeat more and give more detail.

Decide with your teacher how you would continue after using the expressions above.

9.7 Exercise

Tell your partner how to parallel park. Use the phrases above. Your partner should pretend that he or she cannot drive (teacher may wish to model this with a student).

Copyright

Copyright exists to legally recognize creators' rights to control the uses of their works and to be compensated for those uses.

Budget restraints of many organizations and institutions put teachers in a difficult position in terms of copyright—the need to provide, on short notice, relevant material responding to your students' needs and interests versus keeping within the materials budget.

Teachers who do not use a set textbook, with a copy for every student, often find themselves copying one page each from two or more textbooks, seeking to provide the best from both for their students. This is illegal. To avoid copyright infringement, find out about copyright laws in the country in which you work. Also find out what arrangements have been made by your institution regarding copying published materials.

One way to minimize breaking copyright regulations is to choose a textbook that will provide a good backbone for your course. You can also encourage your institution to buy multiple copies for your students rather than a single teacher's copy. Supplement your textbook as much as possible with student-generated materials or with materials you have adapted. And remember: Textbooks are usually written by hard-working, moderately paid ESL and EFL teachers like you. They lose money when you choose to photocopy rather than invest in more copies. Chapter 3 provides more information on this topic.

Written Texts

LEARNING OR SLACKING OFF?

The teacher's supervisor knocked and walked in. She caught the students with their feet on their desks and a radio blaring. Some were browsing through *Sports Illustrated* or *People* magazines. Others were reading a novel. Two of them appeared to be doing a personality quiz in the popular journal *Psychology Today*.

"Reading period?" she asked. The instructor smiled shyly and nodded. "Sorry to disturb you," said the supervisor. "I just have a message for one of your students."

What is your assessment of what is happening here? What does it tell you about how this teacher deals with materials? What does it tell you about the students and their choice of materials? What does it say about accepted classroom atmosphere in this school?

Not much teaching and learning is possible without interesting texts. Well-planned and executed activities require motivational written texts to involve students and to promote active and experiential learning. In your teaching and professional development, you have undoubtedly discovered a variety of techniques for teaching reading and working with written text. This chapter focuses on the characteristics and types of written text available and how to choose appropriate written text for your English language students. Sometimes, teaching material won't be as captivating as a favorite novel or magazine, but if it's relevant to your students' needs and interests, is at an appropriate level, and is combined with an engaging task, then the odds are that students will become involved and learn from it.

This chapter includes:
- how to choose written texts for your ESL or EFL class according to defined criteria
- the benefits of literature and newspapers as written text
- the benefits of student involvement in the production of written text
- the advantages and disadvantages of simplified text
- ways to simplify a written text for your ESL or EFL class
- the wide range of written text types you can buy
- written text types you can create on your own or with your students
- respecting copyright in your choice and use of written text

Some Challenging Questions

Before you begin, answer these questions:
- What are your favorite things to read?
- What kinds of materials are you required to read?
- Which types of reading do you find most difficult? Why?
- What characteristics or qualities make these types of written text difficult for you?

Now, think of two different students groups—for example, ESL adult students with limited literacy skills living in an English-speaking environment and students in a university EAP program. Which materials will each group most need to understand?

Written Text as Language Teaching Material

Matching Text to Student

Make a list of all the types of written text available to you and your students. All of these items should be on your list: newspapers, magazines and journals, novels and storybooks, short stories, cartoons, textbooks, poetry and songs, manuals, charts or maps, graphs, essays, business letters, greeting cards, labels, bills, ads, memos, billboards, and the variety of written text available on the Internet. Don't forget the wide variety of written text designed specifically for ESL, EFL, and literacy students in the form of textbooks. How does a teacher choose wisely from this wealth of written materials? To assist, we outline nine aspects to consider when choosing written text for your English language students, regardless of whether the written text is available in hard copy or digitally.

First, we consider program and learning objectives, then three aspects related to students, and finally, five aspects related to the text itself. Lotherington-Woloszyn (1988) identifies the nine aspects as:

- knowing your teaching and program objectives
- students' interests and ages
- students' background knowledge
- students' reading abilities and English language proficiency
- text layout and presentation
- linguistic difficulty of the text
- text genre and writing style
- sociocultural context
- text length.

Knowing Your Teaching and Program Objectives

"Being able to read a little story about a circus is not a priority for a student who cannot identify a public washroom or read the destination sign on a bus" (Burnaby 1990). This quotation illustrates the importance of choosing written text according to learning objectives. Because your objectives should be based on your students' goals and needs, they will have a primary influence in your choice of written text. For example, if your main lesson focus is a particular grammatical structure, then make sure the text you choose illustrates the ways the selected structure can be used. If you are looking for written text to promote reading for pleasure, avoid overly technical or academic texts.

Many of us start from the reading rather than from the objectives. That is, we find an article we like and then devise a way to use it within a particular theme unit or as the basis for an activity such as scanning or role playing. If we don't have an immediate use for the reading, we file it for future use. Actually, both starting points are legitimate. You wouldn't want to bypass a text that is timely or of interest to your students because it did not meet your immediate learning objectives. But you also need to weigh the most appropriate time and way to use the text if it digresses too much and takes you too far from your objectives.

Written text can help meet many learning objectives. Some of the more apparent uses of written text are to develop specific reading skills—such as, skimming and scanning, predicting, inferring, and recognizing words. You may also want to use written material to provide information about culture or a particular subject as a springboard for discussion or writing, or to introduce a thematic unit or grammatical structure. In academic programs, for example, essays are useful writing models for students at all grade levels. Of course, written text is necessary to develop overall reading skills through extensive reading (discussed later in this chapter), as well as through academic reading and improving more discrete reading skills.

If you teach ESL students in employment-readiness programs, your students need to become familiar with written materials such as job application forms, trade manuals, workplace signs, and memos.

If you are a content-area teacher with ESL students in your classroom or an ESL teacher working with students who are or will soon be in content-area classes, you need to find and use the texts used by mainstream students, in addition to those designed for ESL students. If you teach students in college or university preparation programs, expose them to university textbook material, journal articles, essays, literature, and case studies.

If you teach in an EFL setting, you will have a special set of considerations depending on the program goals, ranging from programs for children who may be taking English as an academic subject in school or in a post-secondary institution to programs for adults that range from business English to English for travel and communication. Your biggest challenge in EFL contexts may be finding locally available material, particularly in places where you are isolated or do not have Internet access.

Students' Interests and Ages

When possible, it makes sense to provide students with reading that interests them for two reasons: (1) topics of interest are motivational and (2) students may more readily pursue challenging texts if the material interests them. Extensive reading is instrumental in developing fluency and speed (Krashen 1998). It also helps students focus on gist, thus indirectly contributing to the development of vocabulary, grammar, and writing.

Even the most creative, engaging text-based activities do not compensate for reading material your students don't like or don't consider relevant. A colleague once tried to engage her teenage students in what she thought was a poignant and culturally appropriate story entitled "A Secret for Two." It was about a milkman and his horse and was intended to teach prediction skills. The source was from a course for adults. Initially, the students were very interested in the title, since everyone loves secrets. The students enjoyed guessing what the secret might be. At the bottom of each short page was a little STOP sign indicating the students should stop reading and reassess what they now thought the secret might be and what might happen next. The first time they stopped, students wrote their predictions and discussed them with a partner. The second time, they discussed them as a class. However, interest in the activity and the story waned when students said the new vocabulary made the text difficult and that they preferred adventure stories. Apparently, a story about a milkman and his horse at the turn of the 20th century simply didn't hold the interest of a group of 16- and 17-year-olds (the secret, by the way, was that the milkman was blind and couldn't do his milk route with any other horse than his own).

Children's Literature for Adults

In an effort to provide material at a suitable level for adults of low proficiency, teachers sometimes resort to children's books and stories. Some children's stories are suitable for adults, but many are not. Ann Silverman (1990) discovered that students who are parents of school-age children sometimes find children's literature valuable in understanding the cultural content and context of their children's classrooms while improving their own reading skills.

Literature, in general, is valuable reading because of its concern with the deepest human preoccupations and its ability to inspire reader involvement. Some children's literature can be valuable for adults for these reasons, but not all children's reading material is literature. This distinction is important to ensure that the children's literature is not condescending or overly immature. Silverman explains that good children's literature expresses ideas more simply than adult literature, has more explicit plot development, avoids the complexities of flashbacks and digressions, and has more illustrations. This, she asserts, can be better than using simplified readers.

We recommend starting by having a look at the books from the Newbery or Caldecott Award list and The Canadian Children's Book Centre (*www.bookcentre.ca/*). Take the time to browse through children's books and talk to librarians and kids to find out what they like. In her presentation at TESL Canada 2002, entitled "Multicultural Literature Circles in Your Classroom," Elizabeth Coelho, known for her work with ESL children, uses well-chosen children's books that address cultural themes as a way to promote reading as a "pleasurable and exciting way to spend private time and encourage students to share ideas and experiences with others." She suggests the following process, which can also be used with adults:

1. Choose appropriate short books or stories related to a common theme, such as friendship, making peace, family, growing up, or overcoming adversity.

2. Model a short presentation using one of the books or readings. Ask questions and ask for predictions about the book. Encourage students to respond to the books they read in their journals or orally using the retell, relate, reflect approach. In retell students are asked to use their own words to explain the content of the reading. This is followed by the relate stage in which students are guided in connecting what they have read to their own experiences. Finally, students are asked to reflect on what they have read in terms of how well they liked it or its effectiveness in getting a point across to them.

3. Have groups of four students read a selected book or reading, making sure they cover a range of levels and topics. Structure the reading by providing a process for discussion of a specific number of pages each session and developing questions or activities for each session.

4. Showcase the books or readings by having each group present aspects of it to their classmates in a creative way, such as a dramatization, creation of illustrations, or reading their own stories on the theme of the book or reading.

5. Assign independent reading. Have students reflect on the reading in their journals using the retell, relate, reflect approach.

Students' Background Knowledge

Newspaper articles and other expository texts are usually considered more difficult to read than narratives. But students are often able to read more linguistically complex materials if they are familiar with the subject matter of the reading because it is from their own culture, from their academic background, from a reading you have done orally, or based on shared experiences. For example, inviting a storyteller from the community is a wonderful way to introduce a story to students, thus providing a shared experience. You should also select reading material that uses the English variety most familiar to your students. That is, if you are teaching in North America, be aware that written text from the United Kingdom may use unfamiliar English expressions, for example, *lift* instead of *elevator*, *lorry* instead of *truck*.

If you are working with North American Indigenous students, another way of tapping background knowledge is to collect similar stories from Indigenous groups in other countries. You may also find appropriate translations from the students' cultures.

One teacher took the chance of relying on her students' background knowledge and chose a newspaper article about a celebrity singer from their culture. As a result the students enthusiastically attacked the new idioms and vocabulary and became totally engaged in the follow-up discussion questions. They said that the article was just right in terms of challenge, yet the linguistic complexity was at least as difficult as the short story "A Secret for Two," mentioned on page 38, which students said was too difficult.

Students' Reading Ability and English Language Proficiency Levels

Reading and exposure to books and written texts are important to English language students at all proficiency levels. You will need to consider the students' literacy levels, reading skills in their native language(s), confidence, and backgrounds. You want to challenge them—not overwhelm them—with the written text that you present.

Beginning readers will benefit from LEA or the language experience approach (described later in this chapter), in which students' oral language is the basis of the written text. This approach develops word recognition and comprehension skills. ESL students in school systems who will eventually study academic content in the target language are not ready for content-area reading until they have developed good word-recognition skills and can comprehend the material with some support. Most students in fact, benefit from support. Bridging support includes pre-reading activities such as class discussions on the topic of the reading and new vocabulary, during-reading activities such as think-alongs and comprehension checks, and post-reading activities such as cloze exercises, problem-solving, information gaps, and summary writing.

Mary Ashworth (1992) describes three different comprehension levels that will influence the texts and tasks you choose:

- Literal comprehension—readers can answer questions dealing with detail at the surface level of the text. For example, after reading a current event, you can ask students who, what, where, and when questions.
- Inferential comprehension—readers can make inferences from the ideas the writer presents. For example, ask students how and why questions as well as prediction about the outcomes of a news story.

- Critical-evaluative comprehension—readers can evaluate and make critical judgments about what they have read. These judgments, for example, might include whether the text expresses fact or opinion or how the knowledge might be applied in different situations. (94)

Reading material is important for non-literate students as well as for literate students. Non-literate students need to learn how to hold a book and turn pages. They need to learn about left-to-right orientation, sequencing, and what words are. However, do not let students' lack of background knowledge hinder your use of written material, as text is a valuable way to present new linguistic information and cultural content. Just remember when choosing readings that it is more difficult for students to read new information than to read about familiar subjects. If you are interested in materials for ESL literacy students, refer to the article by Barbara Burnaby (1990) in the References.

In content-based programs such as K–12, citizenship programs, and employment-related ESL where written text presented in various forms (e.g., on paper, via the Internet, in signs) is necessary for presenting important concepts and information, you will want to choose texts that facilitate the reading process in other ways.

Text Layout and Presentation

Whether presented on hard copy or digitally on the Internet, layout and presentation of a text are important factors in facilitating reading. Layout and presentation attributes include: paper quality (no glare), thickness, and durability; use of white space, such as sufficient margins and space between paragraphs; font size, clarity, and choice of font; and illustrations that enhance readability and comprehension (Wong 1993).

A visually inviting text can influence students' perceptions of text difficulty and of their ability to read it. To help you imagine your students' reactions to the appearance of a text, Lotherington-Woloszyn (1988) asks teachers to consider whether or not students are "faced with an unbroken wall of tiny print." Layout with sufficient white space, illustrations, and subheadings facilitates reading for both native and non-native speakers.

It is important to also consider if the font is too small and if it is appropriate for your students' abilities. Jean Campbell (2006), for example, suggests that ESL literacy students be provided with texts for readings in Comic Sans 12 point and that there are two spaces between each word. She also recommends large amounts of white space surrounding sections of print. Such standards would not be appropriate for advanced readers who may be prepared to read authentic text. Therefore, you can help your students by gradually presenting them with print that is increasingly more like the authentic text that their English-speaking peers would read.

Linguistic Difficulty of the Text

Ashworth (1992) uses these features to determine difficulty:

- number of multisyllabic words that are new to the student
- whether vocabulary is concrete or abstract
- sentence complexity, including number of sentences
- kinds of figures of speech (94)

As mentioned earlier, students can often deal with greater linguistic difficulty in a text if they are familiar with the subject matter of the reading. They may be able to read with an idea of what is coming next, comprehending the general idea better than they would with a more unfamiliar subject. So remember that linguistic difficulty should not be isolated from other factors in considering readability level for a particular group of students.

Text Genre and Writing Style

Genre is used in this book to mean the different forms or categories of text such as memos, letters, essays, narratives, and so on. The genre, as well as the style in which a text is written, contribute to the challenge of teaching written text. In this section we will look at the following genres: signs and documents, literature, case studies, and expository and written text.

SIGNS AND DOCUMENTS

Signs do not involve sentences or paragraphs, as do many other text genres. Bring sign genre into the classroom by:

- taking your students on a field trip to record the kinds of writing they see on signs
- making replicas of signs and notices and posting them in the classroom or school
- asking students to collect print samples from home—cereal box labels, stickers, classified ads or headlines, posters, magazine covers, or CD jackets—and sharing them with their classmates

Discuss the underlying or cultural as well as the explicit meaning of these materials, and don't forget to talk about the images that support or, in some cases, replace, the words/phrases.

No Smoking   Wheelchair Accessible   Poison

LITERATURE

Materials that provide information, particularly those that help students survive in a new culture, are important and necessary components of many English language programs. However, at most levels beyond basic literacy, it is also valuable to include material that students can react to intellectually or emotionally. This is what makes stories, novels, poems, and human-interest stories from newspapers, magazines, or other sources so valuable. These kinds of texts should be of enough consequence to students that they want to read-write-react to them orally or in writing.

Marilyn MacLean (1990) notes that for children as well as for adults the stories presented in literature enhance the development of writing, speaking, and listening. Through hearing stories, beginners become familiar with the sound of the language and are later able to use the presentation of stories as patterns for their own early speech and writing. Because story exists in the literature of all cultures (in the form of tales, myths, and legends as well as story itself), it can also act as a bridge from students' native cultures to the culture of English speakers. Students can compare stories and in doing so compare the customs and values of each culture non-judgmentally. The Cinderella story, for example, exists in a large number of cultures. It is worth seeking out stories with universal messages that students at all proficiency levels can relate to. Story telling, story reading, and sharing of stories are familiar to everyone; they contribute to a positive classroom environment in which students are more comfortable taking risks. For these reasons, stories can be presented at all proficiency levels and ages. Seek out storybooks with good visuals that enhance the story to make it more comprehensible. Pantomime, puppet shows, and role play are other ways to present stories and aid understanding and student involvement.

Stories may present cultural difficulties, but they are rich in cultural learning through the cultural mores and customs inherent in them. In addition, they often touch on universal themes to which students from many different backgrounds can relate. Using an ESL textbook based on human interest newspaper stories, a teacher assigned a group of intermediate-level adult ESL students a story about two lovers, one from Czechoslovakia and another from Russia. They had met when they were in their twenties but were separated for many years by geographical boundaries. It was only after emigrating separately to North America many years later that the two were reunited. Reactions to the text indicated that students were engrossed; one student even had tears in her eyes. Texts such as this allow students the thrill of entering into worlds of experience in the way that reading in our first language offers us. If you want students to develop the desire to read in English, you need to provide this type of engaging written material. ESL publishers' catalogues and websites can be a source of simplified novels, story collections, and other engaging reading material at a variety of levels. Young adult sections of public libraries and teen/young adult book lists are also useful references for high-interest readings at an intermediate level. Your local newspaper is, of course, another source of human interest stories. Finally, books you or other teachers have read and judged suitable for your students' level and interests are fair game.

If you do choose literary texts, check whether the language of the text reflects natural usage or is exceptional (for example poetry or English from a past era). Contemporary literature is more suitable in most cases than classical literature. Shakespeare or even Charles Dickens should probably not be your first choices in ESL or EFL classes unless you are teaching in a bridge or introductory literature course for university or college-bound students. Literature can be inspirational and accelerate language development.

CASE STUDIES

The case study is gaining popularity as an authentic type of textual material. Case studies are used not only for academic preparation (e.g., in fields such as business and sociology) but also for cultural investigation. They are written in a variety of styles to meet a variety of student interests and program objectives. Case studies are compactly written scenarios that are "rich in content and sufficiently open-ended to encourage meaningful discussion and sharing of similar experiences" (Lam and Henriques 1991, 22). EAP reading textbooks sometimes feature case studies, as do Business English textbooks such as the Millennium Edition of Myra Shulman's *Selected Readings in Business* (2003), and other books referenced later in this chapter. University and college textbooks in several fields such as geography, psychology, sociology, and commerce or economics often present case studies that you can use as is or adapt, keeping in mind copyright restrictions. You can also write your own case studies, ensuring that what you write fits with your curriculum and learning objectives and matches with your content focus if you are theme teaching. Don't forget to check the Internet for case studies as well, particularly in the area of business. A quick Internet search will reveal many sites from which you can get ideas. Case studies are most suitable for teaching adolescents and adults at higher proficiency levels. When presenting cases, be sure you have clear objectives for using them, for example, to promote discussion by solving a problem raised by the case. Also ensure that you clearly explain the purpose to students, including what a case study is.

WRITING STYLE—NARRATIVE AND EXPOSITORY TEXT

Offer students samples of a wide range of styles, registers, and types of text that will better prepare them for authentic reading. Fraida Dubin and Elite Olshtain (1986) suggest moving students from popular writing (e.g., newspaper human interest stories and simplified contemporary novels) to textbook writing (e.g., chapter excerpted from a high school or first-year university geography textbook) when they are at the intermediate and advanced stages.

For lower levels, narratives are preferable to expository (information-laden) text because in narratives, authors usually describe events in chronological order. Narratives also represent a universal genre, so many students will already have experience with them. Narratives often contain redundancy, which helps readers to comprehend through repetition and rephrasing.

There are different levels of complexity in the narrative style—the degree of repetition, differences in the amount of information provided or withheld, and the ways characters and events are developed. A complex narrative is one in which the reader needs to infer information from the text. As a teacher, you can judge a narrative's complexity in these areas and use less complex ones for lower-level students, gradually increasing complexity. Complex narratives requiring inference include genres such as mysteries, while less complex narratives include straightforward genres such as descriptions.

In expository texts, the writing conventions are sometimes culture specific and require higher levels of competence. When using expository texts, make students aware of the organization and style, for example, knowing whether an academic text describes a process, supports an argument, proves a hypothesis, provides comparison, or demonstrates cause and effect. These help students understand a text's overall purpose. Footnotes, indexes, tables of contents, abstracts or executive summaries, graphs and charts, and bibliography are parts of expository text that some students may need to become familiar with.

SOCIOCULTURAL CONTENT

Consider your students' "sensibilities as people and citizens of the world" (Silberstein 1987) when selecting a written text. Sandra Silberstein describes how she developed a series of exercises around an article about an earthquake in the Middle East. Happy to have found a text about an area of the world familiar to many of her students, she only later realized that the text was not appropriate for another reason—she was using a tragedy, one that many students felt personally (the earthquake), as the basis of impersonal exercises in vocabulary development.

When using literature, do not limit yourself to the literature of the dominant English-speaking countries. British and American classics are not the only ones worth reading. India and Africa, Australia, New Zealand, and the Caribbean produce excellent English literature. Writers from the area in which you are teaching will obviously be relevant, so consider good translations of written works from other linguistic backgrounds. What you present to your students suggests what you consider valuable and can validate a wide variety of writing traditions.

TEXT LENGTH

Longer texts are not necessarily more difficult. Sometimes shorter texts pose more problems for the reader because they do not provide the repetition and the "extended conceptual support" (Maley and Duff 1990) of longer texts. Brief news updates in the paper, for example, can be harder to follow than longer magazine articles that provide the background information required to understand the described events.

Authentic versus Simplified Written Text

Should you use only authentic (unedited) texts, or should you also use simplified and abridged texts? While this remains an issue, many language teaching professionals advocate authentic texts for college-level ESL students, citing the satisfaction and sense of cultural belonging that come from reading authentic materials. Dubin and Olshtain (1986) suggest using authentic texts as soon as possible, though abridged and edited texts may be necessary bridges to learning.

In elementary and secondary classrooms, ESL students must usually learn some English and academic content simultaneously. One approach is to simplify texts, find alternate readings, or do away with textbooks if appropriate. This approach may help to ensure content-area learning, but it may compromise content in the process.

Simplifying materials can also deny students access to the very language they need and limit their learning opportunities. As an alternative, some experts encourage teachers first to

> exploit the materials they use every day, with all their students, to the benefit of the ESOL students they teach. Second, in exploiting materials, the modifications that count are elaborative adjustments, rather than simplifications. . . . Giving ESOL students more than one word, more than one reading, or more than one avenue for understanding a concept can be more useful than watering down content. . . . Allowing students to approach content from several angles—by reading and writing or by reading and doing—allows them to show comprehension without having to have the control needed in speech. (Teemant, Bernhardt, and Rodriguez-Munoz 1996, 17–18)

Providing charts, labeled visuals, and pre-reading activities also aid comprehension of key content.

Keep in mind that the readings in ESL and EFL textbooks are not necessarily simplified (recall the discussion on authentic materials, which are now popular in textbooks). Textbooks often use excerpts from magazines, academic material, and newspapers and contain strategies and activities to support students' understanding. Read the book's preface or introduction to find out the type of readings provided. Are they authentic or simplified? If simplified, is enough detail and new information present to respect the students and maintain interest? A mixture of both simplified and authentic texts can be useful for students at intermediate levels, building their comfort and skills through simplified texts and preparing them for greater use of authentic texts at advanced levels.

Selecting Books for Extensive Reading

Involving students in extensive reading, in addition to development of discrete skills, is a good way to develop reading skills. However, students may not know what is available to them and might be intimidated by the prospect of reading authentic materials, especially long ones. Therefore, it is important to tell students the value of extensive reading—a sense of achievement, improved confidence in reading, and the satisfaction of reading something real from the target culture. In addition, providing challenging, comprehensible input through reading, as Steven Krashen (1993) contends, helps students improve in all of the other skill areas. There is evidence that by reading texts of novel-length—and even being seen carrying a novel—creates a boost of confidence and achievement. Novels and longer readings are less intimidating and allow students to believe they can tackle more on their own.

When selecting books for extensive reading, Dupuy, Tse, and Cook (1996) suggest authentic books that are available, affordable, and accessible to students. They suggest that books be of reasonable length of "30–50 pages for low intermediate, 100–150 pages for intermediate, and 200 or more pages for advanced-level students" (11). If students preview a movie based on an assigned book, it will aid their understanding. Research shows that knowledge of the basic plot and characters assists students in reading longer texts. Some examples are *The Joy Luck Club, Like Water for Chocolate,* and *Harry Potter and the Sorcerer's Stone.* There are many others available for a variety of age levels. If you are selecting one book for the entire class to read, you will need to cover a broad range of student interests. Conduct interviews or surveys with students about their interests, hobbies, recreational activities, or books that they liked to read in their native language. Some publishers have companion texts for ESL students based on popular or widely available novels.

Dupuy, Tse, and Cook suggest the following ways to incorporate extensive reading: a survey course in which all students read and discuss the same book; directed reading in which the teacher helps and individuals or small groups read and discuss the same book; sustained silent reading in which students have time to read during class; and literature circles, similar to book clubs. Reading should not be evaluated; but students should keep logs of their readings or present oral or written book reviews (12–13).

Books in Students' Native Languages

Although many teachers allow only the use of English in their classrooms, there is a place for written text in students' native languages. In order to support reading in the content areas for ESL elementary and secondary students, encourage extensive reading regardless of the language. Ask school librarians to order content-area books in students' native languages to support learning in mainstream classes. Mary Ashworth (1992) reminds us of research showing that bilingual students "may do better academically in the long run than monolingual students and that they may be more creative . . . maintaining reading skills in the first language has a beneficial effect on reading skills in the second language" (87).

Written Text on the Internet

The proliferation of sites on the Internet, whether or not they are specifically developed for English language instruction, provides a rich source of textual material. Motivate students through engaging online activities, such as webquests (such as those found at *www.world-english.org/* and at *www.nelliemuller.com/*), online scavenger hunts (such as those found at *www.pitt.edu/~poole/eledScavenger. html*), and other searches that involve students' choosing what to read. Often the images, audiovisual elements, or interactive elements that accompany the written text enhance students' understanding of what has been written, enabling them to read at a higher level than might be the case in text alone. For example, this site provides audiovisual support on a variety of topics: *www.historychannel.com/.*

Since the Internet is a largely unmonitored source, you must be prepared for students finding unsuitable textual material, not only in terms of appropriateness of language level, but also in terms of appropriateness of content (e.g., pornography, hate sites, etc.). And remember that your students will not be able to judge this on their own since some of that judgment requires cultural knowledge they may not have.

Student-Generated Written Text

According to Virginia Sauvé (1988), "the stories one writes or tells from one's own experience" are superior, especially for adult students and those with low literacy skills and little or no previous exposure to textbooks as a learning tool. In describing the weaknesses of textbook readings, she states that students' own stories are often more personally meaningful and easier to relate to than are commercial textbooks readings. This is because some form of story is found in all cultures. According to Sauvé, published textbooks that seek to appeal to the widest possible market cannot hope to intimately incorporate content that is specific to a region or community, as life texts do (182).

According to Sauvé, teachers are story weavers who can help students create and use life texts in the classroom that help them represent and reinterpret their lives and develop their identities in a new world. Seeing their own words in print validates their experiences. Sauvé further states that for other students in the class, one student's story can be far more gripping than textbook material designed to illustrate language. How is a life text created?

> Life text comes from the student in whatever form she or he can offer at a given time and is given back to the student in forms more articulate and complete than the original. I do not mean that the teacher corrects the errors and hands it back, but that the teacher and the class work with the student to find the words and structures that student wants and needs to tell the story in her or his own way. (184)

Some sources of life text are journals between a teacher and student; spoken stories informally shared at coffee time or in a structured story circle in which the story of one person provokes a story from another; pictures, drawings, or collages; or stories collectively developed through a shared experience. (A technique for collective story writing known as The Language Experience Approach is described later in this chapter.)

Barbara Burnaby (1990, 165–86) recommends use of student texts for literacy students. Intermediate-level readers and even those literate in their first language(s) can also benefit because background knowledge and meaning in the text are assured if the text is student generated. Such text will be interesting and linguistically appropriate because students are using words from their own vocabularies and will be writing what they can already say. Depending on student needs and level, the teacher or students with the teacher's help will do the writing. That is, the teacher may act as a scribe while students develop the story orally. Furthermore, they will learn that written text has different conventions from spoken language—it is more grammatically formal and focuses more on content and detail. However, for beginners, using spoken words in print may be an easy way to start reading.

Even intermediate students can sometimes learn more complex word and sentence patterns if the content comes from their own spoken words that are written down. Student-generated texts allow you to combine reading, writing, and speaking practice. If students know their writing will have a purpose—as a reading text for themselves or other students—they may be motivated to invest more in their writing and to revise and rewrite.

Following are ten examples of student-generated texts. Most of them are group writing projects. You might want to pair a student with strong writing skills with a student with weaker skills. You may also want to design some of the activities for individuals or for the entire class. For example, a picture book, environmental print book, and personal dictionary for lower levels may be produced by individual students. The activities are described as paper based, but you may have students create their products on a computer.

LANGUAGE EXPERIENCE APPROACH (LEA) STORIES

A brief description of the steps involved in writing an LEA (Language Experience Approach) story from Lee Gunderson's *ESL Literacy Instruction: A Guidebook to Theory and Practice* (1991) follows. You can, of course, vary these steps.

- Students relate an experience, usually one shared by other class members, to the teacher. Story content may be a field trip or a special event at school or in the workplace. Individual language experience stories can be based on any kind of experience, in or out of class.
- The teacher acts as recorder, writing down the story exactly as students tell it. Students are not corrected, so that the story-writing experience is a positive one for them.
- The teacher reads the story aloud. Students read it aloud also, or they can identify and read individual words and phrases instead, according to their abilities.
- In another lesson, the teacher and students read the story again and talk about it. You can develop reading and writing further using new and difficult language from the story. For example, write the words on flashcards, in student dictionaries, or use new words in games.
- Students can copy their stories.
- Students practice reading their stories to a partner, a small group of students, the teacher, friends, or the whole class. (65)

After writing and reading their stories, students can illustrate them and keep them in a notebook or folder. Stories can also be typed up by either the teacher or the student. The notebook or folder of stories will become a class reader.

In the language teaching method known as Counseling or Community Language Learning, transcripts of student conversations are often taped and then written on large sheets of paper. Teachers use the story as a basis to develop language.

STUDENT NEWSPAPERS, MAGAZINES, OR E-ZINES

English language learners of all proficiency levels can learn from newspapers, magazines, and e-zines. Use them with beginning readers and writers by using LEA as a starting point to generate articles. Janice Isserliss (1990, 272) suggests using a format similar to that of real newspapers, so that students become accustomed to the organization of the press. Some of the regular columns that you might include are school news, news from individual students, weather reports, travel column, events calendars and classifieds ads. Once you have created a newspaper, you can use it for exercises to improve student reading.

More advanced students can take more control of the writing and publication process. If you have artists and humorists in the class, encourage them to do artwork and cartoons for the paper. Sports enthusiasts can write a column about local or school sporting events.

You and your students may also want to consider including letters to the editor, announcements, and an advice column.

Keep in mind the purpose of your course—if this type of writing is too different from what students will have to do, you may elect not to use it.

TALES

Students can develop a number of types of tales, including fairy tales, folk tales and fables, myths or fantasy, from their own culture. Begin by helping your students to establish characters and a setting for the tale:

- Make a list of possible characters and settings. Cut up the lists. Ask students to pick these beginning elements of the tale out of a hat. *Advanced Communication Games* by Jill Hadfield (1997) has ready-to-use, reproducible lists and instructions for student tales.
- As a class, brainstorm character and setting ideas and record them on the board. Pairs or small groups of students can then choose from those listed.
- Ask each writing group to develop its own characters and settings. Students may prefer to make up various elements of the story themselves. Allow class time over several days for the writing of the tale.

Writing modern-day versions of well-known tales such as "Little Red Riding Hood" with "Little Red Riding Hood on a Motorbike and the Wolf in a Lamborghini" can be quite successful.

STUDENT BIOGRAPHIES

Biographies and autobiographies can be written by students at all proficiency levels. Help beginners using a fill-in-the-blank form such as:

My name is _____. I am from_____. I like to _____.

More advanced students can interview each other and write about the person they interviewed. The stories can be typed up, accompanied by a photo of each student, and placed in a photo album or on a bulletin board.

Those preparing for academic study can do research and write about famous people.

PHOTOSTORIES

Photostories are cartoon-like books (Burnaby 1990), but students use photographs rather than drawings. Students can make their own photo stories by taking pictures or finding magazine pictures to help them build a story. You can also take pictures on a field trip to create a true story on a shared experience. Students write a caption under each picture. They can present the story in book format or as a poster on a large sheet of poster board. You can find an example in the book *Getting There: Producing Photo-Stories with Immigrant Women* (Barndt, Cristall, and Marino 1982).

ENVIRONMENTAL PRINT BOOKS

Used primarily with lower-level students, an environmental print book is made up of words from the students' immediate environment that they prepare themselves (e.g., in the classroom words include ceiling, floor, walls, whiteboard, pictures, door, windows, chairs, tables, etc.). You can also ask students to cut out all the ads they recognize, such as fast-food restaurant, cereal, and soft drink ads. To help the student build a sight vocabulary of these environmental print words, the teacher can circle words in the book and discuss them with students. The teacher then writes several circled words on index cards and places them on the appropriate page of each student's book. These words can be reviewed during each class until they are learned.

PICTURE BOOKS

Picture books are best used with students of lower-level English proficiency. Each student finds a picture of interest and mounts it in a notebook. The student writes a description of the picture on a sheet of paper. If the student writes only one or two words, the teacher or another student can transcribe the description as dictated orally by the student who chose the picture. Students hand in the written work, and the teacher corrects it by giving enough guidance so the message is comprehensible. Students rewrite the description under the picture in their notebook.

PERSONAL DICTIONARIES

Personal dictionaries are also best used with students at lower proficiency levels. This kind of dictionary can be a notebook, an elaborately bound hardcover book with blank pages, or one made with heavy construction paper for covers and newsprint for pages. Laminated covers will last longer. Ring binders allow for pages to be added or removed. Tabs on the edge of pages can indicate the letter of the alphabet.

Students put new words learned in or out of class in the dictionary. When a student asks how to spell a word, the teacher asks the student what letter the word might begin with. The student then finds the right page in the personal dictionary and writes the word as the teacher spells it.

Sometimes the teacher may know that the student already has the word in his or her personal dictionary or that other students have the word in theirs. Then the teacher only has to say, "It's in your dictionary" or "Ask Chris, it's in her dictionary" (Gunderson 1991).

BIG BOOKS

Big books are enlarged versions of original literature, usually stories or poems. Each page consists of one to three sentences with accompanying illustrations. The storyline is predictable, with a strong rhythm or rhyme and repeated patterns. The process for creating and teaching a big book is:

- Choose a book with an easily understood pattern and concepts that your students understand.
- Familiarize students with the story.
- Print a sentence or two of the exact text in large print at the top of large sheets of paper. Do the same for a title page. Color code vocabulary you wish to focus on.
- After discussing how the illustrations were made in the original text, brainstorm with your students alternative ways of illustrating the text, for example using crayon, fabric, cutting and pasting. Then, let them create the pictures.
- Help the students to reorganize and number the pages.
- Display the pages on a bulletin board or story clothesline, or bind them with staples and bookbinding tape, rings, or coil binding.
- Make an inside cover page. Include the names of the artists, publishing group, and the date. Additional features you can include are a picture of each student, extra pages for future reader comments, and a loan pocket. (Heald-Taylor 1986, 37–40)

Big books are typically for children, but you may have some success with them for older students. For example, a group of 12- and 13-year-old students may enjoy putting together an illustrated Signs of the Zodiac big book. The class can include the names of all the students in the class under the appropriate zodiac sign.

THEME BOOKS

In theme books, students write stories around a particular theme. For example, students could retell stories or legends introduced by a guest storyteller.

The stories are compiled into a book format. You can use a Duotang, laminated construction paper covers, or bound books with blank pages. Children enjoy making shape booklets, using a cover cut into a shape related to the theme (e.g., a rabbit, an apple, a coat). Some literacy organizations have published theme books of student stories. Themes may range from "my grandmother" to "my future plans," "job experiences," and "my greatest accomplishment."

Recipes are another possibility for a theme. If you have students from different countries, festival or holiday recipe books provide a way for students to learn more about one another.

Teacher-Created Written Text

It is not realistic to expect busy teachers to write a lot of original text, especially since authentic texts may be, as we've seen, the most useful materials and since graded readers and texts for ESL or EFL may be adequate in many instances. As a result, most of these suggestions for teacher-created text involve adaptations of existing material to produce interactive and simplified texts for your students.

First, be sure to select an existing written text that is of appropriate length and interest to your students and that meets class objectives. Ensure that it is organized in a way that is easy for students to follow. Each paragraph should have one main idea. Write simple sentences in the active voice. Retain some variety in sentence length to get students used to natural writing. Replace jargon and difficult and vague vocabulary with easier words, or provide context clues, including definitions, to help students. It is often content words for which you may need to provide context clues. Five ways to provide such clues are described by Lotherington-Woloszyn (1988) and Epstein (2001a) with examples of each and with the difficult word italicized and the clue underlined:

- **by definition.** For example, The Hebrew word *shalom* means peace in English and is also a greeting.
- **by restatement.** For example, *Katakana*, the Japanese writing system usually used for foreign words, is relatively easy to learn.
- **by example or illustration.** For example, It is said that the *circumflex accent* in French words, such as forêt, château and arrête, replaces a former s in the word.
- **by cause-effect.** For example, He caught *malaria* from mosquitoes carrying the disease.
- **by summary or explanation.** For example, In many Asian countries, people wrap a long, attractive piece of cloth around their lower torso, rather than wearing pants or skirts as we do in the West. This cloth is known as a *sarong*.

Lotherington-Woloszyn points out that long words are not necessarily difficult words (116). This is important to remember. A word like *hippopotamus*, for example, is not difficult because it has a very specific meaning and students can be shown a picture as an explanation. However, a short, common word like *use* may be difficult because it has many meanings and is harder to show or describe. In this case, you should use a more specific word.

While short texts do not overtax students' memories, a shorter text is not necessarily easier than a longer one because sufficient background information to aid understanding may not be present. Be sure that you provide this background either when adapting a written text or when presenting it in class through discussion and pre-reading activities. Address implicit information that requires inference; make sure that you replace between-the-lines information with explicit explanations, if that is needed for your students to understand the text. For example, a short article on Mahatma Gandhi may assume students know about his life and work. You may need to explicitly explain who he was and what he stood for to ensure they can make sense of what they are reading. Finally, be sure the layout and presentation follow the guidelines outlined earlier in this chapter.

Using Written Text

BIG BOOKS REVISITED

If you are ambitious and artistic, you can produce your own big books using the guidelines described on page 52 for student-created big books. Now you, not the students, draw the illustrations. Remember, however, that children enjoy participating in the creation of big books and may use them more if they have had a hand in making them.

CLOZE TEXTS

There are many variations to cloze texts. Commercial cloze texts usually leave out every sixth or seventh word, usually key words. Depending on your objectives, you can also choose to leave out punctuation or word classes such as adjectives, function words, or linking words. You could even delete the names and genders of characters and allow students to reconstruct the content of a text to assess their comprehension.

Lee Gunderson (1991) suggests beginning with individual cloze sentences before you ask ESL literacy students to complete cloze paragraphs. Remember, however, to put the sentence in some kind of context for students, perhaps through an oral discussion of the topic of the sentence. Following is a sample of sentence-level cloze:

"Angela made an appointment with the _____ because she has a toothache."

Note that this sentence contains information that is probably common knowledge to the students. It does not contain new or unfamiliar material.

Gunderson suggests that cloze passages for literacy students should be under one-half page in length initially, suggesting that very short stories with clear beginnings and endings are ideal for literacy students. He notes that cloze texts are difficult for students because some important context clues may have been removed. Because of this, he recommends that cloze passages should be at least two years below students' reading levels. He adds that they should not be used too often because they quickly become tedious. Both of these points are true for students at all proficiency levels. Cloze is suitable for students of all proficiency levels and for many purposes. For example, the CanTEST, a Canadian test similar to TOEFL®, includes cloze passages.

You can easily turn LEA (Language Experience Approach) into cloze passages by covering up target words on the chart paper with sticky notes. Students can read the text, predict what words go in the spaces, and remove the notes to verify their predictions.

STRIP STORIES

Strip stories are usually successful and, as Folse (1996) points out, require students to work together for a solution, or completed story. On separate slips of paper, write the sentences or paragraphs from a student-generated text, from a published text, or from a story you have written. Ask the students to read each slip and then put the sentences or paragraphs in order to make the original text. If you want to focus on sentence syntax, print parts of sentences on separate slips of paper. Ask students to read each section, and then put the parts together to form each sentence. You could even combine the sentences from two different texts and have students disentangle and order them.

JIGSAW READING

Jigsaw is a teaching strategy that promotes cooperative learning. The focus of cooperative learning, as the name implies, is setting up activities where students work together in groups or teams to accomplish a task. Cooperative learning contributes to academic achievement, language development, positive social attitudes and behaviors, intercultural and interracial relations, and self esteem. Jigsaw is a highly interactive technique that capitalizes on interdependence within groups. Jigsaw reading lessons are content based and use realistic or authentic readings or texts.

Materials for jigsaw reading involve three or four readings related to one topic. The best topics are motivational situations that lend themselves to being presented by three or four characters, each with a different point of view. For example, a story related to construction of a casino run by an Indigenous band in a small city could be told from the following four viewpoints: non-Indigenous citizens who oppose it (Group A), the Indigenous band members who support it (Group B), addiction counselors who oppose it (Group C), and politicians who both support and oppose it depending on their political motives (Group D). In a unique jigsaw, you would either have to write the stories (you can write at either one or at several proficiency levels depending on student needs) or find stories presented in a textbook, magazine, or newspaper that lend themselves to this technique. Here is the procedure for presenting the viewpoints from this example as a jigsaw.

1. Explain the topic of the jigsaw and engage student interest. For example, ask if they have ever gambled in a casino. Brainstorm casino vocabulary. Introduce new vocabulary from the reading before distributing handouts. Tell the students that each team is a city advisory group and that the aim of the jigsaw is to make a decision on whether or not a casino should be built.

2. Tell students that they will divide into four advisory teams. Each team will consist of representative stakeholders in the casino project—one citizen (from Group A, pink), one Indigenous Band member (from Group B, blue), an addiction counselor (from Group C, yellow), and one politician (from Group D, white). Divide the students into these advisory teams of four (mix proficiency levels if that is an issue in your classroom). Note that color coding using colored dots on each reading or colored paper will help you and the students keep track of what group and what advisory team they should be in.

3. Provide one reading to each student in an advisory team so that all of the group stakeholders are represented (i.e., Group A, pink; Group B, blue; Group C, yellow; and Group D, white). Each reading will be different,

according to what that particular stakeholder group believes. Also, each reading can vary in difficulty so that weaker students receive easier readings. When you create the readings, also create a vocabulary list and some comprehension and analysis questions to accompany each reading.

4. Tell students that they will need to break up their advisory team for 20 minutes so that experts from each group can analyze the evidence. Then have students physically move to stakeholder groups so that all of the students with Group A readings are together, all the students with Group B readings are together, all the students with Group C readings are together, and all the students with Group D readings are together. (You can see how color coding will help).

5. Tell the stakeholder groups (A, B, C, and D) to read their evidence, define the vocabulary, and answer the questions as a group. Explain that they will have to provide their view and teach vocabulary to their advisory team in 20 minutes. They should work together in their stakeholder group to make sure that they understand their viewpoint. They can rehearse with each other so that they do not have to refer to their handout too often when they return to their advisory team. You circulate and offer assistance as required.

6. In 20 minutes, ask students to reassemble into their advisory teams. Note that there again should be handouts of four different colors in each advisory team. They have 40 minutes to share each stakeholder's view and develop a decision on whether or not the casino should be built. The solution can be presented by the team in a written or oral report. You can assign a team grade. You can also have each student write a quiz to test individual learning.

It may take a few tries for you and your students to become familiar with the procedure and groupings. However, you will find the technique extremely effective to promote skills integration, a high degree of interaction, and reading benefits.

A major advantage of cooperative activities is that stronger students can be grouped with weaker students in multilevel classes. Furthermore, everyone has the opportunity to participate. An unintended outcome is often improved confidence in reading and in speaking.

When creating materials for a jigsaw reading, keep this in mind:

- create or adapt readings that focus on a problem, task, or controversy
- be sure that the reading addresses learner goals and needs, is interesting and engaging, and is age appropriate and of appropriate language proficiency
- divide the written text into manageable chunks that offer different viewpoints or solutions to a problem
- make vocabulary lists to accompany each reading
- make exercises to support comprehension of each reading
- color-code the reading for each stakeholder group
- give clear oral and written instructions when presenting the activity; have students repeat back the instructions to you to be sure they understand what to do

Published Written Text

Publisher catalogs and displays at conferences are the best places to look for written text designed specifically for ESL and EFL students; this includes books with simplified traditional literature that is accompanied by exercises and audiovisual supplements and associated websites. Browse a copy of a publisher's catalog to look for the types of texts listed and for those suitable for your students.

Online catalogs often contain more information about materials to help you. Remember to peruse your local library and bookstore for authentic texts. Variety in text is important in developing reading skills and in meeting students' interests and needs. Different text types also serve different teaching objectives, so don't limit your students to any one type of published material.

Newspapers

Your local newspaper is an excellent teaching and learning resource. You should be able to find material of interest to children as well as adults in the visuals, ads, and in some columns of a paper. It is worth incorporating newspaper reading into the curriculum, even at beginning levels. Basic readers can use the newspaper to become familiar with numbers, the alphabet, recurrent symbols, punctuation, and upper and lower case. James Patrie (1988) asserts that beginning students will gain confidence using the newspaper and will learn newspaper writing conventions through early exposure.

Immigrants can gain a great deal of useful information: advertisements, for example, allow price comparisons that will help them in their shopping. Patrie suggests newspaper activities related to comparison shopping, combined with a field trip to a grocery store, will be relevant and interesting to newcomers. Information on holidays, seasons, and entertainment is usually presented succinctly and introduces students to local culture as well. One of the advantages of newspaper writing is that articles contain all of the main information (who, what, where, when, why) in the first paragraph or two. Also, North American newspapers often include clear, eye-catching visuals with captions supporting what is written in the column that can be used as springboards for pre-reading discussion. It is important to take note of international news, especially news coming from students' countries of origin. Or students can select articles of interest to them, clip them, and post them on the bulletin board for the interest of others in the class. Students may be reading similar news from newspapers in their native language (remember that international newspapers are often available on the Internet). For example, comparing how a sports or political event is covered locally and in the country of origin is interesting for students.

Patrie also suggests that when using the newspaper with students at lower-proficiency levels, use it in the same way a native speaker does. That is, selectively read columns of personal relevance and immediate concern. This is why it is important that the newspapers that you or your students bring to class are current. Fortunately, newspaper publishers may make the newspaper available at a reduced rate or even free for educational purposes. Some newspaper publishers welcome tours of their plant. Some larger newspapers offer educational exercises and supplements to accompany their paper.

For intermediate and advanced students, the ability to choose relevant, up-to-date articles makes the newspaper a rich resource. You might choose articles that refer to immigration and employment issues that may affect students or articles that refer to news in the students' countries of origin and to their interests, such as sports, entertainment, or recipes.

ESL and literacy newspapers like *Easy English News* or *News for You* are available online and in many jurisdictions. These newspapers may be graded for different proficiency levels. The articles may be shortened and simplified with additional visuals and a layout designed specially to meet the needs of ESL and new readers. Some of these newspapers even contain supplementary activities or teaching suggestions for classroom use. Check your local libraries, literacy and ESL institutions, and government education offices for information on these newspapers.

You may not have easy access to newspapers if you are teaching in an isolated EFL context. In larger centers abroad, you will find some news agencies that sell English papers. You can also find a large variety of newspapers on the Internet. If you are planning to teach in an EFL context, consider taking a few newspapers or a file of recent clippings with you. You may find that tabloid newspapers are hot items with students, even though you may not want your students to spend all of their time reading this type of material.

Other Published Materials

- **Magazines**—Remember the reading period anecdote at the beginning of this chapter? Adult and teenage students at any level often enjoy browsing through magazines, much as they do in their first language. Many magazines contain pictures and photo advertisements that aid inference. It's a good idea to have a selection of magazines on hand in your classroom for students to browse in spare moments or during time set aside for pleasure reading. Choose magazines that will interest your students from the wide variety available—sports, news, car, computers, beauty and fashion, cooking, science and nature, and geography. Some schools subscribe to ESL magazines and magazines for school-age students. Students may enjoy these as a change from their textbooks. Compilations of student writings are also available in magazine format.

- **Short stories, fairy tales, fables, myths, and legends**—Authentic texts and ESL/EFL readers are readily available. Check bookstores and publisher catalogs.

- **Novels and storybooks**—Authentic, abridged, simplified, and graded versions are available. Again, check bookstores and publisher catalogs.

- **Life texts**—Collections of student writings about life experiences are increasingly being published in book form. Often they are written around a theme. You can find these items in local libraries or in a variety of non-governmental organizations (e.g., settlement agencies and literacy organizations), such as the "grandmother" and "my first job" theme books described earlier.

- **Jigsaw readings**—As previously outlined, you can make your own jigsaw readings. However, many ESL and EFL textbooks now include them.
- **Questionnaires**—You can find questionnaires, surveys and human interest self-tests in magazines and newspapers. Consider students' comfort level with topics when choosing. Students can do them on their own, in pairs, or as the basis of a class survey.
- **Picture dictionaries**—Picture dictionaries for elementary, high school, and adult students are available from publishing companies. Some publishers have bilingual picture dictionaries in several languages.
- **Real world text**—These realia include recipes, cereal boxes, how-to manuals, medicine containers, and manuals.
- **Recipe books**—Believe it or not, recipe books are popular choices for pleasure reading with some adult students. Books with pictures are even better. You may notice students busily copying recipes during free reading periods.
- **Case studies**—ESL and EFL textbooks sometimes contain case studies. *Business across Cultures* by Laura English (1995) is just one is example of a textbook that uses case studies.

Don't forget the big books, strip stories, and photo-stories described earlier in this chapter.

Developing Activities for Written Text

So, you've selected or developed a suitable text for your students. How are you going to use it? Lotherington-Woloszyn (1988) notes that it is important that you provide a purpose for student reading and that you match the task to the written text that you are presenting. Some of these tasks include following instructions, finding references, obtaining information, entertaining or helping someone, summarizing course notes, or taking a memo or phone message.

Sandra Silberstein (1987) suggests giving realistic reading tasks in terms of both context and level of difficulty. For example, don't ask students to carefully read material that we ordinarily would just scan in real life. Reading passages should determine appropriate reading tasks; a text typically scanned for one piece of information is not suitable for extensive grammatical analysis of the verb tense in which it is written.

A personal subject response activity, such as response journaling (Shih 1999), is more suitable after reading certain kinds of text. In this type of writing, students are asked to record their own reactions to the story or article.

Copyright

As mentioned in Chapter 2, copyright law exists to legally recognize creators' rights to control the uses of their works and to be compensated for those uses. Copyright regulations apply to most forms of written text. You must learn about copyright restrictions for your teaching context, whether it is in North America or abroad.

The United States, for example, has a fair use for education policy. Canada's copyright laws have permitted educators to make single copies of periodical articles, short stories, and chapters from books. However, the law does not permit multiple copying of works for teaching purposes, so you must apply to the copyright holder listed in the title page of the book or journal and sometimes pay a fee for copying.

Some ESL and EFL activity books allow photocopying of pages. Look for whether or not the material is reproducible. This is usually indicated on the pages that can be reproduced or in the marketing materials. With these books, you may photocopy as needed. Look for grammar tests or other activity books, such as *Testing Academic Reading Processes* (Altano 2005) or *101 Clear Grammar Tests* (Folse, Ivone, and Pollgreen 2005).

CHAPTER 4

Visual Aids:
Pictures, Charts, and Realia

THE DUAL IDENTITY OF LANGUAGE TEACHERS

By day they are ordinary people, by night they are scavengers—picking up and storing in plastic bags and in boxes unusual and everyday objects and pictures. You might find them ferreting through closets, medicine cabinets, or the fridge and flipping through piles of old magazines and calendars. Suddenly, a gleam comes into their eyes. With a swift movement they reach quickly for an object or deftly rip out a picture. You know who they are—they are English language teachers! Begging, stealing, borrowing, taking, and creating visual aids themselves. Why? Because they know the truth of the Russian proverb, "It's better to see once than hear one hundred times."

We hope that working through this chapter will help you improve your scavenging and creative skills in order to provide and use effective visual material in your classroom.

This chapter includes:

- how to select and classify pictures for use in the language class
- how to use pictures, charts, and realia
- how to use key visuals to aid in teaching language and content

Some Challenging Questions

Before you begin, answer these questions:

- Have you ever found yourself scavenging for visual aids? Why did you do this? What were you looking for?
- Do you recall a learning experience when the teacher used visuals? Did this help you learn? In what way(s)?
- Do you use visual material in your teaching? How?
- Do you keep files of images? If so, how has this helped your teaching? If it has not helped, why not?

The Importance of Visual Aids

According to Doff (1990), Curtain and Dahlberg (2004), and our own experience, visual aids are an important part of effective language teaching because

- They can focus attention on meaning in a concrete way.
- They can simplify and provide focus on the core content in a language and content class.
- They can give students something to look at, holding their attention and adding interest (Doff 1990).
- Some students may feel less self-conscious and more ready to speak up in class if their attention is focused on an image.
- A visual aid can often represent an idea or demonstrate the use of a grammatical structure more efficiently than a verbal explanation; students may remember images longer than lengthy verbal or written explanations.
- Visuals can demonstrate how and why to use a particular type of language. For example, Larsen-Freeman's (2000) "form, meaning, use" pie charts clarify structures to students visually.
- As speaking cues, visuals help students to produce the forms expected without unnecessary memory work.
- Visual materials can provide a context or function as an advance organizer for dialogue work and for certain reading and listening texts.
- Images can support and clarify reading and listening texts for students.
- Visual aids can help students think in English by encouraging them to relate language to the meaning inherent in the visual, rather than relating language to their mother tongue.
- They can stimulate the imagination and arouse interest in a topic.
- Visual material provides a link between the classroom and the world outside the classroom.

Characteristics of Good Visuals

As you hunt for visual aids, look for a variety of characteristics, such as being

- attractive, bold, and clear
- motivational, adding outside interests into the classroom
- adaptable to many language levels and various teaching objectives
- suitable for your students' age, interests, and experiences
- large enough to be clearly visible to everyone in the class or the group
- simple, without too many distracting details

For example, to illustrate the concept of "same and different," one ESL teacher we know uses four colored squares of paper—two pink ones placed side by side and one black and one pink placed together. There is genius in simplicity!

Types of Visual Aids and Their Uses

Reflect on your own teaching or language learning experience, and then place a check mark beside those visuals that you use or have used as a teacher or have used as a language learner. Briefly describe how they were used in the space provided in the chart.

Visual Aid	✓	Uses
drawings		*to explain expressions, vocab.*
magazine pictures		
photographs		*family tree*
flash cards		
wall charts		
graphs		
maps	✓	*giving directions.*
forms, such as hospital registration or job applications		
real objects (realia) such as clothing, food, medicine bottles		

Old calendars and sales flyers, as well as magazines, are excellent sources of pictures. If you don't subscribe to magazines yourself, garage sales, friends, colleagues, and libraries may be sources of back issues that you can cut up. Some English language teaching institutions have developed picture files for teachers—inquire at your workplace. There are also English language teaching resource books containing photocopiable pictures or series of photos to cut out for activities. The Internet is another source of pictures. Clearly, there are many ways to use teaching aids. This chapter will examine each of these types of visual materials. You may wish to return to this chart at the end of the chapter to add more ideas for using each type of visual.

Drawings

There will be times when you are unable to find an image in a magazine or from some other source or when spontaneity demands that you draw something on the board for students. This is when you will want to be able to make simple line drawings. The goal is to quickly create and reproduce line drawings once you know the content you want. If possible, arrange to observe other teachers who are well known for their skill in creating effective drawings for their students.

Many of us *think* we can't draw. You can draw simple illustrations to help students construct meaning. You can draw something that looks like a person—even a stick figure. You can draw features on a stick figure to make it look like a cat versus a dog. The trick is to keep it simple. Too often, teachers try to add too many details to drawings in an attempt to make them realistic rather than representative. You really can draw almost anything with a few simple lines and shapes. Don't worry if you can't create "perfect" drawings. Allow yourself to make mistakes, to have fun, and to experiment, and you'll probably be pleasantly surprised with the results. We will not attempt here to teach you how to draw because there are resources to help you to do that. However, we do encourage you to take some paper and pencil and try the following:

- draw a face using only a round circle for the head and experimenting with changing the shape of the eyes and mouth
- draw a stick body, again experimenting with changing the positions of the arms and legs
- draw a stick snake, cat, dog, pig. For the ambitious, try a cow or horse.
- draw the map of your school or neighborhood
- copy a few simple magazine pictures (You may want to start by tracing!)

If you want to learn more about doing simple line drawings, refer to Andrew Wright's (1984) book *1000 Pictures for Teachers to Copy* or Bruce M. Watson's (1983) book *Drawing in the Classroom: A Handbook for Teachers of English as a Second Language*.

Magazine Pictures

Sources

Magazines, calendars, brochures, postcards, greeting cards, catalogs, clip art, flyers, and the Internet are all good picture sources. Different kinds of magazines—fashion, science and nature, travel, sports and hobby—will yield different kinds of pictures. Today, an Internet search will result in a plethora of images useful for the classroom. Pictures from these sources are usually authentic, colourful, clear, and attractive. The element of realism they provide can make them an appealing change from board drawings or cartoons.

Occasionally you will find pictures that are clear enough and large enough in the newspaper. This is especially important if current affairs is part of your curriculum. Pictures the size of a magazine page are large enough to use with a class of 15 to 20 students. With larger classes, you can show the picture to different sections of the class at a time. You can use smaller pictures for small group work and games.

Selecting Pictures for a Picture File or Library

When developing your image collection, it is not important to know exactly what you will do with each picture; you don't want to reject pictures that could prove useful later (McAlpin 1983). What is more important is to apply the six characteristics of good visuals mentioned earlier.

When collecting small pictures, include more than one of most items because students may use them in groups or pairs. In this way, you can avoid frantically searching for one more image when preparing a lesson or game for several groups of students.

Classifying and Storing Pictures

Devising a system for classifying illustrations will make your pictures much more accessible to you when you need them. If you have been teaching the same course for a long time, it is possible to organize your pictures according to your syllabus. However, this can limit their use and, as McAlpin notes, assumes that you know precisely what you will do with each picture once you have selected it. We suggest classifying your images according to content. This system is versatile, especially if you are teaching many different levels and types of language courses.

Some useful categories for pictures are described, based on McAlpin and our own experience. When you are beginning your collection, these categories may also prove helpful in selecting pictures. In each category, look for pictures that are representative of your students' culture and the target culture.

- **People portraits**—Look for pictures that focus on individuals, couples, families, or small groups of people. Look also for pictures of old and young, big and small, poor and rich, and people with interesting expressions. Avoid fashion pictures because the range of personalities and characteristics that can be illustrated by the models is limited.
- **Famous people**—Look for pictures of famous people from the target culture and the students' cultures. An Internet search will facilitate finding these. Include politicians, musicians, actors, artists, athletes, and historical figures. Write who they are on the back of the picture.
- **Landscapes and places**—Look for variety and write the location on the back of the picture.
- **Buildings**—Collect different types of structures, such as office towers, historic monuments, different types of homes, churches, and factories.

- **Transportation**—Look for cars, buses, trains, planes, bicycles, and baby carriages.
- **Animals and plants**—Collect different kinds of plants for talking about likes and dislikes; comparisons; and various descriptions related to size, shape, colors, and patterns.
- **Sports**—The possibilities here are endless, and sports magazines and the Internet are the best sources.
- **Occupations**—Look for pictures of people of both genders involved in different occupations. Peruse publishers' products of work-related pictures.
- **Everyday situations and activities**—Look for illustrations of people eating, shopping, playing, or dancing.
- **Ceremonies**—Look for wedding, funeral, and graduation pictures.
- **Food and drink**—This large category is especially useful for teaching partitives, count and mass nouns, as well as names of different foods. These pictures are also a source of substitution prompts for shopping and restaurant situations, and most students are interested in talking about food!
- **Unusual situations and curiosities**—You may find oddities and fantasy pictures in advertisements or art sources. Pictures that are ambiguous can be used to provoke discussion, speculation, surprise, and amusement. Such pictures could include almost anything—a person peeking out from behind a door, someone in handcuffs, a man on the phone with a disconcerted look on his face, a demonstration, a fire. You and your students can also cut and paste to make your own collages of ambiguous or unusual situations.
- **Other objects**—This could develop into a large category that you may want to subdivide into other categories, such as appliances, clothes, furniture. You can compare color, number, size, function, and characteristics, or describe spatial relationships with the variety of objects in your collection of other objects.

Some of these categories overlap, so you may want to file them beside each other (e.g., all the people pictures together and all the everyday situations and activities together). Or, you can arrange your categories alphabetically. Depending on the size of your collection, you can use file folders and a box for your collection. If file folders aren't big enough, you can use hanging files and a file cabinet. For small pictures, use envelopes placed inside file folders.

Preparing Pictures

Many pictures include captions. Captions usually distract from your purpose for using the picture. Cut off the words or cover them with a colored pen.

To cut out your pictures as cleanly as possible, put a thin card under the page and using a razor knife or box cutter, follow the shape you want. If you are cutting through thick card for a backing, using many light strokes will eventually cut through. If children are helping, use only scissors. For straight edges and larger pictures, a paper cutter works best. (McAlpin, 20–21)

Mount pictures on a surface stiffer than paper to make them last longer and to prevent light from shining through when you hold them up in class. Use a backing larger than the picture to protect the edges. Taping all the edges with plastic tape adds strength and helps to protect the pictures. Another way to ensure image longevity is lamination, but the shiny surface can obscure pictures somewhat. You can use clear plastic folders instead and take them out of the folders, if necessary. You only need a few plastic folders, enough for the pictures you will be using during any one lesson.

Activities for Using Drawings and Pictures

There are endless ways to use pictures. You can use pictures to present new language to your class and in practice activities in which students use visuals to practice language already presented. In this section, we include the following uses: teaching meaning, practicing grammar, practicing descriptions, enhancing writing, and posing problems. We also discuss picture stories and using pictures that students find.

Developing Picture Activities for Teaching Meaning

Usually a single image is too ambiguous to teach the meaning of a new item. Instead, we suggest that you use several examples to direct students' attention to similarities, such as three people reading to show "reading" or different people working at different tasks to show "working." It can also be easier to use pictures to teach contrasting concepts rather than teaching one meaning by itself—a man and a woman contrasts gender, images of happy situations and unhappy situations contrast these emotions, white and black images contrast light and dark.

Some concepts need to be illustrated in a sequence of events. For example, the concept of a process, such as how to make an omelet, can be illustrated by a picture or series of pictures. Also cause and effect relationships such as *he went to jail because he robbed a bank* need two visuals—a robbery and a jail. For sequences or stories that you create, you usually won't be able to show the same person doing things in each scene, but you can find pictures of objects and places to represent the actions. Books such as *LexiCarry* by Pat Moran (2002) contain picture sequences depicted in simple drawings.

Many teachers like to present new language to beginners in story form, using the Natural Approach to language teaching (Richards and Rodgers 2001). In a typical lesson for beginners on stating personal information, choose pictures of two to three individuals from the People Portraits category. Develop the identities of the people according to whether you want to focus on the action or on the people and on the target culture or on the students' culture. Your choices will depend on teaching goals, student interests, and picture availability. A lesson on describing daily activities of people may require different images than a lesson on describing physical appearance and clothing. With a group of immigrant women, you might choose pictures of women from various countries. Or in an EFL context you might choose pictures of individuals who are representative of the students' own and the target culture(s). You might also choose pictures of the places where the picture characters live. Create links among the characters to create interest as in a real story. For example, they might all work for the same company or they might all be related in some way. Repeat the same structures and type of information about each person in order to provide repetition in the structure on which you are focusing. Here is a sample story:

Picture 1: This is Rosa from the Philippines. She loves dresses. She hates jeans.

Picture 2: This is Michel from Quebec, in Canada. He loves jeans. He hates ties.

Picture 3: This is Tolik from the Ukraine. He loves ties, but he hates t-shirts.

Repeat the information at least once before proceeding to controlled practice with the pictures. For this step, ask questions about the people in the following sequence:

- Yes-No questions, for example, *Is this Rosa? Is Rosa from Quebec?*
- Alternative questions, for example, *Does Tolik love ties or jeans?*
- Information questions, for example, *Where is Michel from? What does he hate?*
- Personalize questions by asking students to provide the same information about themselves as that presented in the story, for example, *Do you like t-shirts? Are you from Ukraine?*

After further practice with language used in the story, you may choose to extend the activity. For example, you may want to show another picture of someone and have the class make up a story about that person. Free practice with different people pictures can follow in a later lesson, with pairs of students choosing a people picture from your collection and making up their own stories using your model as a guide. Students then present their character to another pair of students. The activity can end with a writing exercise. In our experience, students usually enjoy using pictures in this and other ways that allow them to use their imagination to create a story, description, or dialogue.

Developing Picture Activities for Grammar and Vocabulary Practice

Some examples from the variety of activities that you can develop for presenting and practicing grammar with pictures follow.

"WHO AM I?" TO PRACTICE SIMPLE SENTENCES

Choose a category, such as famous people. Give each student a picture of someone such as Oprah Winfrey or Tiger Woods. In small groups, students play 20 Questions. Teams of students take turns asking yes-no questions in order to determine who the person is. Students can ask no more than 20 questions (we suggest limiting this to 10 questions per student). A variation on this game is, "What am I?" in which students have a picture of an object.

MODALS

A way of using pictures to practice modals of possibility (e.g., *could, might*) is to introduce the activity by asking students to suggest possibilities for an ambiguous picture: *What do you think the man is going to do next? How do you think the accident happened?* Or, show only part of a picture as in the example that follows, and have students guess what the entire picture depicts. Reveal more and more of the picture as the activity progresses. You can do this activity with drawings by having students guess what you or another student is in the process of drawing on the board. Try this one with a friend to see what kind of language it generates. In *Recipes for Tired Teachers*, Ian Butcher (1985) provides an interesting series of pictures for modal practice.

WH- QUESTIONS

For use of *wh-* questions you can use newspaper photos without the article or captions (like the one above) and ask students to discuss the news event. Ask them to answer questions in small groups or as a class: *Who is in the picture? What is happening or has happened? Where is this event taking place? When do you think this is?* Then pairs, small groups, or individuals will write a story about the news event. You can post these on the bulletin board for the entire class to read.

COMPARATIVES

A friend who was teaching in Japan used pictures of sumo wrestlers to practice comparisons. Student groups decided who was the youngest, oldest, largest, smallest, heaviest, lightest, most skilled, most popular, and cutest wrestler. Of course you could do this with picture series of many sports figures or other internationally famous people . . . or not use famous people.

CONCENTRATION/PICTIONARY®

Play Concentration to help students practice and remember new vocabulary. Have a set of pictures and then duplicate it so that you have an identical set (e.g., in a review of clothing vocabulary you would have two pictures of dresses, two pictures of shoes, two pictures of jackets, etc.). To play the game, lay the cards face down on a table. Students take turns turning over two cards, reading or saying aloud the word represented in the picture. If the cards match, the student who found the match takes the cards from the table and makes up a sentence with the word in it. That student then gets another turn, continuing until a mismatch occurs. A student who fails to get a match turns the cards back over again. The student with the most pairs at the end, after all cards have been matched, is the winner. From two to four players are best for each card set.

ESL Pictionary can also be used for vocabulary development and generates student drawings that you may be able to use as materials for future lessons. In this game, the teacher writes vocabulary items on separate pieces of paper or cards. Students work in teams. One student takes a card and tries to illustrate its meaning to team members by drawing it within a time limit. Team members must guess the word and use it in a sentence.

Developing Picture Activities for Practicing Descriptions

SPOT THE DIFFERENCE

"Spot the difference" pictures are common in ESL and EFL books. Or you can draw them yourself or find them in other sources (our local newspaper includes these weekly). Give pairs of students almost identical pictures with a lot of detail. They must look for and describe the differences between the two pictures.

PICTURE PUZZLES

Cut up several pictures into a three- to four-piece puzzle and then have students describe their piece of the puzzle to each other without showing their piece. They have to find the other pieces of their picture. Landscapes and groups scenes such as parties or picnics lend to this kind of picture activity. Hadfield's *Advanced Communication Games* (1997) contains several cartoon-like scenes to cut up and have students reassemble.

EYE WITNESS

Eye Witness is an amusing activity for practicing reporting and recounting. A picture of a crime, a fire, or an accident from your unusual pictures file works well for this activity. Find a busy street with many people because of the number of characters and possibilities the picture presents. The activity works like this:

- Divide students into groups. Display the visual.
- Explain that one person from each group was at the scene and witnessed the entire episode. If you are using an image with several people near the scene, the witness can identify himself or herself and the culprit in the picture.
- A second person from each group is a reporter who finds out what happened.
- Each group is responsible for assigning the two characters and helping them create the story and the questions to be asked by the reporter. Reporters from each group also need to interview eyewitnesses from another group. In this way, stories will not be known and there will be an element of improvisation.

Developing Picture Activities for Writing

Use pictures as the basis of writing activities, such as descriptions, narrations, personal responses, and cloze passages.

DESCRIPTIVE WRITING FOR EARLY WRITERS

In this activity, the teacher shows a picture of someone performing an action—for example, children playing in the snow—and writes on the board: "The children are playing."

The students add to it:

- "The happy children are playing."
- "The happy children are playing in the snow."
- "The happy children are playing in the snow in their colorful snowsuits." (Cassar 1990)

Guide students in the type of descriptive words or phrases to add, depending on your teaching objectives, for example, single-word adjectives or adverbs, or prepositional phrases to describe places or time. Students can take turns adding descriptors, or they can work in pairs with a list of types and number of descriptors to add.

COLLABORATIVE WRITTEN BIOGRAPHIES

One collaborative writing activity that combines narration and description is based on portrait pictures. The goal is to write biographies of the people in various pictures selected by the students.

- Each student chooses a picture of a person and attaches a sheet of paper to it.
- Divide the class into small groups. Each small group sits in a circle.
- Students assign the person in their portrait a name and write a sentence about the person.
- Students then pass their pictures to the right, and the next person adds one sentence of further biographical information (age, occupation, hobbies).
- Students continue passing the pictures and adding details until they receive their original picture back.
- Now that more is known about the people in the pictures, students begin a narration by contributing two sentences before passing it on. Narration topics can be a typical day, yesterday, tomorrow, or a special event in the life of the character.
- Possible follow-up might include using the narration as a source of common errors on which to work or for role plays (Grace and Pigott 1991).

Developing Picture Activities for Problem-Posing

A problem-posing approach to language teaching, based on Paulo Freire's (1981) approach to literacy instruction, involves the use of pictures or objects to represent problems of vital importance to the students. We suggest that you use pictures of different local housing conditions in the area to provoke a discussion of rent, problems with neighbors, security issues, and so on, as an example. The teacher uses the picture and a series of questions to guide students through a process of identifying and describing the problem, analyzing its causes and proposing solutions. Drawings, films, posters, objects, and role plays can also be used to present a problem.

Language and Culture in Conflict by Wallerstein (1982) and *ESL for Action: Problem-Posing at Work* by Auerbach and Wallerstein (1987) have problem-posing activities.

Picture Stories

Picture sequences are useful for describing a process, but they also work well as the basis of a story. Ambiguity in terms of how the story can be sequenced provides additional reason for discussion. Picture stories work well with literacy students and students at low-proficiency levels. Often a page in length, a series of about ten pictures can help students generate the meaning and main ideas of a story without direct translation. Through picture stories, students will learn to recognize sequences and make connections between images and written language. It is often effective to choose or make picture stories that have a conflict and realism to maintain interest and aid in retention.

The steps that follow are a general outline for using picture stories. They can be adapted to accommodate various levels:

- Students look at pictures and generate related vocabulary they know, while the teacher jots down this vocabulary on the board. The teacher might begin by asking students, *What do you see in the first picture?*
- The teacher reflects back students' comments about the picture in correct English.
- Students progress through the pictures and try to guess the story.
- Students practice retelling the story in pairs or collectively.
- Students are then given written words that accompany the pictures and do various activities to connect a word or phrase to the appropriate picture.
- Students read the text, in order, with the associated pictures.
- Follow-up activities can include scrambled text and cloze activities, concentration with pictures and descriptive sentences or with selected words from the text. You can also remove all the words and have students rewrite as much of the story as they can using only the pictures. (Based on Ligon and Tannenbaum 1990)

The pictures used in picture stories are usually drawn. Red Riding Hood, for example, can be illustrated as on page 73.

The advantage of drawing the illustrations yourself is that you can adapt them to make the story more meaningful to your students. In the example, the story is modernized by having Grandma watching TV with a remote control in her hand rather than lying in bed reading a book, as illustrated in traditional renditions of this story. You may, for example, change the bowls of porridge to rice in a culturally adapted version of "Goldilocks and the Three Bears."

Well-produced and relevant commercial pictures stories are also available. *Picture Stories: Language and Literacy Activities for Beginners* by Ligon and Tannenbaum (1990) is a good source of amusing picture stories based on situations especially relevant to new immigrants. You can also use cartoon strips and white-out the captions. Children's picture books are another excellent source. If you are making copies of cartoons, make sure you adhere to copyright law.

Students might also enjoy creating their own picture stories and illustrated storybooks, using characters in a book, a famous character, or an invented character. You may want to specify a situation such as being at the zoo, Thanksgiving, or visiting grandmother. Provide each student with a paper divided into squares (six squares is an appropriate number) for creating their sequence of pictures.

Student-Found Pictures

You can have students find their own magazine pictures for vocabulary review.

- To practice descriptions, feelings, colors—Students find pictures of a room they like and one they don't like. They list adjectives that describe the rooms and then give oral descriptions of each room to another student. They can describe and compare why they like one room and not the other and discuss this with their partner.

- To learn the names of objects that appeal to different senses—Students find pictures of something they like to eat, hear, smell, touch, or taste. They then find the names of these items and label them. Some of the items can be displayed on a table with their labels for class vocabulary development.

- To review previously taught vocabulary—Students find pictures and write related sentences under them. The sentences must illustrate the meaning of key vocabulary from a unit or week of study (Hart 2000).

In several of the other chapters of this book you will find other ideas for using pictures, as prompts for drills, to provide a context for dialogue practice and to aid in character development for role-play activities.

Photographs

Digital cameras and images available on the Internet now make it more feasible to use photographs. Photographs of students and their experiences provide a wonderful basis for oral and written language practice. It is also gratifying for students to work with photos of themselves. Because of the relevancy photographs provide, it's often worth putting up with the inconveniences of size if you are not able to project the image. Digital cameras in combination with computers and data projectors result in excellent teaching materials, but you may not have access to the equipment. High-tech options are discussed in more detail in Chapter 6.

Here are some suggestions for using photographs:

- Students write captions for pictures taken on a field trip and pasted on a large sheet of poster board. They can also mount the pictures individually on small sheets of construction paper or in a photo album to create a storybook.
- Take pictures of a story or process that students act out. You or the students can write captions for each picture and, again, create a storybook or poster.
- Use school pictures or take pictures yourself of each student to accompany student biographies. Compile them in a photo album or binder, or display them on the bulletin board. You might decide to feature a number of student biographies monthly on your bulletin board.

The activity that follows, originally suggested for use with projected slides, can also be done with projected digital photographs. The activity promotes the use of scenes or actions such as a hockey player who has just passed the puck to a teammate, or a swimming pool full of children playing (Duncan 1987, 20–21).

- You can ask your students to imagine themselves in a projected image and describe the context and how they feel.
- Let them ask for the vocabulary they need to discuss their feelings.
- Students prepare a skit in which they will act out what goes on in the slide scene. As many students as possible will participate. You can divide students in small groups for this activity.
- The students role-play the slide beginning with a still scene and moving into a 1- to 2-minute skit that includes sound and movement.

Flashcards

Preparation and Classification

Flashcards are useful for showing simple pictures of objects or actions. The size of cards you select depends on how you plan to use them. They need to be a size that is easy to handle and store. If you are going to show them to the class and describe some feature of the pictures, the cards need to be big enough to be seen at the back of the class. You can make cards from boxes, notepad backs, or card stock paper. You can use small pictures from magazines or brochures or line drawings for flashcards. Buckby and Wright (1981) make these suggestions for flashcard preparation:

1. If you are drawing the pictures, make bold lines.
2. If the line drawing is complicated, try filling in some of the areas with color for ease of recognition. Remember, however, that color can be distracting. Use it to help make something more recognizable (e.g., yellow for corn) or to direct attention to a particular detail.
3. If you are using magazine pictures, fix them to the cards with glue or self-adhesive putty or cover them with self-adhesive clear plastic.

As with larger magazine pictures, you can divide cards into categories. These categories might include hobbies, geography, travel, people, food, sports, and shopping. Keep your flashcards in large envelopes or a recipe box, according to category.

Uses of Flashcards

You can use flashcards for teaching pronunciation, vocabulary, structure, and functions. The most basic way of using flashcards to introduce new language is:

- Show the flashcard and describe some aspect of it (e.g., "It's cloudy and rainy.").
- The class repeats the description.
- You ask a question to elicit the original description again (e.g., "What's the weather like?").

You can use flashcards as vocabulary drills. After presenting the new vocabulary, put cards associated with the new words face up on the table. When you say the word, the first person to grab the card gets to keep it. The person with the most cards at the end gets to be the caller in the next game. If you have a duplicate set of picture cards, you may use the flashcards to play Concentration (described earlier).

The types of questions described for working with a Natural Approach picture story work well for flashcard practice. You can ask these types of questions based on the story:

- Yes/No questions, for example, *Is she hungry?*
- Alternative questions, for example, *Is she hungry or angry?*
- Open questions, for example, *How does she feel?*

You can use these three types of questions in a multilevel class to challenge students according to their abilities.

You can also use flashcards to practice grammatical structures. For example, students can practice the past tense in a drill with flashcards. Ask students, "What did you do yesterday?" according to activities depicted on a series of flashcards. This can be a teacher-controlled activity or done as pair work.

There are many innovative ways of using flashcards for pair and small group practice after you have presented a specific language point. Here are some examples:

- People and Weather Flashcards—the two categories of cards are placed face down on the table in two separate piles. Student A takes a card from each pile. The student may pick, for example, a picture of a rain cloud from the weather category and a line drawing of a little girl from the people category. Student A then asks the other students in the group, "What do you think she does when it's raining?"

    Other students: "I imagine she watches TV." or "I think she plays inside." (Responses will vary.)

    Student A: "Yes, you're right." or "No, I don't think so."

- Food Flashcards—One student plays the role of a server in a restaurant and holds all the cards in the food category. The other students take turns trying to order food. The server responds according to whether or not he has a picture of what is asked for.

    Server: "What would you like?"

    Customer: "I would like some ice cream."

    Server: "Oh, I'm sorry. We don't have any ice cream." or "We're all out of ice cream." or "Yes, of course."

- Hobbies and Weather Flashcards

    Student A: "What do you want to do?"

    Student B: (takes a hobby card of a bicycle or of someone cycling) "Let's go cycling."

    Student A: (takes a weather card) "Sounds great. The weather's perfect for cycling." or "No, we better not. It's _____." (makes a statement about the weather based on the picture that is picked, e.g., "too cold").

- Use the two sides to contrast two concepts or verbal forms. For example, on one side of the card show a picture of a pregnant woman to illustrate the phrase, "She's going to have a baby." On the other side of the card show a woman holding a baby to illustrate, "She had a baby." Or, you may use two sides of a card to illustrate "over" and "under.")

- Use a longer, rectangular card with two folds to illustrate and practice three tense forms or use separate cards as illustrated.

Flashcards for Language Learning by Buckby and Wright (1981) created these activities and contains many other practice activities for flashcards.

Charts and Graphs

Charts and graphs contain more complex visual information than flashcards or single images. They may combine photographs, drawings, symbols, graphs, and written text. Charts are effective teaching tools. Displayed charts, often called Wall Charts, enhance the classroom environment, are good references, and act as memory aids for students. They are big enough for students to refer to easily in class.

Wall Charts

GRAMMAR WALL CHARTS

Grammar charts focus on a particular structure, with or without the aid of pictures. You can make them according to needs as in this example:

I am

You are

He is

She is

We are

They are

LANGUAGE LADDERS

Language ladders are charts for teaching classroom expressions as shown.

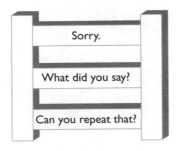

You can post the language ladder, adding to it as necessary.

TOPIC AND VOCABULARY WALL CHARTS

A number of government agencies and publishers offer illustrated vocabulary charts. For example nutrition, weather, maps, and body parts wall charts are common. Your students can make their own illustrated vocabulary charts by topic or theme using magazines pictures or their own drawings.

IDIOM WALL CHARTS

You can create a running list of idioms that students are learning on a chart. List the idioms in three columns: one for the idioms, one for definitions of the idioms, and one that states when and when not to use each idiom. Associated visuals and student participation in making these charts will facilitate retention.

PROCESS CHARTS

Process charts are similar to the sequences of pictures used for showing and describing how to do something such as how to change a tire, how to use a pay phone, how to make a pot of tea. Here, the sequences or processes are all on one chart. They can be used to practise sequencing words or vocabulary for a specific activity. They can also be used for tense practice by asking specific types of questions, for example: "What will he do next?" "What did he do after he arrived?" They may also be used for Total Physical Response activities in which the teacher or a student instructs students to carry out the sequence of actions indicated on the chart.

ACTIVITY WALL CHARTS

Activity wall charts depict four to eight activities in the life of one person, drawn by the teacher. The time of each activity is indicated on the chart. Ensure that the chart is large enough for all to see clearly. Activity charts are extremely useful for practicing verb tenses. The sample chart for the character named Lily is suitable for a beginning class to show the following type of information in pictorial and written form. For beginners, you might present the story first, referring to the appropriate picture, and have the students listen. Students can repeat the story after you. Then they can ask questions about the chart. You can direct practice with the chart to certain tenses by asking different types of questions (Celce-Murcia & Larsen-Freeman 1983):

- What does Lily do every day at 6:30 AM? (simple present)
- It's 9:00 PM. What is Lily doing now? (present progressive)
- What did Lily do yesterday at 7:00 PM? (past)
- It's 1:00. What has Lily already done? (present perfect)

6:30 AM • get up

7:30 AM • prepare food for supper
         • get kids ready for daycare

9:00 AM • go to work

7:00 PM • do housework
         • spend time with children

9:30 PM • study English
         • watch TV

CULTURAL INFORMATION CHARTS AND POSTERS

Posters can depict aspects of life in the target culture, or students' cultures. Travel agencies and government offices are excellent sources of tourism posters. They help to give students an awareness of the people and places associated with the language. This brings language to life and can be a stimulus for questions, discussion, or writing. Furthermore, they brighten up a classroom.

Posters with Captions

Students can make their own posters using magazine pictures, poster board, proverbs and dialogue exchanges to create a pleasant classroom environment. They can create Personality Posters with pictures of activities and things they like and add captions about themselves. Or, they can design covers for their favorite books, movies, or CDs and display them.

Charts versus Board Drawings

Some charts such as the activity charts and charts to accompany reading passages can be drawn on the board. However, because they often contain a lot of information in picture, written, or symbolic form, they take time to prepare. Carefully preparing a chart beforehand means you can use it over again with another class or with the same class in different ways.

Displaying Wall Charts and Pictures

Doff notes that the method you choose for displaying images depends on class size and your purpose. For example, if you have a small class sitting around you in a semicircle, it may be most acceptable to sit holding the picture in your lap. If you have a large class, projection may be the most appropriate. Consider the visibility and ease of use of each of these display methods:

- The teacher holds up the visual aid or sits with the visual aid on his or her lap.
- The teacher posts the visual to a wall or the blackboard.
- The teacher passes around visual aids to students or student groups.
- The teacher projects the image using a data projector or opaque projector.

Realia

Realia refers to actual items that we bring into the classroom, such as food, maps, menus, stuffed toys, puppets, articles of clothing, household items, puzzles, tickets, globes, model cars, or a medical kit. An advantage of many types of realia over other visual aids, such as pictures and charts, is that they are authentic, bringing relevancy to your lessons. If you are doing role plays, realia—a hat, scarf, or money—add greater realism. Students can manipulate realia. This renders learning more concrete, especially for young learners. With children, laminated circles and shapes are teacher-made realia useful for Total Physical Response activities and content instruction. Realia allow students to use more of their senses to learn; adding touching, tasting, smelling, seeing, and hearing accommodates more learner styles.

Students will be pleasantly surprised to see realia from their culture as well as the target cultures used in the classroom. A postcard or money from your students' home countries will pique their interest and can still be discussed in English.

If you are teaching in an English-speaking context, it will be easy for you to find realia. However, in EFL contexts, you may need to take a supply of realia with you. Make a list of possible themes before you leave. Then explore toy stores, educational stores, bookstores, souvenir shops, and novelty shops for useful items that will illustrate your theme and bring it to life. Take forms, such as banking forms, ticket stubs, airplane or bus schedules, menus, and candy packaging. You should also make audio and video recordings of news, weather, and sports casts, role plays, and conversations (you can make these with friends or colleagues before you leave). Be sure to take a variety of magazines. Once you are in the teaching context, explore local stores for items that will supplement your realia collection. Many larger cities have news agencies with newspapers and magazines. You should also try to get brochures and posters from travel agencies and airlines tourist bureaus, embassies, and consulates. Local libraries may be another source (Shih 1999). You will also be able to find realia on the Internet, although it is most often in the form of written text. Helena Curtain and Carol Ann Dahlberg (2004) suggest that you correspond with a teacher from home and exchange realia (300). Of course, there will be a time delay, but this may be a good way to get items free of charge.

Forms and Schedules

Forms and schedules are authentic materials that you can use for language practice. When teaching a unit or course on English for the workplace, gather work-related forms such as parts order forms, bills, restaurant order forms, housekeeping checklists and medical history records. Then, use these forms for vocabulary, spelling and pronunciation, reading and writing practice, and even in role plays. You can also fill in different parts of the same form for information gap activities in which a pair of students each has different information on the same form and must question each other in order to fill in the missing information.

Job application forms, bills, pay stubs, and checks are more general types of paper realia. Be sure to take these types of realia with you if you intend to teach in a foreign country. Checks, for example, are a good medium for practicing both writing and reading dates and numbers. Here are two ideas for household bills:

- Photocopy a number of household bills (e.g. phone, rent, utilities). Students work in groups to sort bills by type, by date (due this month, due next month, overdue), or by amount. Be sure to cross off/black out any personal data!

- Give each group of students a set of bills and ask them to complete a chart:

	Bill amount	Due date
rent		
credit card		
utilities		
phone		
cable		

- Students match bills with pre-printed envelopes.
- Students write a check for one of the bills, put the check and return portion of the bill into the correct envelope, and fill in their return address. (Adapted from Bell and Burnaby 1984, 106)

Post Office Items

In ESL settings, have students collect realia at the post office to practice making requests and to provide the class with items for further language practice. Some post office realia include change of address cards, stamps for domestic and overseas letters, and airmail stickers. Another post office realia activity is to put material you are handing back to students in self-addressed envelopes that they supply to you. You can assign a letter carrier to hand them out, or you can give out all the envelopes at random and let each student find the appropriate recipient.

Menus

Menus are good practice for reading food names and prices. They add reality to a restaurant role play, and most people like to talk about food. You can use menus for Community Language Learning (CLL) lessons (Larsen-Freeman 2000, 120–36). In these lessons, students point to what they want on the menu. You can act as the server, telling them in proper English how to say the item, for example, "I would like a grilled halibut steak with rice and mixed vegetables." Each student repeats the sentence(s) until he or she is comfortable with it. Then we record the sentence. Other students in the class observe, trying to learn the sentences as well. Once all of the students have had a turn, we transcribe the recorded sentences on the board and look for language patterns, ways to extend language, and discuss other ways to place an order.

Here are some other ideas using menus:

- Groups choose a low-fat, heart-healthy meal for a set price.
- Practice skimming and scanning by asking questions such as, "Do they serve fresh fruit?" "Is there a children's menu?" "What is the soup of the day?" "How much is the special?" (Bell and Burnaby).

Food and Related Items

When you are working with people from diverse cultural backgrounds, sometimes pictures alone aren't sufficient to communicate meaning. With children, a concrete object may hold their attention most effectively. Food is one area where the real thing works best. Here are some ways of using food:

- Set out various food items and teach their names by pointing and naming each (a box of _____, a can of _____, a bag of _____). Name each item at least twice. Have different students point to or pick up items as you name them. You can instruct them to place the food items in various places or instruct them to give them to other students. Ask yes and no questions to reinforce vocabulary: "Is this a box of cereal or a can of cereal?" "Is this a jar of peanut butter or a bag of rice?" Finally, point to items and ask a student, "What's this?" Note that with perishable items such as fruits and vegetables, you may need to find plastic representations.

- Ask students to describe what you are doing step by step as you prepare a meal or snack such as a bowl of cereal or a cheese sandwich.

- Have the students follow oral or written instructions (recipes). We know of a teacher who taught a group of rowdy ninth-grade students how to make sandwiches. It was easy, it focused the students, and it satisfied their large appetites!

- In an ESL setting, take a trip to the grocery store or a restaurant. Ask your students to write down the names of ten unfamiliar food items. Follow up in class. You can do the same in an EFL setting, but in that situation ask students about items with which you are not familiar.

- Have a food-tasting party where students describe or categorize food by taste, for example salty, sweet, and sour.

- For younger children, a food theme can also include making macaroni or food picture collages, writing in flour or gelatin crystals in trays, or setting up a supermarket with food boxes and cans and having children "shop" (Richard-Amato 1996). For children, a large box can be cut and decorated to be the store entrance. You can also put up posters of nutrition or other food charts and discuss them.

Maps

Map-reading is a practical skill that students need to learn. For those who already can read maps, you can use maps of a city or region to familiarize them with the local area and provide a pretext for language work. If you are teaching a geography class, maps and globes can allow you to combine language and content. Many teachers display maps of the world or city on classroom walls, so that students can indicate where they live with a stick pin. This can lead into language practice on modes of transportation and travel, with students showing their transportation routes on the map while describing their trips: "I come to school by bus. I get on the bus on 22nd Street at 8:25 AM." or, "I left my country in a little boat. We traveled to Thailand. I stayed there for two years. In 1989 I left my country and came to the United States by plane. We flew to San Francisco. Then I took another plane to Vancouver."

You can use maps for pronunciation practice of street and place names and to develop skill in giving and following directions. For example, "You are at the northwest corner of 22nd Street and 3rd Avenue. Go two blocks west, turn left, go one block south. Where are you?"

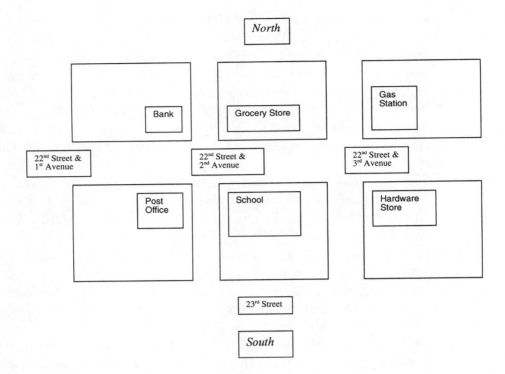

You can fill in different landmarks on two different copies of a map (shown above), and students can do an information gap activity in pairs to find the location of places not marked on their map:

Student A: "Where is the post office?"

Student B: "On the corner of 22nd St. and 2nd Ave."

Other map ideas are included in Chapter 7.

Puppets and Toys

Children will particularly appreciate you using toys and puppets in the classroom. In fact, on occasion you may be able to make judicial use of them in teaching some adult classes. Curtain and Dahlberg (2004) use puppets or stuffed animals for these reasons:

- to take on roles of personalities not in the classroom, such as an adult male if the teacher is a female, a special friend or visitor, a pet, or an unruly child
- to create a personality with which the teacher can model conversations and meaning and consequences of breaking classroom rules
- to take the place of students who are hesitant to speak by speaking on behalf of the student
- to use in student-created role plays or mini-dramas (261)

Can you think of some other uses of puppets or toys in language teaching?

Cultural Artifacts

Artifact study is designed to help students discern the cultural significance of certain unfamiliar objects from the target culture. The activity involves giving descriptions and forming hypotheses about the function of the unknown object. If possible, the teacher brings in the article in question or obtains pictures of it. Once the article is displayed for all to see, students answer these kinds of questions given as a handout or written on the board:

- What are the physical qualities of the object? Give as complete of a description as possible.
- How was it made, by hand or by machine?
- What is its purpose? For example, is it supposed to be decorative?
- What role does it play in the culture? What is its social meaning, if any? Does it have associations with status, wealth, power, prestige?
- What facts can be determined about the culture from this object?
- If this object were yours, what would you do with it?

After a suitable amount of time for discussion, briefly provide facts about the artifact and its use in the society. The students then examine how closely their own hypotheses conform to your explanation. Students determine to what extent their own cultural biases played a role in the formation of their hypotheses about the unknown object.

As a possible pre- or post-activity, students may bring something from their home that is meaningful or important to them. They sit in a circle and place objects in front of them. The teacher picks up his or her own object and briefly describes its story and its meaning. Students pose questions about the object. Students then proceed, one by one, describing their objects. After each student speaks, questions can be asked about the objects (Jerald and Clark 1989, 52–55).

Collections of Objects

Lee Gunderson (1991) suggests that using collections of real objects can be helpful in developing verbal sequencing, categorizing, and pre-reading skills such as the ability to recognize similarities and differences in shapes and the ability to arrange items in a sequence—smallest to largest, beginning to end, left to right. This includes categorizing and arranging pictures into a logical narrative order.

Real objects that can be manipulated are recommended for providing practice in these areas and are more effective than worksheets. Here are some collections of items that can be useful for sorting according to size, color, shape, texture, flexibility, order, and numbers:

- buttons, rocks, shells, leaves, flowers
- stones, nuts, beans, marbles, metal objects
- cloth, feathers, corks, bottle caps
- ice cream sticks, straws, toothpicks, blocks.

You can use collections of articles for numeracy development, such as weighing, measuring, graphing, comparing, counting, and estimating. You can also use them in more general language practice such as defining and describing (118).

Rods

Cuisinaire rods, sometimes called algebrics, are wooden or plastic rods of different colors and lengths. They were first developed for teaching mathematical concepts and were later used by Caleb Gattegno in his *Silent Way* approach to language teaching (Larsen-Freeman 2000, 53–72). They are tangible objects that can be used to represent as many different things as your imagination allows. You can use them to encourage students to talk about their lives and the contexts in which they live (shown here). After representing their homes or a specific room and furnishings— either where they are currently living or in their country of origin—they can use a

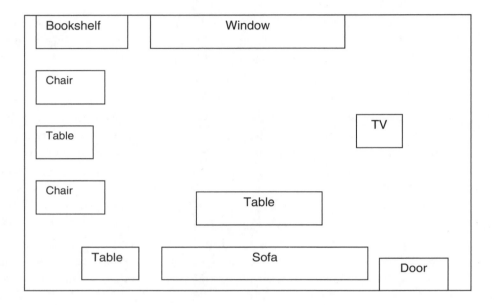

rod to represent themselves and describe their daily routines. Rods are also useful for teaching and practicing telling the time because you can make the "hands" movable as shown here.

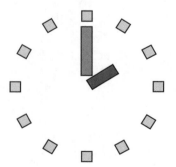

In the Silent Way approach, rods are used to present and practice almost any language structure. By using only a single noun (rod), Silent Way proponents say we can more easily focus work on linguistic structure and meaning. Teaching comparatives and prepositions are examples. If you are interested in using rods, *Communication Starters and Other Activities for the ESL Classroom* by Judy Winn-Bell

Olsen (1977) is a good resource. You can search schools supplies catalogues or stores if you wish to purchase rods or algebrics.

Key Visuals for Language and Content

If you are teaching ESL children and teenagers in mainstream schools, you can help them with their school subjects during English language instruction. Key visuals are graphs, charts, and other items that support content area teaching. A diagram of our planetary system, for example, would be a key visual for teaching astronomy. By examining school curricula or working with content area teachers, you will discover what your students are studying in their regular classroom. Knowing this will help you systematically support and reinforce their content learning in your language class. The use of graphs, charts, pictures, and objects are all excellent ways to teach and reinforce content visually. In addition to nonverbal clues such as gestures, key visuals help students understand content (Ashworth 1992, 105). Key visuals are also useful in many other English-teaching contexts, for example, in academic preparation courses to facilitate reading comprehension.

Curtain and Pesola (1988) note that it is important for language teachers to remember these three areas as they help mainstream students with their school subjects: (1) the language skills needed, (2) the content-area skills that will interrelate with the language skills, and (3) the cognitive skills that are necessary to perform the tasks in the lesson (104).

According to Mary Ashworth (1992, 116), key visuals bridge content, language, and thinking by facilitating understanding. Key visuals also help teachers and mainstream students by

- presenting content clearly and directly
- simplifying cognitively demanding information
- organizing content at the start of a lesson ("advance organizers")
- focusing on the core content of a lesson
- facilitating pre-teaching, such as introduction of new or difficult vocabulary
- providing material for practice activities
- focusing attention and motivation
- allowing for review

Many ESL reading textbooks and textbooks in content areas (e.g., science and history books) use key visuals extensively to support written text. You can also find key visuals, such as charts, to support explanations in grammar books. Academic preparation texts also provide authentic readings with key visuals to support comprehension. Some books provide organizational flowcharts illustrating how the book is set up to help both you and your students follow the intended sequence. Information for developing your own key visuals is provided later in this chapter.

The development of cognitive skills involves not only helping students develop ways to learn the content area and keep up with mainstream students, but also helping them manipulate information. They can do this through assessing what they know, critical thinking, making judgments, planning, trying a variety of learning strategies (Curtain and Pesola 1988, 111–12). This is especially important in cognitively demanding subjects such as math and science.

Royce (2002) states that key visuals are effective in enhancing academic content for English language students in all four skill areas:

- **Reading**—reading development is enhanced when students ask questions about key visuals that accompany an academic text; the visual provides students with a schema to help them relate more easily to academic writing. Students make predictions about what they will read based on the key visual. When they read the actual academic text that accompanies the key visual material, they test their assumptions and predictions. The key visual becomes the focus for further reading.
- **Writing**—students can write about what they see in the key visual or a sequence of visuals as an aid to understanding the structure of narratives and other genres. They also write more creatively about the key visual, if creative writing is the objective.
- **Speaking and Listening**—using key visuals, students can give classroom reports or other short presentations, including explanations and descriptions; the teacher can check oral presentation as well as comprehension during these student reports.
- **Vocabulary**—students can associate words with vocabulary, giving them a mental image that facilitates learning vocabulary.

Three Ideas for Developing Key Visuals

Curtain and Pesola (1988) suggest that you start with short units and wait until you gain experience in planning content-based lessons before you plan academically based extensive units. Studying curriculum documents or working with content area teachers is the best way to find out what your students are studying and how you can systematically support and reinforce their content learning in your language class. Watch particularly for content that you can teach using key visuals.

Developing Thinking Skills with Key Visuals

Although teachers may need to create their own key visuals, Ashworth (1992) says that doing this will ultimately save you time, especially if you involve students in their creation (116). Student involvement helps them learn the content and the language and cognitive skills associated with it.

Ashworth suggests that you first get a gist of the academic content and structure of that content. Next segment the information into manageable chunks. For each segment identify the key concepts, discourse structures, vocabulary, and thinking skills the students need to understand or develop. Finally, select visuals that will facilitate student learning of each segment. You can obtain or adapt some of these visuals from students' academic textbooks, or create them with your students. Ashworth describes some key visuals for the six areas of thinking skills development identified by Moran (1992). The theme of "My School" for elementary or secondary students has been used to provide you with examples:

- **Description** involves using or developing pictures, maps, or drawings. For example, ask students to identify places in their school on a blank map based on an audio recording you supply to them.

- **Sequencing** involves using or developing flow charts, timelines, or recipes. For example, ask students to develop a timeline showing school development and special events at their school from oral or written information that you supply.
- **Choosing** involves using or developing flow charts or tree charts. For example, ask students to make an organization chart of school staff, from principal, to teachers, to support staff.
- **Classifying** involves using or developing lists, tables, graphs, or databases—for example, lists for the current year the subjects are taught at each grade and who is teaching them. Students are instructed to develop a table or simple database using this information. Create a worksheet for students to facilitate their understanding of the concepts.
- **Developing** involves using or developing diagrams, graphs, or tables. For example, together with the students use an overhead transparency to graph anonymous student grades on a science test to show how a bell curve works or trends in grades over the year.
- **Evaluating** involves using or developing rating scales, worksheets, or grids. For example, provide students with a sample course evaluation. Have the students rate their satisfaction with the course content and instructional methods. This can be a springboard for discussion and also provide you with valuable feedback.

Thematic Webbing

Curtain and Pesola (1988) suggest thematic webbing and semantic maps as two ways to organize content-based instruction and guide your selection of key visuals and appropriate activities. Thematic webs "provide for integrated holistic instruction and at the same time incorporate subject content in its interdisciplinary dimensions so that students can see the relationship of the theme or unit to many areas of the curriculum." (105). An example of a teacher-created theme web using the "My School" theme is shown on page 90. Note how the four language skills—speaking, listening, reading, and writing—are addressed and how cultural components are included. Note that new vocabulary will need to be taught or clarified throughout the theme unit.

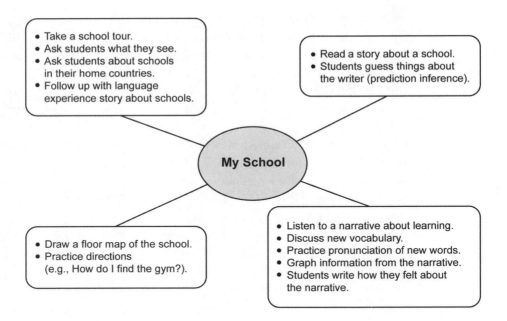

Semantic Maps

Theme webs are possibly best developed through semantic mapping since students contribute to the topic via brainstorming. The teacher and students then categorize the student responses into secondary categories that the teacher can use to develop activities and associated key visuals. A semantic map, again based on "My School," follows. As you look at the semantic map, try to think of some key visuals activities to address the brainstorm.

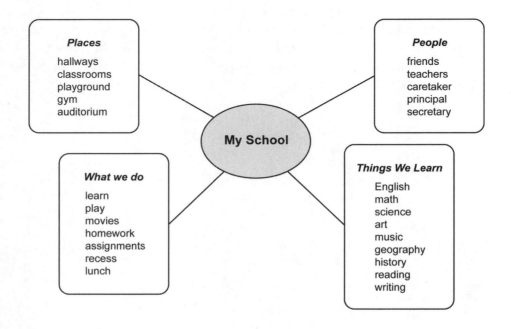

Example of a Graphing Activity

Charts and graphs are common types of key visuals. Graphs can combine math with many different themes. Here is a very basic graphing activity for children in lower elementary grades:

Teacher: "Everyone who has brown shoes on, stand up. Hold up your left foot so we can see your brown shoe." (The teacher walks around class checking for shoes and commenting.)

Teacher: "Yes, Maria has brown shoes—they look new, Maria! Look, Thomas has brown shoes. Let's see how many people have brown shoes." (Counts 1-2-3-4-, or children may count along.) (The teacher goes to a prepared grid on the overhead projector. She plots that seven children have brown shoes using the appropriate colors on the grid. For example, seven squares are filled in with brown marker.)

Teacher: "Everyone who has brown shoes, sit down. Everyone with black shoes, raise your hand. Wave your hand back and forth! Lift up your feet so we can see your black shoes." (Continues in this way, changing things slightly with each color.)

At the end of this activity, there will be a completed graph that the children can talk about. If you use this activity with more than one class during the day, the graphs for the different classes can be compared to raise and practise the concept of "more" and "less" (Curtain and Dahlberg 2004, 254–55).

Advanced students can do similar surveys of their classmates or in the community on relevant topics and graph the results. A group of advanced adult students in a university academic preparation program surveyed seniors at a nearby seniors' apartment complex as part of a unit on the elderly in North American society. They graphed the results to provide an overview of these seniors' lifestyle and attitudes. Content included the frequency of family visits, amount of time spent watching TV, and degree of satisfaction with living in the apartment complex. See the earlier examples in this chapter of how you can use graphs and charts as key visuals to support content area teaching.

CHAPTER 5

Basic Classroom Resources

LEARNING TO TEACH WITH THE BASICS

Joan found herself teacher training in Mozambique. She was given a science lab with tables screwed to the floor and virtually no supplies. There was a cracked chalkboard with poor quality chalk, a ripped screen, a broken overhead projector, a tape recorder that was out of order, and a video machine that would not play the format she had brought from North America. The only media available were paper and pens and a local newspaper willing to supply large sheets of newsprint. Fortunately, she'd brought colored pens and masking tape for group activities. And, believe it or not, there was an old Gestetner machine (pre-photocopier technology) with all the consumables, such as ink. The local teachers were used to the dearth of materials and willing to help Joan adapt the high-tech materials she had brought with her to locally available hardware. It was a wonderful learning experience for her, as most teaching is.

This chapter includes:

- the advantages of basic classroom resources, including the chalkboards, chart paper, boards and charts, worksheets, overhead projectors, audiovisual equipment, and basic language laboratories
- how to develop and use low-tech media and materials effectively in your class
- how to produce worksheets for your class
- materials and activities for the overhead projector
- the advantages and limitations of using audiovisual technology in language teaching
- a variety of ways of using audiovisual equipment and materials in language teaching
- sources and types of audiovisual materials

Some Challenging Questions

Think back to your own teaching experience or your own experience as a language learner. Did you or the teacher:

- erase the chalkboard well before teaching something new on the same surface?
- develop legible, well-organized chalkboard instruction or chart material?
- make worksheets to provide extra practice?
- learn to effectively use overhead projectors and audiovisual equipment for language teaching and learning? Do you feel confident in selecting, adapting, and creating materials for these technologies?
- identify when and under what circumstances you should use audiovisual equipment in your teaching? Consider how you feel about using audiovisual equipment in your teaching?

These questions are all related to effective development and use of basic classroom technology. This chapter elaborates on how to exploit various low-tech media effectively, but for all you techies, don't despair—the next chapter addresses the more sophisticated areas of current teaching technology.

What Are the Basic Classroom Resources?

Digital technology and the Internet are here to stay, but basic classroom resources are by no means obsolete. Effective development and use of the chalkboard and chart paper, display boards, overhead projectors, and audiovisual equipment as well as well-designed worksheets are important in teaching. They are especially important in language teaching, as students struggle to make sense of new symbols, words, and meaning. In this chapter we will cover these basic classroom resources: boards (chalkboard, white board, other types of boards; chart paper; display boards such as felt boards, magnet boards, and Velcro®; worksheets; overhead projectors; audiovisual equipment and materials; radio; and basic language laboratories.

We will start our discussion with boards and charts. A list of resources from Curtain and Dahlberg (2004), our own experience, and the experiences of others that you might use in a language classroom follows. As you read through this list, think about how you might use these resources and for what age group they are most appropriate. Of course, even this list is not exhaustive.

- realia (real objects)—maps, mirrors, clocks, menus, stamps, calendars
- books—song and rhyme; coloring and crafts; picture books and picture dictionaries; easy readers; books of plays, poetry, tales, and fables; books of photocopiable material
- magazines and newspapers
- boards—poster boards, felt boards, magnet boards, peg boards
- individual slates—chalkboards, white boards, or other erasable boards

- cards—postcards, recipe cards, flashcards
- paper—large as well as small sheets of paper, light and heavyweight paper, newsprint and high-quality paper, colored and plain paper
- posters and charts, including pocket charts
- labels—sticky notes, name tags
- worksheets
- games—board and card games, including regular playing cards
- toys—puppets, stuffed toys, dolls and doll houses with furniture, toy cars, planes, boats and soldiers, paper dolls, toy dishes, construction blocks, toy phones, toy cash register, toy money (bills and coins)
- boxes and containers of various sizes—empty food containers
- musical instruments—electronic keyboard and bells
- sports equipment—such as balls, racquets and nets, skis, skates, and jump ropes
- craft materials—yarn, beads, sparkles, glue, and colored markers
- miscellaneous—inflatable figures, rubber stamps, magnetic letters and numbers, plastic fruit and vegetables, flags, suitcase, clothing.

The Board as Language Teaching Material

In this section we will discuss the advantages of the chalkboard or white board, selecting the best board for your class, and using the board in general as well as for specific uses such as for tables, prompts, and dialogues. We have combined our ideas with those of Mugglestone (1983), Wright (1981), Doff (1990), and Curtain and Dahlberg (2004).

Advantages of the Board

No matter where you teach, you usually will have access to a chalkboard or white board. Because of this, we as teachers have traditionally relied on the board, which does have advantages.

- It's constantly at hand, usually placed near you at the front of the classroom.
- It's spontaneous and can serve the needs of your lesson from moment to moment.
- It's cheap, durable, and long lasting (Mugglestone, 11).
- It can help to maintain and vary the pace of your lesson, allowing you to provide new material quickly and to make changes immediately by drawing, erasing, and rewriting (Mugglestone, 32).
- Students can draw and write on it.
- It can be used for various purposes without special preparation.
- It focuses attention and allows you to control what students see and when they see it (Mugglestone, 32).
- It can be used as a magnet board if it has a metal core.
- It allows you to reinforce oral language with visual and written cues, benefiting learners who need to see as well as hear in order to make sense of new language.

Considerations in Board Selection and Use

The main purpose in using the chalkboard is to make things clearer to your class and to focus their attention. If you do have a choice, consider the following when choosing a board:

- The board should be high enough for you to write on comfortably and for all students to see. The center of the board should be about level with your shoulder (Mugglestone, 21).
- Consider the visibility of coloured chalk on a black or green chalkboard.
- Request board space along the walls as well as at the front of the class so that several or all students can use the boards at the same time. You may decide to use board space for small groups to play games such as hangman and Pictionary. Some students like to doodle at the board and practice their writing. If you are teaching younger children, consider a side board or an additional board placed lower for them to use.
- If you have a choice, consider the relative advantages of white boards versus chalkboards. White boards and pens are more expensive than chalkboards and chalk, but they may be more visible and less messy. Chalk dust can exacerbate allergies and get into equipment. White boards can also be used as projection screens. White boards cannot be erased if the wrong kind of marker is used on them, and they can be difficult to erase. Some people may also be allergic to the chemicals used in the markers.
- If you have a choice, consider the advantages of movable or portable boards. This will depend on the class size and portability needs within or between classrooms.

When developing your board space, Mugglestone emphasizes the importance of erasing each item as soon as you and the students have finished with it. Sometimes, she notes, in our haste to move on to something else and to save time, we only erase part of an item—as much as we need in order to make room for the next item. This confuses and distracts students because they usually copy down things exactly the way the teacher writes them. Using colored chalk (or colored markers if it is a white board) to highlight such elements as structural patterns, spelling patterns, and sounds is also effective in developing your board space. (30)

Dividing the Board

If you do have an appropriate board, Mugglestone and others recommend you exploit its possibilities most effectively by dividing it into two or three sections. Use them as follows:

- Use one section as a reference area for key words and phrases that will stay up for the whole lesson. You can make a column along one side of the board for this. If the section gets full, then you already have enough new material for one lesson. Students will quickly learn that this column includes key vocabulary they must write down and review for the next quiz. If you do not have a lot of chalkboard space, use a large sheet of paper taped to the wall. This works well because you can leave it up for future lessons. Don't be afraid to use this section for things like a large *s* to remind students to pronounce the final *s* when using the third-person singular form of regular verbs in the present tense.

- Use a large central section for presenting the main material of the lesson such as grammatical examples or drawings that set the context for a dialogue. Clean this section as required throughout the lesson.
- Use a second small section (i.e., another side panel) for doodles and unexpected things that come up in passing, if you want to keep the central area only for the main teaching material. This second section will be erased constantly.
- Use a corner of the board for the lesson agenda. Students like to know what they are going to be doing or learning during each lesson. Studies say that people learn more when they are prepared for what they are supposed to be learning.

It requires some discipline on your part to consistently divide your board, but it's worth the effort. To encourage you to try dividing your board, stand at the back of your room after your next class or observation and look at the board. Ask yourself, "Is what I see really helpful to students?"

Writing on the Board

Adrian Doff (1990) and Andrew Wright (1981) suggest that teachers keep these principles in mind when writing on the board:

- Stand sideways so you can at least see the students in your peripheral vision and so students can see what you are writing, rather than your back.
- Maintain eye contact with students as you write by turning occasionally and interacting with them. For example, keep their attention by saying the words as you write them or by asking them what the next word will be or how to spell it.
- Write clearly. Your writing should be large enough to be seen at the back of the class. The letters should be open and clear, but fairly close together. Keep a space equivalent to the height of two letters between lines.
- Write in a straight line. This is easier if you are writing on a section of the board and not across the entire board width. Try to keep the left-hand edge of the lines vertical.

Here are some considerations from Mugglestone (1983, 26–27) related to the script you use when you write on the board:

- Printing is usually more legible than writing. With students who are learning the Roman script, your writing style should be the same as that being learned so that students have consistent models as they learn. The board can be useful for demonstrating the movement of the hand in forming letters, which is less easy to do with the overhead projector.

- Spelling is often more difficult at the board than on paper. If you are unsure of the spelling of a word, write it quickly on a piece of paper before putting it on the board.
- Use upper-case and lower-case letters in standard ways. Using capital letters to emphasize words and syllables can confuse students. Instead, use colored chalks, underlining, and symbols for emphasis.

Developing and Adapting Substitution Tables for the Board

Some student textbooks present substitution tables for structure or drill practice. Tables can be confusing, especially for beginning students. One way to help students is to make your own tables or copy or adapt textbook tables on the board (you can also predraw a chart) to show the different forms of a structure together (see below). Be sure to copy the chart neatly and accurately and keep dividing lines straight.

Model Sentence	Instructor's Cues
Do you like to <u>read</u>?	travel? (student says: "Do you like to travel?") swim? study? drive? etc.
<u>Do you</u> like to read?	He (student says: "Does he like to read?") She They Your friends Their parents etc.
Etc.	

Involve students by having them suggest what to write in some of the columns. If the table is long, write it on the board before class and cover it with a large sheet of paper until it is needed, or write it in advance on another medium, for example on flip-chart paper or on acetate for the overhead projector (Doff 1990).

Developing Simple Prompts on the Board

Following is a way of writing word prompts on the board as an outline for written or oral composition. The word prompts may come from a picture story or series of pictures. Here is an example from an introductory activity from *Taking Sides: A Speaking Text for Advanced and Intermediate Students* by Kevin B. King (1997, 1) that shows images of a variety of different people with the question, "What are the most important characteristics for assessing the compatibility of a roommate?" You can ask students to write a composition (story or essay depending on your goals and needs) based on clues from the picture and prompts you list on the board, as shown:

---

found an apartment—expensive—two bedrooms—
want company—roommate advertisement—
many applicants—interview—final decision

A resulting student narrative may be as follows:

> I finally found the perfect apartment. It was very large and it had two bedrooms. But it was too expensive. I decided to advertise for a roommate. I interviewed many applicants. The first was a tall woman, like me, but she smoked! The second was too old and made too much noise with her tuba. The third practised yoga all day and chanted too loudly. I could not live with the others because they were men. I especially didn't like the man with the snake! Finally I decided to get a part-time job and just get a dog for company!

Developing and Adapting Dialogues on the Board

Dialogues written on the board can provide more controlled practice than dialogues in the textbook. Here are some things you can do with a board dialogue:

- Use the vanishing technique—erase words from the dialogue and have students perform the dialogue without all the words to help them learn fixed expressions and structures. For example, in the dialogue that follows, erase the most familiar words or phrases first:

Model:

    Mary: Hi, Ruth. How are you?

    Ruth: Fine, thank you, and you?

Erasure 1:

    Mary: Hi, Ruth. How are _____?

    Ruth: Fine, thank you, and _____?

Erasure 2:

    Mary: Hi, Ruth. _____ are _____?

    Ruth: _____, thank you, and _____?

- According to need, use the following visual cues to show:

  —linking of sounds

  > He likes it.

  —intonation

  > Where did he go?

  —silent letters

  > chocølate

  —syllable and word stress

  > What time is it?

- Write a dialogue collectively with your students.
- Adapt a textbook dialogue to make it more appropriate for your students.

Developing and Adapting Drawings on the Board

You can use stick figure drawings on the board to quickly illustrate meaning. Students usually love to see you drawing a picture before their eyes, so the board is an ideal surface. However, if you know you are going to be doing a particular drawing, practice it first. As with charts and tables, if you are drawing a long picture sequence and aren't confident in your drawing abilities, you might want to draw your picture sequence beforehand on overhead projector acetate or on chart paper. You don't need to produce a large number of complicated pictures for stories. Recall the illustrations for Little Red Riding Hood in Chapter 4.

One type of impromptu illustration that language teachers often draw on the board is a side view of the human face and position of mouth, tongue, and lips for pronunciation of various sounds. On the board, you can easily change the tongue position to show contrasting sounds, as shown here.

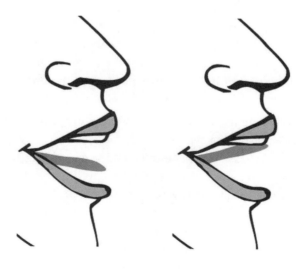

Student Drawings on the Board

Remember that students often like to draw an illustration for you. For children, drawing on the board can be an excellent way to practice following and giving instructions. For example, you can ask students to draw the day's weather as the teacher describes it. Or, you can ask them to collaborate on a monster or other drawing. For example:

> **Teacher:** Draw a big head. Draw an ear. Do you want large ears or small ears?
> (Curtain and Dahlberg, 335)

Developing Student Handwriting on the Board

For ESL/EFL literacy students, using a lined board is a way to model and have students practice their handwriting. Ruth Mowat (1990) finds this method far more effective than simply copying letters and words onto a piece of paper. Mowat states that students can stand beside the teacher at the board and see the large example. The board allows them to erase easily and correct errors.

Chart Paper as Language Teaching Material

In this section the term *chart paper* refers to large sheets of paper such as paper torn from rolls of wrapping paper (usually brown or white), butcher paper, newsprint, large sheets such as flip chart paper, and poster board. We will examine the advantages and development of uses for chart paper in language teaching.

Advantages of Chart Paper

In *Technology Assisted Teaching Techniques*, Janie Duncan (1987) lists these handy qualities of large sheets of paper:

- The sheets of paper can be kept, either displayed or rolled up for future use.
- They can be easily posted around the room using masking tape, thumbtacks, or Fun-Tak®.
- They can be prepared and hung in advance, rolled up like a window shade, pulled down, folded, or flipped over at the appropriate moment.
- They can focus class attention on one central spot instead of on individual student copies.
- All the students can work simultaneously on individual sheets of paper, whereas only a few can write at the board at the same time.
- Students seem more inclined to express themselves freely or to illustrate in greater detail on a large sheet of paper than they do at the board. (1)

Individual static sheets are available at some school supply stores and work in a similar fashion to a white board. They are more expensive than paper, but reusable. As well as being erasable, static sheets cling to the wall or chalkboard without tape. This makes them useful for covering the chalkboard or as a projection screen for slides and transparencies. After awhile, however, they lose their cling and are not totally erasable. They work best in dry rather than humid conditions.

With all kinds of large sheets of paper, take care that you don't start using them as a replacement for the more economical and ecologically sound chalkboard and that you don't allow them to clutter your classroom.

Uses of Chart Paper

Following are items that you might like to keep and therefore will record on chart paper. This is particularly useful when you don't have an overhead projector or much board space:

- language experience stories
- activity, verb, vocabulary, and idiom charts
- key vocabulary from a lesson or theme unit, written by either you or your students
- jazz chants
- longer tables and charts

You can also write up student grammar errors by category on chart paper and post them on the walls around the room. In groups of two or three, students circulate from paper to paper, discussing and correcting the errors with markers that you leave near each sheet of paper.

Other Types of Boards and Charts

In this section we examine the advantages and uses of other types of boards, such as felt boards, flannel boards, magnetic boards, peg boards and Velcro® boards, which are similar to uses of the chalkboard or chart paper. You can also purchase ready-made boards and charts, such as maps and posters, in educational supply stores.

Advantages of Other Types of Boards

Here are the advantages of these kinds of boards:

- Most allow for the movement of pieces that adhere to them. This means you and your students can develop a story or narrative in a step-by-step manner. Extension activities related to the story can be repeated over and over.
- Using colorful figures and allowing students to place them on the board makes the felt, flannel, and magnet board especially appealing to children.
- Several students can work on these boards simultaneously.

Developing Uses for Other Types of Boards

These activities take advantage of the moving of pieces this type of resource offers:

- sequencing the alphabet, scrambling sentences and letters or numbers, illustrating prepositions of place and spatial relationships
- giving and following directions (e.g., put the canoe in the river)
- developing stories, narratives, or step-by-step processes and routines
- displaying pictures and student work or products, such as one-page stories or poems
- illustrating phrase structure and word formation. For example, you can have *John, is,* and *studying* on separate cards. By changing the order of the cards on the felt board, you can illustrate the phrases, *John is studying.* and *Is John studying?* For word formation, for example, you could print *er* on one card and print root words on other cards to which ~*er* can be added at the end such as *teach* (teacher) and *sing* (singer).

These kinds of manipulations can also be done using pieces of card stuck to the chalkboard with Fun-Tak®, or Poster Putty® (available in most stationery departments), pocket charts (which can be purchased or made), or index cards arranged along the board ledge. However, it is not as easy to move things around with these materials. Sticky adhesives may stain your chalkboard. Also there is less visibility using the board ledge.

Making Boards

The boards listed in this section are all available commercially at office supply stores. However, Curtain and Dahlberg (2004, 311–12) suggest a number of ways that you can make your own boards, often with little cost:

- magnet boards—First, check to see if your chalkboard or white board is magnetized. If not, you can use a cookie sheet or a piece of steel. Magnets are available at hardware, hobby, or school supply stores. Magnetic figures, numbers, and letters are also available at school supply and toy stores.
- flannel or felt boards—Find a suitably sized board or frame (about 2 ft. by 3 ft. or smaller for individual or group work), stretch the flannel or felt around it, and secure with thumbtacks or a staple gun. The board can be any rigid material. Corkboard works well for tacking up visuals. You can have students make letters or story figures out of any felt, interfacing, sponge, paper backed with sandpaper, or flannel. Yarn and pipe cleaners will stick to felt and can be used to divide the board into spaces such as rooms of a house. Educational supply and toy stores may have figures that you can purchase for felt or flannel boards.
- pocket charts—use poster board or cardboard for pocket chart backing and glue on either one long pocket or several pockets in rows. Envelopes work well for pockets.
- Velcro®—Available in strips, circles, or various pieces, this material is sold at sewing supply and sometimes hardware stores. If you have permission from your school, glue the Velcro to a wall, bulletin board, or chalkboard with the soft side up to avoid other material such as flannel or fluff sticking to it. Then, glue a piece of the hook or sharp side onto the figures or cards that you want to use.

Laminating pieces to be stuck to boards stiffens and protects especially paper materials. Also, you can write on laminated materials with erasable markers. If you don't have access to a laminator, use plastic or acrylic protective sprays from hobby stores. You can also extend the life of your paper productions by binding the edges with masking tape, available in several colors.

Worksheets as Language Teaching Material

Worksheets contain exercises that are distributed for in-class individual or group work or for homework. The worksheets are often checked by the teacher. You can use worksheets for oral practice in pairs or groups, and for reading and writing practice in pairs and individually.

Work cards are more permanent and reusable than exercises written on paper.

They are only reusable if you ask students to write their answers elsewhere or if you laminate them with plastic and have students use erasable pens. A student can work through several short work cards in a self-access center or during individual study time. (Ur 1996, 192)

Why Develop Worksheets and Work Cards for Your Students?

Some advantages of using worksheets (Doff 1990) are:

- They encourage students to work in pairs and small groups and provide focus on the activity. Students do not have to turn to the board to look at information and prompts.
- They save time in the lesson—the teacher does not have to spend time writing or drawing on the board.
- When students are absent, they provide a record of activities missed.
- They provide a change of pace and something new to look at.
- When done on the computer, they are easy to modify and reuse.
- They provide written instructions and examples for tasks that may be easier to understand than oral instructions alone.
- Their clear instructions and self-check answers promote learner independence so students can use worksheets on their own or at their own speed, possibly in learning centers.
- They support skill development in areas not covered by the textbook. They also allow extended practice such as controlled oral practice, freer oral practice, reading, writing grammar exercises, and vocabulary development.
- You can build up worksheets with similar tasks, but with varying levels of difficulty to meet the needs of a multilevel class.
- The exercises in the textbook may need to be adapted to make the context more relevant and personal, to relate the language being practiced to a particular theme or for other reasons cited in Chapter 2, Textbooks. You can do these adaptations on worksheets or cards.

Making Worksheets

Consider the following when you make worksheets:

- Your worksheet should contain at least four or five minutes of practice.
- Worksheets should practice language that students already know. Use them to supplement and extend practice activities such as those provided in the textbook or use them for review.
- A worksheet should provide more practice than presentation. If including some presentation and modeling in your worksheets, do not overwhelm students with too many variations. Ten ways of saying each function, for example, is overwhelming.
- Use simple instructions and an example or model so that students can carry out the activity without much of your help. This means using short, active sentences that do not contain unfamiliar vocabulary. Depending on your teaching context, you might choose to write the instructions in the students' language.

- Make your worksheets <u>attractive and inviting</u>, but keep them simple. Use clear, bold printing; use underlining or italics to focus on important items. Illustrations may help.
- <u>Refer to textbook</u> and activity book exercises for ideas for worksheets. You can use a textbook exercise format, but substitute your own vocabulary or other language that your students need to practice.
- <u>Make the tasks self-checking</u> when possible by <u>providing answer keys</u>. You may want to distribute answers after the students have completed the task.

These considerations are based on Doff (1990), Ur (1996), and our own experience. Barbara Burnaby (1990) and others recommend these special considerations when developing worksheets for literacy language learners. These guidelines apply to students at all levels:

- Choose a <u>font close to hand printing and large enough</u> for easy reading if using the computer; avoid font variations and novelty. Use only upper case if your students have not yet mastered lower case.
- Don't use symbols such as a CD or a hand with a pencil unless you have previously made students aware of their meanings. They may be more difficult to interpret than words.
- Don't use a <u>two-column layout</u>; it may be confusing.
- Include enough space for handwritten answers. Let students write their answers or notes directly on the worksheet.
- <u>Separate the two parts with a line or borders</u> if your worksheet contains different sections, such as speaking exercises followed by writing. This helps students to concentrate on one part at a time.
- Include <u>several examples for clarity</u> and for reading practice.
- Include critical language items students may need to refer to such as letters of the alphabet across the top of the worksheet or on separate cards.

Sample Worksheets

ORAL PRACTICE WORKSHEETS

An example of an oral interview worksheet is provided. Although the focus here is on oral practice, notice that the follow-up includes another skill area.

Instructions: Ask your partner these questions. Write your answers on a piece of paper.

What is your favorite:

- animal?
- song?
- TV show?
- color?

Use your answers to write three sentences about your partner.

1. _____

2. _____

3. _____

Task-based worksheets, discussed later, are an excellent way to promote motivation and student talk. Considering background knowledge, age, interests, and language level of your students in your choice of worksheet topics and questions will also help to maximize student talk and participation. In the example above, the worksheet contains an information gap—each student must ask his or her partner questions in order to complete the worksheet. This ensures that everyone participates. Designating partners or small groups of individuals that work well together, circulating among groups, and assigning roles for group discussion tasks can all contribute to success with oral worksheets.

When you develop worksheets for oral fluency, Penny Ur (1996) advises ensuring that they are motivational and that they promote a great deal of student talk. Also ensure that they encourage participation by all students, that they don't inhibit risk-taking, and that the language you expect students to use is at an acceptable level of accuracy (120). Ur and Folse (2006) describe two types of speaking activities: topic- and task-based.

> [According to Ur, topic-based tasks ask] participants to talk about a (controversial) subject, the main objective being clearly the discussion process itself; the second asks them actually to perform something, where the discussion process is a means to an end . . . it requires the group, or pair, to achieve an objective that is usually expressed by an observable result, such as brief notes or lists, a rearrangement of jumbled items, a drawing, a spoken summary . . . so within the definition of the task you often find instructions such as 'reach a consensus,' or 'find out everyone's opinion.' (pp. 123–124)

Ur asserts that usually there is a greater amount of talk, more evenly distributed participation, and higher motivation and enjoyment in task-based activities. Many adults enjoy discussion for the sake of discussion, so don't rule out topic-based oral practice worksheets, as in the one on page 104. However, you should tell your students what skill such worksheets will develop so that they don't think they're wasting time. Also, consider designing worksheets that involve tasks such as:

- decision-making—"Which of these candidates should get the job and why?"
- describe and draw—"Draw your favorite place. Then have your partner draw that place following your description of it."
- ranking—"Your community wants to place a time capsule in the new city hall. In it will be 10 items that represent the last part of the 20th century. What will those ten items be?"

The activities that follow illustrate a sample ranking or decision-making task for beginning to intermediate students involving pictures on which to base the discussion. The worksheets from Folse (2006), designed for intermediate and advanced students, promote discussion as they seek to fill in the grid.

Example of Information Gap: Simple Completion

Student A

Who Is Who? At the United Nations

Four people are eating lunch at a cafeteria at the United Nations in New York City. These four people are from four different countries. They have four different jobs and four different hobbies.

Directions: Work with a partner to find out who is who. Ask questions such as "What is Pablo's job?" "Where is _____ from?" or "How old is the man from Senegal?"

Name	Age	Country	Work	Hobby
Jason	33			
Pablo		Mexico	interpreter	
	31		operator	chess
	35	Kuwait		

Source: Folse, K. (1993). *Talk a Lot: Communication Activities for Speaking Fluency.* Ann Arbor: University of Michigan Press.

Example of Information Gap: Simple Completion

Student B

Who Is Who? At the United Nations

Four people are eating lunch at a cafeteria at the United Nations in New York City. These four people are from four different countries. They have four different jobs and four different hobbies.

Directions: Work with a partner to find out who is who. Ask questions such as "What is Pablo's job?" "Where is _____ from?" or "How old is the man from Senegal?"

Name	Age	Country	Work	Hobby
		Canada	English teacher	traveling
	37			reading
Pierre		Senegal		
Saleh			translator	tennis

Source: Folse, K. (1993). *Talk a Lot: Communication Activities for Speaking Fluency.* Ann Arbor: University of Michigan Press.

Name _____

Address _____

WINTER DRIVING KIT

ACTIVITY

A. Match the words with the pictures.
Do this by yourself.

_____ a shovel

_____ blankets

_____ nuts

_____ a candle

_____ matches

_____ extra clothes

_____ a pen & paper

_____ an ice scraper or snow brush

_____ sand

_____ a bottle of windshield washer fluid

_____ a first aid kit

_____ chocolate bars

_____ jumper cables

_____ a bilingual dictionary

_____ a good book

_____ a flashlight

_____ a rope

_____ flares

_____ a knife

_____ a thermos of coffee

A	B	C	D
E	F	G	H
I	J	K	L
M	N	O	P
Q	R	S	T

B. Find a partner.
   Compare your answers for Part A.

C. Do this with your partner.
   You need 10 things in your car for winter driving safety.
   Choose 10 important things from Part A.
   Write them here:

1. _____   6. _____

2. _____   7. _____

3. _____   8. _____

4. _____   9. _____

5. _____   10. _____

D. Show your list to another group.
   Tell them why you choose each one.

E. Check your list with your teacher.

Source: Ormiston, M., R. DeCoursey, and S. Fredeen, *The ESL Toolbox: Ready-to-Use Enrichment Activities for LINC Classes* (Saskatoon, SK: University Extension Press, 1994). Reproduced by permission of the University of Saskatchewan Language Centre.

Talk it over . . .
Wind, or windchill, can feel very cold.

WINDCHILL
900 - 1600	-Wear hats, coats and gloves.
1600 - 1800	-Wear very warm clothing.
1800 - 2300	-Skin can freeze in 1 to 5 minutes. Wear layers of clothing.
2300 or more	-Going outdoors is dangerous.

What do you tell people in your first country about Canadian weather?

Source: Ormiston, DeCoursey, and Fredeen, 1994. Reproduced by permission of the University of Saskatchewan Language Centre.

GRAMMAR AND ORAL PRACTICE WORKSHEETS

Sometimes your worksheet can include the correct grammatical form. In the worksheet that follows, students are required to choose the correct grammatical forms themselves (*few* or *a few, little* or *a little*). When designing worksheets, be conscious of the input you want to provide students in terms of structures and vocabulary and what you want them to produce on their own.

Optimist or Pessimist?

(a few/few, a little/little)

Instructions: *Ask your partner the following questions. Your partner chooses from these answers:*

- **few, very few/a few + noun**

- **very little, little/a little + noun**

> Example: Is there enough time left in the course to improve my English?
>
> "Yes, there is still a little time." (An optimistic answer.)
>
> "No, there is little time." (A pessimistic answer!)

- How many people have you noticed downtown in the evenings?

  _____ people.

- How many opportunities do you have to practice English outside of class time?

- Do you do any interesting activities on the weekend?

- How much money do you have left for this term?

  I have _____ money.

- Do English speakers you meet try to understand your English?

  They try _____.

- Has your English improved in the last 3 weeks?

  _____

Source: M. Ormiston, *TESL 32: Materials Selection and Development* (Saskatoon, SK: Extension Division, University of Saskatchewan, 1998).

The worksheet that follows illustrates grammar and oral practice, as did the previous one. It was developed to compensate for a textbook that clearly presented prepositions and gerunds but did not provide sufficient practice. Like the preceding worksheet, it includes personalized practice to encourage students to use the structures to talk about their own experiences.

Preposition Plus Gerund Review Worksheet

Instructions: *Fill in the correct preposition and the correct form of the verb. Then ask your partner the question.*

> Example: **study:** What subjects are you most interested **in studying**?

1.   **do:** What activities are you most looking forward
    _____ _____ during the holiday?

2.   **have:** If you decide to get married someday, what qualities will you insist _____ your
    spouse _____?

3.   **do:** What activities are you opposed _____ teenagers _____?

4.   **eat:** What kinds of food are you excited
    _____ _____ _____?

5.   **do:** What things are you good _____ _____?

6.   **visit:** What kinds of places are you most fond
    _____ _____ when you travel?

7.   **ban:** What do you think _____ _____ smoking in bars?

8.   **speak:** Who are you nervous _____ _____ to in English?

Source: Ormiston, 1998.

You will find more ideas for oral practice worksheet ideas in Chapter 7, Project and Community Contact Materials.

A SAMPLE WORKSHEET FOR GRAMMAR PRACTICE

There is plenty of textbook material available to practice the use of *going to* for expressing future plans, particularly in written form. Following is a worksheet that integrates *going to* with a holiday theme. Notice these worksheet features:

✓ clear, simple instructions
✓ lines for writing on
✓ self-check features at the bottom
✓ form fill-in practice at the top, which is helpful for literacy students
✓ borders separating sections of the worksheet.

Holiday/Vacation Match

Surname: _____

First Name: _____

Address: _____

Write the names of your classmates for the Numbers 4, 7, and 8.

Beginning

1. The class
2. The teacher
3. I
4. _____ and _____
5. You
6. We
7. _____
8. _____

   _____

   _____

End

A. is going to take a good book.
B. is going to take lots of money.
C. am going to take sunglasses.
D. are going to take their bathing suits.
E. are going to take a dictionary.
F. are going to take her boyfriend.
G. am going to take a warm sweater.
H. are going to take the children.
I. is going to take some skis.
J. are going to take a camera.

Check: *Read your sentences.*
Did you use the right form of the verb to be *in each sentence?*   ❑ YES   ❑ NO

To Be	
I am	She is
You are	We are
He is	They are

Source: Ormiston, DeCoursey, and Fredeen, 1994. Adapted by permission of the University of Saskatchewan Language Centre.

WORKSHEETS FOR READING TASKS

When developing your own simplified reading texts or when using authentic readings, you will usually want to develop tasks to focus on specific reading skills or content. Information transfer tasks involve the reader in transferring information from the reading to another form, such as a chart, a cloze text, or a summary. You can start doing this at early stages as shown in the example that follows, based on a written text analyzed into chart form for early readers (Beaumont 1991). Four worksheets are provided to illustrate the development of skimming, scanning, intensive reading, and inference. You can easily develop this type of exercise for your students' needs, interests, and age group.

SAMPLE TEXT

Avi has a small red dog. The dog is quiet and good. It likes to go for walks. Daniel has a large white dog. The dog barks loudly. It is lively. It likes to play with a ball. Jay has a fat brown cat. The cat purrs when it is happy. It is sweet, and it likes to sleep. Max has a thin black-and-white cat. The cat meows when it is hungry. It is friendly. It likes to hunt mice.

Analysis Chart

Master's Name	Pet Type	Pet Size	Pet Color	Pet Noise	Pet's Likes
Avi	dog	small	red	quiet	going for walks
Daniel	dog	large	white	loud bark	playing with ball
Jay	cat	fat	brown	purrs	sleeping
Max	cat	thin	black and white	meows	hunting mice

Skimming Worksheet

Instructions: *Read the text quickly. Write a word or two on each line.*

How many paragraphs does the text have? _____

Each paragraph talks about a boy's _____

List the colors of the animals. _____

List two sounds from the text. _____

List two animal noises from the text. _____

Source: Adapted from Mike Beaumont, "Reading in a Foreign Language at an Elementary Level," in *At the Chalkface: Practical Techniques in Language Teaching,* eds. A. Matthews, M. Spratt, and L. Dangerfield (Walton-on-Thames, UK: Thomas Nelson, 1991), 84–88.

Scanning Worksheet

Instructions: Look at the text quickly. Write a size description in each blank.

Avi's red dog is _____

This cat likes to sleep. Its size is _____

This cat is black and white. Its size is _____

List two sounds from the text. _____

Avi's dog is quiet. Its size is _____

Source: Adapted from Beaumont, 1991.

Intensive Reading Worksheet

Instructions: On the sheet of paper below, draw a picture of each boy's pet.

Avi's pet	Daniel's pet
Jay's pet	Max's pet

Source: Adapted from Beaumont, 1991.

Inference Worksheet

> *Instructions:* Write the name of the pet's owner in each blank.
>
> This boy likes to spoil small, quiet animals. _____
>
> This boy likes large, lively animals. _____
>
> This boy likes two-colored animals. _____
>
> This boy likes red. _____

Source: Adapted from Beaumont, 1991.

You can develop other worksheets for reading by:

- making a cloze exercise from the text
- rewriting the text with factual mistakes. Students have to write the correct version.
- rewriting the text with sentences in the wrong order
- developing questions based on understanding main ideas, inference, or critically evaluating information in a text
- finishing a partially completed semantic map.

WORKSHEETS FOR LISTENING

When you are asking students to listen for specific information on an audiotape or during a movie or lecture, a worksheet helps them to focus and record their information quickly while they are listening. You may also instruct students to make their own worksheets for this purpose. You can create information transfer tasks that are similar to the reading information transfer tasks described on pages 113–14. Even a worksheet that is as simple as the one that follows, used to record main ideas from the news, can help students.

> *Instructions:* Listen to each of the three news items and write brief notes about each to answer the following:
>
> 1. Who ?
>
>   What?
>
>   Where?
>
> 2. Who?
>
>   What?
>
>   Where?
>
> 3. Who?
>
>   What?
>
>   Where?

Source: Ormison, DeCoursey, and Fredeen, 1994. Reprinted by permission of the University of Saskachewan Language Centre.

Many listening textbooks provide listening activities that you can adapt into worksheets suitable for your students.

WORKSHEETS FOR WRITING

To demonstrate to beginners that writing is an enjoyable way to communicate, Donn Byrne (1991) proposes a letter-writing task to follow related oral practice. With simple instructions, this task can become a worksheet.

Instructions: *Write a letter to a classmate. Fill in the blanks.*
Give the letter to your classmate. Wait for a reply.

September _____, 20_____

Dear _____,

What are you doing this weekend? I'm going to

_____ and

_____.

Yours,

_____

Source: D. Byrne, "Writing in Class" in *At the Chalkface,* 94–97.

WORKSHEETS FOR PRINTING PRACTICE

Go to libraries and educational bookstores to look for literacy books for children and adults. There you will find ideas for workshops for printing practice. You will also find ESL literacy and ESL books available with printing practice exercises. For example, in her book Ur provides several worksheets for beginning readers and writers on pages 156–57.

CULTURE WORKSHEETS

Culture can be integrated into language learning in many ways. Worksheets are one way to encourage active involvement with and reflection on cultural content in a way that is more compelling than lectures on culture.

This culture quiz was developed for EFL teachers who were non-native speakers and had not travelled to English-speaking countries but were proficient in English. They wanted to know more about Canada and Canadian culture. Some of the questions are tongue-in-cheek, some involve inference, and many relate to topics of interest such as nationalism, wealth, and education.

Canadian Culture Quiz

Instructions: *Circle the correct response to each numbered questions. Then check your answers with your neighbor.*

1. When the national anthem ("O Canada") is played, most Canadians:
   a.   stand and sing, then applaud
   b.   stand and mouth the words
   c.   go and get a beer

2. Most Canadians:
   a.   respect and admire the United States
   b.   dislike or distrust the United States
   c.   go shopping every weekend in the United States

3. Canada's population is about 27,000,000. How many people speak French as a first language?
   a.   1 million
   b.   6 1/2 million
   c.   12 1/2 million

4. It's best to call someone you just met (e.g., Carol Peters):
   a.   Ms. Carol
   b.   Ms. Peters
   c.   Carol

5. If you are invited to your friend's house for dinner at 7:00 PM, the best time to arrive would be:
   a.   6:50 PM
   b.   7:00 PM
   c.   7:05 PM
   d.   7:30 PM

6. Your friend invites you and four other friends to a restaurant to celebrate his or her birthday. How will the bill be paid?
   a.   The person celebrating her birthday will pay for all.
   b.   The oldest person present will pay the bill.
   c.   The bill will be divided equally amongst all people there.
   d.   Each person will pay for what he or she ate and drank (Joe had a beer and a hamburger for $10.00; Kim had a glass of wine, chicken, and salad for $14.00).

7. What is considered the usual tip in a restaurant?
   a.   5% of the bill
   b.   10–15% of the bill
   c.   15–20% of the bill

8. Canadians can often be distinguished from other English speakers by the frequency in their speech of the following words:
   a.   like
   b.   maple syrup
   c.   eh

Source: Adapted from R. B. Genzel and M. G. Cummings, *Culturally Speaking: A Conversation and Culture Text for Learners of English* (New York: Harper and Row, 1986).

To complement a theme, quizzes can focus on a single topic such as eating customs or celebrations as in this quiz.

Thanksgiving Quiz

Instructions: *Circle the correct answer in Questions 1–6. Answer questions 7 and 8 in three or four short sentences. Be prepared to discuss your answers to each question with others in the class.*

1. Thanksgiving is a day to celebrate and give thanks for an important part of farming called
   a. planting
   b. harvest
   c. weeding

2. People usually celebrate Thanksgiving by
   a. dancing
   b. having a big meal with their family
   c. going to church

3. What is the traditional meat eaten at Thanksgiving?
   a. chicken
   b. turkey
   c. beef

4. What is the traditional dessert eaten at Thanksgiving?
   a. chocolate cake
   b. carrot cake
   c. pumpkin pie

5. What are the fall harvest vegetables?
   a. squash and potatoes
   b. beans and peas
   c. lettuce and cabbage

6. Thanksgiving is always celebrated in?
   a. spring
   b. fall
   c. the equinox

7. Do you have a holiday similar to Thanksgiving in your country? Briefly describe it.

8. What holiday do you enjoy celebrating most? Why?

Source: Ormiston, 1998.

You can develop short discussion worksheets for your students and keep them at a speaking station at the back of the class. Students who finish their in-class work early can form pairs or small groups to participate in these discussions. For an oral practice worksheet focusing on personal habits, you can provide statistics and facts about how North Americans spend their time and then ask students to compare with their pastimes as in the worksheet that follows.

Pastimes

Instructions: Discuss the following:

"Canadians watch TV about 23 hours every week. They also read newspapers about 4 hours every week. Are you surprised? Why or why not?"

1. How long do you watch TV every day?

2. How long do you read the newspaper every day?

3. How does this compare with what Canadians do?

Source: Ormiston, DeCoursey, and Fredeen, 1994. Reproduced by permission of the University of Saskatchewan Language Centre.

PRONUNCIATION WORKSHEETS

Following are sample worksheets for practicing initial b/v. One student receives Part A of the worksheet, and one student receives Part B.

- Student A asks questions about each person on the worksheet—"What did Betty buy?" or "What did Vincent buy?" Student B listens and chooses a food from his or her sheet. The food item should begin with the same initial consonant as the person's name in the question—that is, "Betty bought butter" or "Vincent bought vegetables." Student A writes the food name given in the space provided. Student B writes down the person's name beside the food.

Self-checking is easy. Partners check their answers by sharing their completed sheets with each other.

Other types of questions suitable for this exercise are, "Where does Betty live?" and "What does Betty like?" Other examples can be found in Knowles and Sasaki (1980).

STUDENT A

Student A: What did Betty buy?

Student B: <u>Betty</u> bought <u>butter</u>.

NAME	FOOD
Betty	*butter*
Brandon	_____
Vincent	_____
Bob	_____
Bin	_____
Vanessa	_____
Vicky	_____
Bonita	_____

STUDENT B

Student A: What did <u>Betty</u> buy?

Student B: <u>Betty</u> bought <u>butter</u>.

NAME	FOOD
Betty	butter
_____	vinegar
_____	brown bread
_____	blueberries
_____	vegetables
_____	bacon
_____	veal
_____	bananas

Source: Ormiston, DeCoursey, and Fredeen, 1994, based on N. Naiman, "Teaching Pronunciation Communicatively," *TESL Talk: The Teaching of Pronunciation* 17, no. 1 (1987): 141–47.

WORKSHEETS FOR TESTING

Teacher-developed paper-and-pencil tests should take into consideration much of what is important in designing worksheets for language practice. Your tests, like your worksheets, should have clear, simple instructions and review material already presented and practiced. As much as possible, tests should follow a format that is familiar to students from their classroom practice activities. Tests should also include examples where necessary.

The Overhead Projector

Advantages of Using Overhead Projectors

As teachers, we may take the overhead projector for granted because, like the chalkboard, it has been such a common piece of teaching equipment. Following are some advantages of using overheads from Shrum and Glisan (1994) and from our own teaching experience.

- You can be flexible in your use of overhead transparencies. Since overhead pens are available in both permanent and erasable ink, you can prepare them ahead of time and keep them for reuse, or you can use them spontaneously during class.
- Creative displays on the overhead projector, such as silhouettes, overlays, and systematic exposure, make it suitable for teaching in a variety of ways.
- It is easier to write on an overhead transparency than on the board or chart paper when you may have to turn your back on the class. This is important for presenting longer texts.
- Students can participate as pairs, groups, or individuals by writing on or preparing transparencies.
- There are few technical problems with overhead projectors.
- The overhead projector is accessible to you and your students.
- The overhead projector is cheaper than most other hardware and more economical than making a photocopy for each student.
- The overhead projector is a better choice than the chalkboard for charts and for drawings that are more elaborate than stick figures.
- The overhead projector is a better choice than the chalkboard for visual material that you plan to use repeatedly.
- Transparencies are easier to store and transport than rolls of paper.

General Considerations in Using Overhead Projectors

Following are suggestions for overhead use based on Shrum and Glisan and on our experience:

- Objectives—Have clear reasons for using the overhead projector. The presentation or activity should match your objectives and be more appropriate to this medium than another.
- Layout—Keep your transparencies simple and bold, avoiding details as much as possible. Limit a transparency to 25 words or less, and don't use too many colors on a single sheet. Avoid using transparencies for presenting a page of dense text such as a story; handouts are preferable for this purpose.

- The transparency—Shrum and Glisan suggest that you use a medium-grade transparency. Of course, if you are photocopying, you will need to use the grade recommended for the photocopy machine. Shrum and Glisan suggest that individual transparency sheets provide more flexibility than a roll of sheets and that you should clean them with spray appliance cleaner. Store transparencies between two sheets of clean paper.
- Pens or markers—When creating a transparency, decide if you want to reuse all or part of it. Use permanent overhead pens or markers for the part you wish to reuse. Use erasable markers for additions done in class or during production for parts that you do not wish to reuse. Use blue, black, purple, or green ink because they are the most legible to students.
- Transparency creation—You can create transparencies with pens or markers, or use a computer application such as PowerPoint or MS Word. Such programs can help you organize your thoughts, add a professional look to the transparency, and ultimately save you time. When you do use the computer, the transparencies will be permanent, but you can still supplement them with erasable pens. When creating transparencies, experiment with overlays, silhouettes, and systematic disclosure of information in which you present the overhead to students one section at a time, starting from the top and covering the rest with paper or cardboard. Number your transparencies to keep them organized.
- Erasing—If you are erasing selective words for cloze or other activities, a correction pen is better than a cleaning tissue. This is because it is difficult to remove text with a cleaning tissue without smudging other parts of the text, unless the rest of the transparency is done in permanent markers or is typed.
- Student involvement—Teach students how to make transparencies so that they can create them for individual, pair, or group presentations.
- Delivery—Shrum and Glisan say that use of the overhead should be limited to 10–15 minutes to avoid fatigue caused by the dim lights and fan noise of the machine.

  When you present material, stand next to the projector facing the class. Use your finger or a pen to point out things directly on the transparency rather than walking up to the screen. We have also seen teachers sitting when using the overhead projector to avoid obstructing the image on the screen. You may require a higher stool for this.

  You can use an acetate roll to slowly reveal language input, or you can use pieces of paper to cover up sections of your transparency. This allows you to control where you focus student attention. Paper can be manipulated while you are talking and looking at the students. You can't do this as easily at the board.

  Rest your hand on the projector to avoid tremor. Check the image on the screen occasionally to ensure that it stays centered and toward the top of the screen. Leave the transparency up for a few minutes after your presentation to let students copy, if necessary.

- Set-up—Set up the projector in advance so the image will be in focus, centered on the screen, and legible to all students when you turn it on. Prepare all supplementary and emergency equipment in advance and be sure you know how to use it. This equipment includes a three-prong plug adapter, extension cord, and spare projection bulb. When you have finished using the projector, turn off the light but leave the fan on for a few minutes to allow the machine to cool down.

Activities with Overhead Projectors

SILHOUETTES AND SHADOWS

You can cut out shapes or silhouettes and move them around on the overhead projection surface. For beginners, you can use cut-outs to illustrate a story or song. For students who don't like to sing, the moving visuals help them to remain involved and interested.

You can also use cut-out silhouettes with children for activities involving accidents and directions. Students move the cut-out of a boy on his bike and a car, for example, according to directions given (Brims 1985), or they create their own story about an accident using figures on a map background.

Students can participate in role plays using shadow puppets on the overhead surface or using the light from the overhead on a screen or large sheet of blank paper.

A roll of acetate can be used to illustrate and tell a story sequentially on the overhead projector (Duncan 1987, 13). You can also use cut-outs, as in the above example, for telling stories and illustrating the action. One teacher taught about the romance of Valentine's Day to her beginning students using a Vietnamese legend. The legend tells of a boatman who gains the attention of a princess by playing his flute on the river near her home. She summons him to appear before her and then banishes him because he is ugly. Tragedy ensues. The teacher drew the figures and objects needed for the story using cut-outs placed on the overhead projector surface. After telling the story once, introducing and moving the figures as needed, students took turns moving the cut-outs as the story was told. This involved students in the story and motivated them to listen carefully. The other students coached the student at the overhead. This technique provided physical involvement and made learning more concrete.

TEXT ACTIVITIES

Large group text activities for the overhead projector include:

- prediction activities in which you reveal a line at a time
- "think alouds"—read the text aloud and voice your reading strategy, that is, how you figure out the meaning of new words from context, guessing what will happen next. "Think alouds" help students become aware of reading strategies
- vocabulary work and reading comprehension questions—the teacher points with a pen or pointer to the area where the answer is found

- students read a short text projected onto the screen instead of reading with heads bent over books. This provides a change of focus, and some students may feel more comfortable sitting up and reading.
- presentation of poems and songs
- correction of dictation, punctuation, and capitalization exercises
- projection of test questions onto the screen that students answer on a sheet at their desks
- group revision—copying short compositions, or portions of a composition, onto transparencies for group work with students

The remainder of this chapter deals with audiovisual equipment, materials, and associated activities for language teaching and learning.

The Power of Audiovisual

As teachers, we recognize and are excited about the richness that audiovisual technology can bring to learning. However, we also may feel anxious or reticent to use it because of the planning time it takes, the need to learn about equipment that may be prone to breaking down, uncertainty about our ability to design effective teaching and learning tasks, and concern about the reaction and ultimate learning of our students. Judith Shrum and Eileen Glisan suggest that when using technology it is important to carefully examine your context, particularly your students' needs and abilities (249). Is technology the most effective and efficient way to enhance learning? How well will it meet your learning objectives? Does it support the content that you are currently teaching? Is it worth the time you will spend preparing an activity using technology in terms of the learning that you hope for? Ultimately it is up to you to decide if and when you will use audiovisual material.

Audio as Language Teaching Material

Attributes of Audio CDs and Audiotapes

Audio CDs and tapes can bring to your students the voices of native speakers that are different from that of the teacher. CDs and tapes are useful for listening to dialogues and discussions with more than one speaker. Audio material, however, has one major disadvantage when compared to live speech and video—the absence of a visual component makes it much more difficult to understand. The same is true of radio. Nevertheless, in life we are often presented with audio only, so it is worth helping students develop listening without accompanying visual cues.

Recording students' own speech may encourage them to practice many times and attend consciously to correctness. But, for recording purposes, the audiotape recorder is less obtrusive and more portable than video. Some learners may also feel more comfortable talking into a tape recorder than being recorded on video.

Audio recording equipment is still less expensive and more accessible than video recording equipment, although that is changing as the cost of digital camcorders becomes less prohibitive. However, if you are working in a developing country you may find that even basic audio equipment is not readily available. Size and expense may make audio cassettes and recorders more suitable than CDs or video equipment for individual and small group work. And audiocassette format is standardized internationally whereas video still is not.

Because CD players and tape recorders are easy to use, students can work with them at their own pace. A teacher can send individuals or small groups of students out of the class to work with prerecorded material. With headphones, one or more students can work in class without disturbing others. Even in large group activities, students can seat themselves around the playback unit and control the buttons themselves, stopping and replaying as needed.

Types of Audio Material

COMMERCIAL TAPES

ESL and EFL publishers produce these types of audio products on CD or audiocassettes: material for pronunciation practice; drills; stories; material for comprehension-based activities; and material that presents functions, structures, and vocabulary, usually dialogues and conversations in context. Most audio materials accompany the students' course book. In general, the value of each of these products for teaching is dependent on audio quality, relevance to curriculum and course or lesson objectives, age-appropriateness, and interest to students. Because each of these types of products is produced differently and for different purposes, you will need to assess for yourself whether or not they enhance your teaching goals. For example, one pronunciation audio product may be simply repeating individual words or phrases with the goal of helping students become familiar with forming the sounds, while another pronunciation product may involve minimal pairs with the goal of developing students' ability to differentiate difficult sounds. Similarly, one audio drill may be produced to develop automatic responses, while another may involve more communicative or authentic responses. The same is true of audio dialogues, grammar, and vocabulary-building products. You will need to weigh the pros and cons of the particular product and its suitability to the needs of your students and your objectives when selecting commercial audio products.

An interesting type of audio material is jigsaw listening in which different versions or parts of the same story or conversation are presented aurally to students. You can use audio jigsaws in the same way as written jigsaw texts. Some listening/speaking texts contain audio jigsaws. Longer listening material—from textbooks, books on tape, radio, or TV—can also be used as jigsaw listening by giving small groups of students different parts of the listening selection.

TEACHER-PRODUCED AUDIO MATERIAL

Produce your own audio material using either the computer and burning a CD or with an audiotape recorder. Involve other teachers, friends, and family to ensure variety in the voices of native speakers to present functions such as different greetings and leave-takings in context. You can also record authentic English input, such as radio phone-in and talk shows, radio news and weather reports, and live conversations. You can also create your own jigsaw CDs or tapes. Note that copyright laws apply to recordings of radio shows, music, and other commercial audio products.

Have young students individually or in small groups listen to their own recordings of their stories and illustrate them. Students then share their illustrated stories with the rest of the class.

RECORDINGS OF STUDENTS

Ask your students to record themselves interviewing or conversing with someone in the target language. In class, ask them to use their audio material to analyze the phonological aspects of the interviewee's language, such as dropped syllables and pronunciation of various sounds. The activity is useful in raising awareness of fluency as well as dialect differences.

For error correction, almost any oral group activity can be recorded. Group members can take the recording home. Then, in class, students can tell you something they learned from listening to the recording. Groups can study a recording together, preparing a transcript to study or simply listening and reporting back on mistakes they noticed and corrected. They can also report on things they did well (Edge 1993, 58).

- Have students record themselves for homework, speaking on various topics. Then you respond on the same audiotape with suggestions and comments.
- More product-oriented student audio recording activities include writing and then recording fairy tales or radio plays, complete with sound effects.
- Instead of student-to-student or class-to-class written letters, students can make and send audio recordings to each other.
- The Community Language Learning Approach uses transcribed recordings of student conversations, up to ten minutes in length, as the basis for a variety of language work. You can read more about this approach in *Techniques and Principles in Language Teaching* by Diane Larsen-Freeman (2000).

RADIO, LIVE AND RECORDED

As with audio CDs and audiotapes, radio allows learners to hear a variety of accents and to hear authentic use of the language. Because the radio is ideal for presenting current events and real conversations, it brings relevance to learning the target language. If you are recording from radio, be sure that what you record is current; don't use a radio broadcast, especially a news broadcast, that is more than two or three months old. An added benefit to the use of radio is that you can combine radio activities with newspaper activities to study current events. These kinds of activities will be easier for you to develop for intermediate or advanced students.

Sandra Savignon (1997) used radio instead of a listening/speaking textbook in her French class. She found that using live radio and tapes of live radio in the target language helped her students develop comprehension and that their language production also improved markedly during the course. She started by having students listen to newscasts for a week. Students were allowed to record the radio programs so that they could listen to them several times. They then brought their questions to class. Savignon found that cultural context—that is, prior knowledge of the topic and context—affected student comprehension more than vocabulary. By providing cultural information to the students, their comprehension improved and they were better able to focus on their language difficulties as they listened. As their comprehension developed, they could begin to focus on unfamiliar topics. During the course, students presented what they heard and shared reactions in class. Savignon summarized written texts of the news on a daily basis to support students' comprehension. She also invited guest speakers to discuss the current events they had heard on radio. She was easily able to evaluate learning based on the in-class discussions.

Considerations in Selecting or Making Audio Recordings

Here are some general considerations when choosing or developing audio recordings (CDs and audiotapes):

- Have clear reasons for using the audio recordings. The presentation or activity using audio recordings or radio should match your objectives and be appropriate to this medium.
- Ensure the sound quality is excellent; since there are no visuals, you cannot afford to frustrate students with poor sound quality.
- Make sure that your playback equipment is adequate. Check equipment ahead of time to ensure that it works and that everyone in the class can hear it.
- To make speech sound natural when recording, avoid reading a text word for word. Spontaneity is more important than accuracy. You can also have speakers make up a skeleton text, controlling the difficulty of the language if you like, but using their own words. Alternatively, you can give them only a basic situation to improvise.
- Using audio recordings may not be the best way to introduce students to a wide range of accents. Introducing unfamiliar accents can be demoralizing for beginning students who need to experience success in the listening tasks that you set for them.
- The degree of authenticity you should look for or strive to create is debatable. The fact that an audio recording is more difficult to follow than a video recording or live speech is a reason for considering semi-authentic recordings. Authentic speech usually contains many colloquialisms and redundancy. In fact, some aspects of redundancy such as repeating the same thing twice, hesitation, and elaboration, facilitate comprehension. It is helpful to include some of these aspects of authentic speech in semi-authentic recordings.

  We by no means suggest that you entirely shelter students from authentic, spontaneous speech, but you should take their abilities into account. You may want to grade some audio listening tasks to make a smooth transition from semi-authentic to genuine speech. Also, limit your use of audio CDs or audiotapes for listening comprehension because they are more difficult to follow than face-to-face speech. Finally, be sure to include pre-listening, while listening, and post-listening tasks.

Audio Listening Tasks

If you are not using a commercial listening package, you will need to develop pre-listening, during listening, and post-listening activities yourself. Even the listening tasks provided in commercial packages may need some adaptation or adjustment to your students' needs.

In language teaching, audio material is most commonly used for listening comprehension. Listening exercises on audio or video recordings are most effective if constructed around tasks or topics that you have been studying in class. In real life, we have a reason for listening. Thus, in the language classroom, we also need to prepare students for listening with sufficient background context, familiar language, preparation for new structural forms, and motivation for listening.

You can design some listening activities to train students. Some training tasks include discrimination of English sounds, identifying stress and intonation patterns, and grammatical patterns. You should also include comprehension tasks such as activities to practice general comprehension, comprehension of specific details, and inference. Types of listening tasks with audio material include note taking, answering questions, expressing agreement or disagreement, marking a picture or diagram according to instructions, and filling in blanks in a cloze transcript of a recording such as a song, poem, story, or other interesting text. Provide some kind of support, such as a worksheet, to accompany listening. Activities should be relatively easy, with success built in.

As with reading, pre-listening activities are extremely important when using audio recordings for comprehension. You can use visuals and discussion to provide context for the listeners. You may need to pre-teach some vocabulary using drawings or real objects.

Language Labs

Advantages of Language Labs

Language labs have had a tendency to come in and out of favor. In addition, with digital technology, there are many more possibilities and complexities in creating and using materials for language labs. Should you find yourself in a teaching situation with a language lab, take advantage of it. These advantages are compiled from Duncan (66–67) and our experiences:

- Language labs can be set up so that several students interact simultaneously, either during class or as independent practice outside of class.
- Students, according to their listening levels, can replay what they hear.
- Each student can control starting, stopping, and repeating functions as needed, since the listening or pronunciation text is usually recorded onto each student's individual recording in the lab. In this way, students can complete many in-class listening and pronunciation tasks at their own pace.
- For assessment and evaluation purposes, you can listen unobtrusively to students as they work in the lab.
- You can give discrete feedback through the intercom system that only the

individual you are talking to will hear, or you can address the entire class. Some labs allow you to address select groups of students.

- You can create individual lessons, addressing remedial work that individuals require.

If you do have access to a language lab, be sure you have a reason for using it. For instance, why would you have two students sitting side by side in a language laboratory engage in a dialogue when they can do so face to face?

Today language labs can be extremely sophisticated, incorporating computer technology and allowing for video as well as audio input. However, you may find yourself using an older lab designed primarily for practice drills. Or you may find yourself with no lab at all. In such situations, analyze the value of setting up a simple lab using several audio playback units and headphones with splitters at small stations around the classroom.

If you have not used a language lab for teaching in the past, you will experience a learning curve. However, over time you will become proficient and may even become very creative in developing language lab activities.

Language Labs for Skills Development

Traditional labs are effective in helping students develop skills in identification, following directions, imitation, listening and replying, and free speech (Duncan, 66–68).

IDENTIFICATION TASKS

In identification tasks, students listen to pick out a sound, word stress, or intonation pattern by underlining, highlighting, or circling the item on worksheets developed to accompany an audio text; typically identification involves drills, minimal pairs, cloze, and dictation activities (Duncan). Here are two examples of identification tasks:

Example 1
Ask students to circle the picture they hear, for example, to discriminate words such as *walking* and *working*. Learners hear: *He's working in the park.* They circle the correct letter choices.

Example 2

Students read along as they listen and trace the contours of what they hear. Model it first, and then have students try with groups of sentences as in the example of the tags that follows. Consider the two different contours of the tags (underlined) and the different meanings that will result (statement versus question). Note in these following examples how the teaching of sound discrimination and comprehension overlap.

> *Example A:*
> You're going to meet us for lunch, aren't you.
>
> *Example B:*
> You're going to meet us for lunch, aren't you?

FOLLOWING DIRECTIONS

Ask students to listen to directions and follow them as they listen or after they have listened. Some ideas include tracing routes on maps, filling in grids, or locating items on a picture (67).

IMITATION TASKS

Imitation tasks have students listen and repeat; they are most often designed for pronunciation improvement. You can increase difficulty by adjusting speed, length of words, kinds of intonation patterns, and mood. You can decrease difficulty by having lower level students tap rhythms and sing songs (Duncan).

Listening and Replying, and Free Speech

Listening and replying can also be practiced in the language lab. Listening and replying activities involve students listening and responding in short phrases or a single word.

Free speech involves longer input from students, such as summarizing what they have heard or telling a story from a series of pictures. In free speech activities, students can take their time, repeat phrases, and hear and correct their errors themselves, while you listen in on individual students and note strengths and problem areas. For example, you may ask advanced students to summarize a story from a newscast or to summarize today's weather from a weather report recorded from the radio. Topics for free speech can include asking students to make a recording about their family, job, or last holiday, opinions on a variety of topics, hopes for the future, etc. Later, you can use these summaries as dictations (Duncan).

You should note that in the past published pronunciation programs for the traditional language lab provided space for students to record themselves. Many newer pronunciation texts and materials do not provide time and space for student recording. They are designed for classroom use and do not lend themselves to traditional lab work. However, with the arrival of the iBT TOEFL®, this is likely to change.

Video as Language Teaching Material

Attributes of Video Technology

Video technology includes DVDs, videotapes, and television. The benefits of video in the language classroom are tremendous. We have combined our teaching experience with that of other language-teaching professionals (Shrum and Glisan; Stoller 1993; Burt 1999) to offer these advantages of using video:

- Video often illustrates authentic communication in real contexts.
- Video combines visual and audio input, contributing to students' development of comprehension as well as nonverbal communication.
- Video often illustrates many of the cultural factors involved in communication, such as gesture, mood, relationships, age, sex, and social status as identified through such factors as dress. These factors are important because they affect communication style and register, for example, making the choice between saying, *Excuse me, sir.* and *Hey, Mike!*
- Video input is motivational; students like watching them and most students are familiar with the medium and relate well to it. Well-produced video has relevance beyond language learning. Because students are eager to know what happens next, they will ask questions about it.
- Video can provide a variety of types of language practice. As well as listening practice, a video recording can be the stimulus and reinforcement for speaking, reading, and writing activities as well as the development and practice of vocabulary and grammatical structures.
- Video provides the opportunity for students to experience a variety of speech variations.
- Teachers can actively manipulate video in a number of ways to address students' needs. This is increasingly possible with the advent of DVD technology and interactive video (video combined with computer technologies).

Types of Recorded Video Material

There are several types of recorded video material for language teaching. Note that copyright restrictions, discussed later in this section, apply to many of these categories:

- material taken from television programs and movies
- video produced for theme-based and content-area classrooms
- commercial video productions made specifically for the language classroom
- teacher-produced video recordings
- recordings of students that allow them to see and hear themselves using the target language and student-produced video recordings, which offer students the opportunity to work together on a video project in the target language

TELEVISION AND MOVIES

Television shows and movies are rich sources of audiovisual input. Consider all of the genres that we watch on TV—ads, news and sportscasts, weather reports, movies, sitcoms, documentaries, and talk shows. Movies, in DVD or videotape format, also include a variety of genres, some of which are more suitable than others for classroom use. Both television shows and movies depict language spoken at normal speed, with real accents, in interesting contexts, thus challenging students to consolidate all their skills in order to comprehend. You can also use television and movies to help students develop critical thinking skills (Burt).

Captioned video, available on television for hearing-impaired people, helps students to comprehend in three modalities: listening, reading, and using visual clues. Movies subtitled in English allow students to read and watch, but the audio should be turned off unless it is in English.

The advantage of television current events programs is that they illustrate to students an authentic use of the language. One advantage of movies is that all, or segments, of them can be reviewed over and over again, and DVDs have quick cueing features. TV can be recorded, but there are copyright restrictions (discussed on page 142). However, some television networks encourage teachers to use their programs and have created written and electronic supports for this purpose.

Miriam Burt cautions that it may take considerable time for you to preview and select appropriate television and movie input for your class and then design support activities and materials. This is because the content of TV programs and movies is not controlled, and so may not work well unless it was specifically developed for educational purposes.

VIDEO FOR THEME AND CONTENT-BASED TEACHING

Fredricka Stoller outlines the following advantages of using video specifically in theme-based and content-area classrooms:

- They can introduce a new theme or content area.
- They can support or develop a theme or content currently being taught through a new medium of instruction
- They can stimulate development of speaking, listening, reading, and writing.
- They can bring a theme or an area of content study to a close. (26)

You can use commercial, theme-based, video productions as well as video recordings or television programs focusing on specific topics, to support theme and content-based teaching. Stoller notes the importance of including previewing, while viewing, and post viewing activities (discussed later in this chapter).

COMMERCIAL VIDEO PRODUCTIONS

Commercial video productions and interactive video (video combined with computer applications) made specifically for the language classroom are increasingly available through ESL and EFL publishers. Some of these products accompany course books. They are usually designed with specific learning goals in mind such as business English, workplace communication, survival skills, and tourism. You can even buy soap opera videos designed for language teaching. There are a greater number of commercial video or video series available for adult students than there are for children.

High-quality commercial video products usually use graded language with controlled vocabulary and structures. In addition, they have been evaluated for language, content, and length and may be packaged together with teacher guides, worksheets, transcripts, audiotapes (Burt), and other suggested activities. However, as with commercial audio materials, you may choose to design your own activities and worksheets to better serve your teaching purposes, the needs of your students, your particular context, and your own teaching style.

Be aware that not all commercial videos and video products for the language class are of high quality. They may be expensive, so take advantage of publishers' demonstration products. As with audio materials, you need to consider differences between North American and British English. Also, consider the authentic versus nonauthentic debate and what is best for your students.

Don't forget to explore the use of authentic audio material that is not specifically produced for ESL. The increased availability of digital material that includes not only CDs and DVDs but also podcasts and other online products, opens an audio world of learning to you and your students. Podcasts alone, for example, allow you to present aural input from music, to comedy, to religious sermons, to lectures on economics and politics. Some of these products may be available at low cost or for free, while others are more expensive. As we have stressed previously, however, it is important to be judicious in your selection of these products to ensure that they are of high sound quality, fit with your curriculum, enhance learning objectives, and are of interest to students.

TEACHER-PRODUCED VIDEOS

You may want to record your own video material in order to present or reinforce specific language functions and cultural considerations. You can also record a video to bring textbook materials to life. Mary, one of the authors, was involved in a materials-development project with a colleague, acting out about 25 language situations from *LexiCarry* (Moran 2002), a book that depicts cartoon figures involved in various language acts such as greetings, asking for directions, apologizing, and complimenting. They played themselves, using few props to establish the context (e.g., desks to show a classroom and a cup to knock over as the pretext for an apology). To facilitate natural spoken language use, they did not use a script. They simply looked at the illustration of the function, which contained no words, discussed the role designations and sequence of actions for a minute or two for each function, and then improvised.

Mary and another teacher also selected acts of communication that posed difficulties for students in a work-related ESL program, such as responding to sexual harassment or asking for feedback on work performance. They made video recordings of the problems for class discussion, problem solving, further language teaching, and role-playing activities. This video project involved scripting, directing, rehearsals, renting equipment, editing, and the help of a professional camera operator who, fortunately, offered services free of charge. Needless to say, the project involved considerable time and expense and could not have been undertaken without a team approach and the full support of the teachers' educational institution.

Video projects do not need to be as elaborate as this, although with digital camcorders and computer applications that allow relatively easy editing it is becoming feasible to produce acceptable videos for teaching purposes. To bring the outside world into the classroom, Duncan suggests recording native speakers in common situations such as pumping gas, sharing a traditional Thanksgiving dinner, ordering and picking up fast food at a drive-in counter. However, whatever the video recording project, be prepared to spend more time on it than on writing a dialogue or developing a worksheet.

VIDEO RECORDINGS OF STUDENTS AND BY STUDENTS

Many learners enjoy performing and seeing themselves on video as much as they enjoy watching professionally produced productions. Others, particularly some adults, are self-conscious and nervous in front of the video camera. With any class, ask the students if they mind being recorded on video before proceeding. If students are interested in performing in front of the camera, this medium benefits students in these ways:

- They will practice speaking many times, sometimes attending to pronunciation and linguistic accuracy more conscientiously when they are going to be recorded.
- Recordings can be used for error analysis and correction.
- Students can observe their own nonverbal (paralinguistic) communication. For example, students can practice and videotape job interviews and then analyze the results. Your students may be surprised to discover that their facial expressions, tone of voice, and gestures do not come across as intended. This awareness can help them adjust their nonverbal communication so that they can present themselves as they wish to.
- In working together to negotiate and prepare the content of a video, students must engage with each other in authentic, free communication that is not rigidly structured by the teacher.

One way to introduce students to video work is to have them do simple introductions of themselves on camera, for example, "Hi, my name's Mary. I'm an ESL teacher at the University Language Centre." Here are a few additional activities you can record:

- student-led aerobic dance routines (a Total Physical Response type of learning activity)
- simple dialogues to which students add costumes and action
- fully developed role plays and simulations
- a news and weather show, based on current newspaper and TV reports, school events, and news. Students take on the roles of anchors, reporters, weather forecasters, or sportscasters.

Other ideas include student-made commercials, music videos, mock soap operas, game shows based on current television game shows, "on the street" interviews on topical issues, and celebrity interview programs using students and instructors as celebrities. Students can also record rehearsals for class presentations, job interviews, and role plays. Such recordings will help them to critique and improve their performance. Be open to student suggestions for video projects and be prepared for a great deal of student investment in their own ideas.

Selecting Video Material

There are a number of factors to consider when selecting video material. You can develop a checklist for yourself outlining which videos to use for which teaching and learning objectives, or you can just ask yourself:

- What are your purposes in showing a video? How will you use the video? Is this video the best way to support teaching and learning objectives?
- What makes the video suitable to meet the teaching and learning objectives you have set? What are its limitations?
- What is the topic of the video? What is the context? What is its purpose—to inform, to educate, or to entertain?
- Is the message of the video clear? Are the language and cultural content appropriate?
- For whom was the video created? Was the video created for English language learning? For what age range is the video and its content developed (i.e., for children or adults) and at what proficiency level?
- Does the video have entertainment as well as pedagogical value? Is it interesting and motivational or inspirational? Will it appeal to most of the students in your class?
- Can the video or video segment stand on its own? Is there sufficient context in short segments to support comprehension? Is it too long or too short? Susan Stempleski (1993) suggests segments of less than five minutes duration.
- Are the picture and the sound quality clear? Is the speech delivery (rate, accent, clarity) suitable? Do supporting graphics help support comprehension and are they on-screen long enough?
- Is the video available and accessible when you need it?
- What support materials accompany the video (print, audio, computer)? Are the supports accessible and easy to use? Are transcripts available?
- How much support material will you need to develop? Is your time investment worth the learning that you think will occur?
- Is the video in the proper format for the playback equipment in your teaching context (see the section on Using Video Abroad on pages 141–42)? (Shrum and Glisan; Burt)

When selecting videos, be aware that some types of videos are suitable for one group but not another. For example, educational documentaries are usually not suitable for students of lower proficiency levels because they are often too linguistically dense and contain little action to motivate students or to help them interpret meaning. Some comedy shows can be extremely difficult for beginners to follow because of the tempo of the dialogue, the play on words, and the cultural context of the humor. However, if the students are already familiar with the story or content in another form from their own culture, they may enjoy the video, despite the linguistic challenge.

The tasks you develop to accompany a video will influence which productions you choose. You may be able to use one video with many different class levels by adapting the tasks.

With adults, you may choose short video segments of videos, sometimes with sound off, sometimes with picture off. Since children initially want to see and understand the entire story, Barry Tomalin (1990) suggests segments between 30 seconds and 4 minutes in length. Each segment should tell a complete story or section of a story. For young viewers, Tomalin suggests cartoons with controlled language and visual input at the children's age and language level.

Options for Presenting Video

Shrum and Glisan (255–56) and others offer some less traditional ways to present video:

- Image and sound together—teachers show a scene with the sound on and develop activities or tasks according to objectives, for example, to illustrate a theme, to develop vocabulary, to illustrate register, or to summarize,
- Image alone—teachers play a frozen image with the sound turned off and develop activities to take advantage of nonverbal communication and cultural elements. By playing the image alone, language does not obscure the visual message.
- Sound alone—teachers block scene (with cardboard or by turning down screen brightness) to help students develop listening comprehension. Students can predict the images through writing or drawing. Later, the teacher plays sound with the image so that students also have visual clues to check their listening comprehension. Students can also predict the visual image from first listening to the sound alone.
- Pause or freeze frame—teachers pause or freeze a frame of the video to develop prediction skills, check comprehension, or to point out a feature of the video. This makes the presentation of the video more interactive.

Activities with Video Material

Most video activities fall into two categories—comprehension-based activities that work with language and content generated by the video, and production-based activities that stimulate students to generate language, usually in the form of discussion and writing. When choosing and designing video activities, decide on your focus.

The following section has been divided into pre-viewing, while viewing, and post-viewing activities when viewing. We have also included a section on using video material with children. The ideas below are from our own teaching experiences and from Shrum and Glisan, Stoller, and Burt. If you are using commercial products, be aware that they often come with their own previewing, while-viewing, and post-viewing activities. Knowing about these activities will help you in your selection, adaptation, and creation of video products. Feel free to adapt these ideas for your needs.

PREVIEWING ACTIVITIES

Use pre-viewing activities to prepare your students for watching the video material and facilitating comprehension. Pre-viewing activities motivate and give students a purpose for viewing the video. They should also activate students' existing knowledge and experience so that the new material is not out of context or totally foreign to them. Here are some pre-viewing ideas:

- **View the title**—Have students discuss the title of the video. A movie title, in itself, may evoke much discussion as students predict the reason for the title. You can brainstorm from the title alone what the video will be about and even create a semantic map of the brainstorm.
- **Summaries**—Provide students with a brief summary of the video and have them skim for the main ideas or scan for specific information that will help them comprehend the video better when you play it for them.
- **Main ideas**—Present the main idea or a problem raised in the video. Have students interview each other about the idea in pairs, small groups, or as a whole class. If the video presents a problem, students may discuss solutions. You may need to develop a worksheet to facilitate this. For example, high-intermediate or advanced adolescents or adults may discuss attitudes toward schooling before watching a segment from *Dead Poets' Society*, or, more recently, *School of Rock*.
- **Activate knowledge**—Provide students with a worksheet asking them what they already know about the topic of the video material, what they don't know or are not sure about, and what they want to know. During viewing, students confirm what they already know or look for answers to their questions. This works particularly well with documentaries and educational programs.
- **Pre-read**—Have students read a review of the video or information on the topic raised in the video material. For example, if the video is *Moby Dick* you might have the students read about whales and whaling.
- **Preview vocabulary**—List vocabulary or phrases from the video on the chalkboard, choosing dialogue or a description of the action that gives good clues about the story. Have students work in groups to figure out the action, plot, characters, and location. Groups present their conclusions and, after viewing, discuss differences between predictions and the actual story.
- **Preview cultural content**—You may need to explain about some of the cultural situations students will see.
- **Preview structure**—You may need to go over some specialized grammatical items.
- **Predict**—Students can look at still images from the video material to predict what it is about. You can have students suggest news items they expect to hear about on the news before listening to a recording of the news. With dramatic segments of characters in difficult predicaments, show the end of the segment and have students predict what occurred before. Finally, play two separate segments of a drama, and have students predict the middle.

Activities during Viewing

Activities during viewing help students attend to specific features of the video material and should relate closely to your objectives. Or, you can have students watch for overall comprehension only. Here are some ideas for activities while viewing:

- **Video interruptions**—Interrupt the video to clarify, explain, or discuss points raised. You can interrupt for a longer period of time and ask students to do something with the information on the video. For example, you may use a video that shows a process, such as how to make a *papier mâché* mask. As each step is explained, stop the video and have students carry out the described instruction.

- **Worksheets**—To guide video viewing for comprehension, use worksheets for listening tasks similar to those for listening comprehension activities used with audio recordings. Make sure the worksheets are easy to follow and don't require lengthy answers. Pause at points during the video to allow students to fill in answers. Instead of making worksheets on which students record answers, you can also write a chart on the board or overhead projector for students to copy. They can do this while you are setting up the video equipment. Later, students can fill in their answers on your chart for others to check.

- **Individual viewing assignments**—Have groups of students view for specific information. For example, have all students in Group A view for nonverbal behavior. Have all students in Group B view for idioms and slang. Have all students in Group C take note of incomplete sentences. Then, discuss these in class. Similarly, you can have half the class view the image with the sound turned off and the other half listen with the screen hidden. Then pairs or groups get together to fill in the missing information.

- **Vocabulary**—For beginners, make up a task sheet that lists words, phrases, or expressions already covered in class and that appear in one segment of a video. Instruct the students to circle the ones they hear during viewing. This is a good activity for beginners because it is not too difficult and because beginners, especially, need to experience success in language tasks that you set for them. With children, you can make a game by having students name as many objects or colors as they see in a segment.

- **Note-taking**—For students who need to develop note-taking skills, you can make up a partially completed lecture outline to accompany a taped lecture. Often students have difficulty sifting out what is important and what is merely an example in longer discourse, so worksheets that guide their listening can be helpful. You can also have students take notes on which to base a written summary of the video.

- **Dialogue comprehension**—Make up a worksheet with a section of the dialogue scrambled. Students listen and then put the lines of the dialogue in the correct sequence. They have the extra advantage of video cues. You may decide to play the tape more than once.

- **Functions**—Students view, without the sound, a short section showing a function, such as introducing someone, ordering a meal, offering condolences. Then they write and rehearse the dialogue for it. Play the soundless segment again with students doing live voice-over or play a tape recording of their dialogue.

- **Register**—After viewing a scene for a particular function and perhaps practicing it, you can have students practice the same function but in a different register. For example, "Do you need a hand?" to "May I help you?" is a change from an informal to a more formal register. Change the setting, ages, or business roles of the speakers. Have your students role-play the scene, taking into account the changes prescribed.
- **Narration**—For production practice, stop the video and have students orally paraphrase or summarize what has happened up to that point. This can involve practice of various verb tenses and reported speech, such as "She said that . . . ."
- **Comprehension development**—Give students a narrative resume of out-of-sequence video events and ask them to reorder the events.
- **Comprehension development and production**—Students can prepare and ask each other questions about the film such as, "Who arrived at the murder scene first?" or "What did he do after he saw the body?"
- **Cultural comparisons**—Use a video to focus on cultural variations, such as architecture, transportation, dress, food, gestures, ways to express emotions. Students who are studying English in an EFL context will learn something about the target culture simply by noting what they see in a setting that is different from their own. If they are watching a Canadian video production, for example, they might note the red mail boxes, cars driving on the right side of the road, and snow.
- **Transcriptions**—Under some circumstances, you may want the students to view short segments of the video with the script. Keep in mind if you do this, however, that as their eyes are on their papers and not on the screen, they are missing all of the visual elements. As students read and listen, they can circle select items, such as words or phrases that persuade. You may also ask them to delete unnecessary words or fillers such as *um* or *well*. Or you may have them fill in missing words that we often drop in spoken language.

Post-Viewing Activities

Post-viewing activities help students consolidate what they have seen and learned from the video. This type of activity can also help students use the verbal and non-verbal language they have learned. Here are some post-viewing activities for video material:

- writing a summary of the video; this can also be done as a speed-writing activity
- describing the characters
- writing a screenplay of a segment, including as much detail as possible such as register, gestures, and props
- writing an alternative ending
- reading material related to the video

- comparing information in class or group discussions on a newscast item with a newspaper article or two different videos telling the same story
- discussing various elements raised in a video, for example, reactions of two different characters, problems presented, issues raised, opposing views raised
- role-playing the story as it is, or with adaptations
- replacing the soundtrack with the students' own dialogues or narratives
- creating student video recordings based on the one that has been viewed in class.

Tips for Presenting Video

Here are some tips for presenting video:

- Show short segments. Avoid analyzing every segment of a two-hour movie or you will take away the joy of viewing. Let the students watch the entire movie without interruptions after you have finished working with several sections of it.
- Make sure your students know why they are viewing the video material. Emphasize that they do not need to understand everything. Language learners who try, and perhaps nearly succeed, in understanding everything may not "see the forest for the trees," because they become so bogged down and frustrated by their attempts to comprehend every word.
- Set specific tasks that are easily done during viewing. Students can view videos on their own time just for pleasure and information. Class time is best used for helping students work with language in ways that they cannot easily accomplish independently. Without a specific task, students may feel overwhelmed by the complexity of the images and language.
- When appropriate and if time allows, repeat showings allow students to check answers to tasks given while viewing the video material and allow them to fully comprehend the video.
- As with other technologies, make sure that the equipment is booked, in working order, and that the screen is large enough and properly placed so that it is visible to all your students. Miriam Burt suggests a 20-inch video screen for a class of up to 15 students. Make sure the DVD or tape is properly cued. If showing a live television show, be sure you double check the broadcast times. If showing an interactive video (video plus computer technology) or multimedia program, make sure you know how it works and that you can properly give instructions to students.
- Turn room lights low, but not off, for safety purposes and so that students can write.

Video Recording Tips

If you intend to use a video of your students outside of the classroom, you should get signed permission from your students at the time of filming. Whether you or your students are doing the recording, Lonergan (1984, 103–5) suggests some basic techniques to keep in mind in terms of picture composition of static shots:

- Head and shoulders—Leave space above the head, so that the top of the head is not cut off.
- Close-up of the face—You can cut off the top of the head and chin very slightly in order to use the entire screen rather than leaving a lot of white space above and below the head.
- Position of individuals—Position people so that they don't look as if they have objects growing out of their heads. For example, have a person stand next to, rather than in front of, a coat stand, which on film could look like an extension of the person's head.
- What to wear—Avoid high-contrast colors such as black and white that fight with each other on camera. Instead, have students wear bright colors as color will wash out, especially if you are using bright lights.

Here are basic kinds of video camera movements for a variety of effects (Lonergan):

- Zoom in and zoom out—The camera remains still; the zoom lens moves subject nearer or farther away.
- Pan right and pan left—The camera remains stationary and is swivelled from right to left or left to right.
- Tilt up and tilt down—The camera remains stationary and is tilted up or down.
- Crane up and crane down—The camera is moved to higher or lower positions on a tripod.
- Track in and track out—The camera is rolled or walked nearer to or farther from the subject.
- Crab left and crab right—The camera is rolled or walked to the left or right.

Be sure that your camera movements are slow and smooth; don't zoom, pan, or tilt too often as this can be distracting. You may also be interested in a couple of useful effects:

- Show time lapsing by fading in and out, using the lens or other camera control to darken and lighten.
- When cutting to a different scene, the picture should look different and usually be from a different angle, which may mean physically moving the camera. You can make the picture look different by changing from a close-up to a long shot, changing the angle or position from which you are recording, or by having people change position slightly.

Using Video Abroad

DVDs will play back on any DVD playback unit. However, videotape systems overseas are not always the same as those in North America, and your tape won't play on the incompatible system. Different countries have different systems:

- NTSC (National Television Standards Committee) is used in Canada, the United States, and many other places in the western hemisphere as well as in Japan, the Philippines, and some East Asian countries.

- SECAM *(Séquence de Couleurs avec Mémoire)* is used in France and other Francophone countries as well as in most of the former east block countries of Europe, although many are switching to PAL.
- PAL (Phase Alternate Line) is used in the rest of Europe and Asia.

Once you know which format you need, have a copy of your tape converted by a business specializing in audiovisual production (e.g., some camera stores can do this for you). Most charge a fee, but shop around to ensure that you get the best price.

Copyright Restrictions Related to Audiovisual Material

Copyright laws related to showing audiovisual materials, including radio and television shows, or films vary from country to country. Find out the regulations where you are teaching.

SHOWING VIDEOS AND FILMS TO STUDENTS IN THE UNITED STATES AND CANADA

If you live in the United States and wish to show a video or film to your students, you must comply with U.S. copyright law. In Canada, entertainment videos rented from video stores can be used only for home viewing, not public or classroom viewing. You can do this in the United States. Videos that can be used in the classroom will state on them that they are "Cleared for Public Performance Rights." Public libraries and some educational institutions have these types of videos available. They are often informational in nature (e.g., travel videos, videos on science), children's films, and some classic dramas.

Canadian copyright law now allows you to record TV or radio news for classroom viewing, subject to the rules described in the Copyright Act, but the same is not true for documentary or entertainment programs. Those require copyright clearance. In the United States you can record for use in your classroom.

If you decide you want to use non-news television or radio programs, or an entertainment or other video or film that is not cleared for public performance, you need to pay the required royalties or get permission from the copyright holder. Your teaching institution should be able to help you find out about paying royalties or obtaining permission.

CHAPTER 6

Computers and the Internet

COMPUTER LAB BLUES

Jay, a well-educated and experienced teacher, landed a great job teaching English at a new secondary school in an inner-city area. The school was well equipped with a large multimedia laboratory, including computers with language learning software and high-speed Internet access. The principal proudly showed off the equipment, noting that while they had experienced a few too many breakdowns, a technology assistant was available within three days to fix any problems. The principal informed Jay that he should spend most of his teaching time in that facility using the available software.

Jay found that his English language students were either refugees with large gaps in their education or English as a second dialect students who were linguistically ill prepared for academic studies delivered in English. Most students had never used computers, and most had experienced trauma either from their home countries or from social problems at home. In addition, many felt alienated from school.

Although he was experienced in using multimedia labs, Jay had two challenges. First, he had to identify appropriate individualized language programs that would address the social, cultural, linguistic, and academic needs of each student. Second, he needed to find a way to deliver these programs in a multimedia lab equipped with individual computer stations with drill-based language learning software designed for beginners in EFL settings.

What would you do in this situation? How would you use the multimedia equipment and software to best advantage? How would you take advantage of the high-speed Internet capabilities of the lab? What would you say to the principal to ensure that your students' goals and needs were being met?

Some educators fear that computers could eventually replace them. According to Elizabeth Hanson-Smith (1997), this is unlikely, although teachers are increasingly using computers to enhance teaching and learning. Educational aspects such as needs assessment, curriculum development, student evaluation and placement, lesson planning, materials selection and development, student support, and advising can only be done by human experts, not computers.

This chapter will not teach you how to use computer technology and the Internet, nor will it provide an exhaustive list of computer software, digital textbook supplements, and websites to support language teaching. This is because computer technology including hardware, software, the web, and the Internet are constantly evolving. For example, today computers are much more user friendly; most people, even those who are reticent about technology, can sit at a computer and navigate using only their intuition. Also, any websites or software packages recommended in this chapter, may move, be updated, or become obsolete by the time you read this. Consult recent books dedicated to computer technology such as DeSzendeffy's (2005) *A Practical Guide to Using Computers in Language Teaching.*

This chapter focuses on the advantages and limitations of various aspects of computers and Internet technology, types of associated materials available for language teaching, practical ways you can use digital materials, selection guidelines for computer- and Internet-based materials, and language teaching activities for computers and the Internet.

If you are particularly interested in keeping up with this dynamic topic, purchase the most recent recommended book you can find on the topic and consider joining CALICO (Computer Assisted Language Instruction Consortium). Consult their website at *www.calico.org* or have a look at online journals such as *Language Learning and Technology.* Appendix C also includes a list of technologies that may support language teaching and learning, but be aware that new developments are constantly appearing.

This chapter includes:

- the advantages and limitations of computers and the Internet for language teaching
- various types of computer and Internet materials, including software programs, electronic mail, and the World Wide Web
- a variety of ways for using computer and Internet materials in your classroom
- testing—computer-based/Internet-based testing and materials to help students with high-stakes standardized tests
- guidelines for selecting computer language teaching software, online communication programs, and websites
- sample activities for computers and the Internet
- computer- and web-based testing

Some Challenging Questions

Before you begin, answer these questions:

- Do you think that teachers who know how to use computers and the Internet to enhance their teaching have advantages over teachers who do not know how to use these technologies?
- Are you reluctant to use computers and the Internet in your teaching? Why or why not?
- Have your attitudes about using computers and the Internet in your teaching changed in the last five years? If so, in what way and why?
- How do your students feel about using computers and the Internet for language learning?
- How do you now incorporate computers and the Internet in your language teaching and in teaching other subjects?

Introduction to Computers and Computer Materials

There are many advantages to computers in language teaching through interactive software programs for drills, simulations, tutoring, word processing, and authoring (writing). Computers are necessary for connectivity to the Internet, which includes both e-mail communication and the wide array of teaching and learning and information resources on the Internet.

No matter what medium you use, computers, the Internet, or even audiovisual resources and textbooks, only you know the goals and needs of your students and the context of your particular teaching situation. Whatever medium you use to deliver your instruction should supplement and enhance rather than drive your lesson objectives and course curriculum. Although this seems obvious, you may encounter pressure from supervisors or colleagues, or you may be enticed by the glamour of technology. Be aware that these influences may lead you to use complex high-tech materials that are inappropriate to your teaching situation.

Be sure to take the time to learn about the hardware and software before introducing it to students. In addition to considering appropriateness and efficiency in teaching and learning, consider cost-effectiveness in light of enhancing learning outcomes. Elizabeth Hanson-Smith cautions that while computer technology is becoming less expensive, it also changes quickly and the latest advancements may still be unaffordable. She suggests that you not worry too much about constant changes, but "go with the best equipment you can afford at present and upgrade in stages" (13). Finally, be sure that there is someone to troubleshoot on both hardware and software concerns on short notice; institutions may be willing to install expensive equipment and purchase associated software but less willing to fund ongoing support and maintenance!

Advantages and Limitations of Using Computers and Computer-Based Materials

Judith Shrum and Eileen Glisan (1994, 259–65) outline these advantages of using computers and computer-based materials:

- Many students like using computers and are motivated by stimulating activities on the computer.
- Students who already know how to use computers can help those with less experience and in emergencies can even troubleshoot hardware and software problems (although you should not expect them to do so).
- Computer-based materials and activities can be individualized to address the particular needs of a student or students.
- Individuals or groups can work on computer-based activities; this includes activities that teachers can develop to test students' learning.
- Computers are tireless tutors; they don't get bored repeating the same activity over and over again until the student is ready to move on.
- Students have some degree of autonomy when working on the computer; they can take a rest when they feel the need.
- The hypertext capabilities of some software materials and of the Internet allow branching activities, such as allowing students to link to increasingly more difficult activities addressing the same language point, or allowing students after having reached a certain level of competency in one area of language difficulty (e.g., verb tense) to link to a new area of difficulty (e.g., prepositions).

In addition to the points above, many computer programs provide students with instant feedback, providing immediate explanations and reinforcement along with quick correction (Hanson-Smith).

Computer-based materials, particularly on the Internet are often authentic and not necessarily developed for language teaching. So, for example, you can have students participate in real reading and writing activities in news or discussion groups, live or asynchronous chats on bulletin boards, web logs (blogs or personal online diaries and journals that are shared publicly), or on listservs (discussed later). Or you can have them do real research using Internet resources or CD programs such as encyclopedias. For example, they can search the Internet for information on a country and cross-reference it with material found on a CD-ROM atlas. If you are interested in learning more about bulletin boards, consult the *TESOL Journal* article by Dawn Bikowski and Greg Kessler (2002, 27–30).

When carefully selected, authentic material, whether on CD-ROM or on the Internet, is engaging and motivational for students (Gaer 1998) and can fit well within theme units. For example, Susan Gaer suggests that within a unit on racism, for example, you can use speeches available on CD or on the web by human rights activists (e.g., Martin Luther King, Jr.). Anne Dahlman and Sarah Rilling (2001) outline the extensive integration of technologies in teaching EFL at a distance. For an EFL unit on housing, they suggest a web search for availability of accommodation, discussion of those findings with peers via e-mail, and development of an e-journal to their teacher to describe their experience finding housing online. Later in this chapter we discuss integrating CALL (computer assisted language learning) programs into your curriculum.

Computer-based materials are often multisensory, simultaneously conveying a message using written text, still and full-motion images, and sound, all of which motivate and activate student imagination. If you are interested in exploring these features further, consult Richard E. Mayer's (2005) book, *Multimedia Learning*. If you and your students have computers and Internet access, you can take advantage of this in your lesson planning. For example, students can take each other on virtual tours of their countries, share the latest news events using sound and visuals, or teach each other about assigned or chosen topics that are presented in multimedia on the Internet. You can even find historical speeches in multimedia such as Dr. Martin Luther King's famous "I Have a Dream" speech.

You can use computer-based materials to supplement many of your course objectives in all skill areas. Computer-based materials are most effective when supported by the teacher and when they enrich other activities in the curriculum. Some programs call for students to practice a combination of two or more language skills—listening, speaking, reading, writing, grammar, vocabulary development, and pronunciation. Deborah Healey (2001) points out that students who do extensive reading on computers improve abilities in scanning and reading for full comprehension as well as get exposure to large amounts of vocabulary that they can learn in context. Computer-based material also addresses a range of learning styles because it is often multisensory in nature and because students can work as individuals or in groups at their own pace.

Recently, educators have realized the value of computer applications in developing cognitive learning strategies (memorizing, rehearsing, imaging, self-monitoring, etc.) and metacognitive abilities. For example, depending on the program or website and how the teacher uses it, it can be a valuable tool for developing self-monitoring strategies that enhance student independence and communicative competence. Examples of activities to enhance student independence include computer research, webquests, online self-access activities, and spell and grammar checks included in word processing programs. Good computer-based materials support meaning-making or constructivist learning (Healey and Klinghammer 2002). Constructivist learning is characterized by active learning, incorporation of new knowledge with existing knowledge, collaborative learning involving the social negotiation of content to build knowledge, contextualized learning, and reflection on the learning process (Opp-Beckman 2002). In addition, because students talk about their computer-based learning experiences, they develop an awareness of how they learn language, contributing to metacognition (Peterson 2002). You should consider these goals when selecting and using computer-based material. We will discuss how to select communicative CALL materials later in this chapter.

An important advantage of digital technologies is the possibility for supporting students with special learning challenges. Dan Mittelholtz (personal communication 2005) explains that screen expanders, special monitors that expand text, and magnifiers are available for sight-impaired students. Screen readers such as products from Kurzweil Educational Systems allow sight-impaired students to hear text and, if alt tags (alternative text tags that appear in place of images and can be read by text readers) are properly coded into the computer languages required to build websites (e.g., HTML), these readers can read images. Mittelholtz points out that sight-impaired students or students with reading challenges such as dyslexia can purchase inexpensive programs to hear text read in their choice of a natural sounding language. In some cases a utility exists to convert these voices to mp3 audio format so that students actually have a recording that they can play back later, similar to a talking book. There is currently not a great deal available for hearing impaired students, although closed-captioning technologies are being utilized in many video recordings and this is being extended to computer applications. If you have students with learning and physical challenges in your classroom, explore some of the increasingly available digital solutions that will help them overcome barriers to their learning

Finally, by working with computers, you will be helping close the digital divide because your students will gain technological skills that they can use outside of class for purposes such as employment and education. They may also introduce computers to family members.

In spite of all of these advantages, you should be aware of these limitations of computer technology:

- The hardware and software are expensive to purchase and maintain.
- Maintenance may not be available when you need it.
- Facility with computers is required, including comfort with the mouse, navigating the Internet, and keyboarding skills.
- There may be compatibility issues with programs (some programs will not work on both PC and Macintosh platforms), hardware (e.g., microphones), plug-in requirements, and browser compatibility.
- Enhanced learning may not result after use; students may not show improvement after having worked with online material.
- Computer-based materials are not necessarily more pedagogically sound than print-based materials. For example, students may be fooled into thinking that abbreviated language in text messaging is acceptable as standard usage for other purposes (e.g., job applications, academic essays).
- Extensive familiarity with computer hardware and software is important, otherwise it may be difficult to select appropriate material for your students; a steep learning curve exists with some of the technology.
- Computer use is tempting, even when it may not match objectives.
- Despite their memory capacity and processing speed, language on computers cannot replace the natural language of live communication.
- Even minor computer problems may prevent students from continuing a lesson or exercise; you cannot assume every student will have the necessary skill set to solve such problems.

CALL

CD-ROM Technology

Computer programs today are usually available on a CD-ROM. Many publishers of ESL and EFL materials now sell CALL (computer assisted language learning) programs or make them available for purchase or as part of a course textbook. A number of publishers are also now including companion websites to accompany their textbook materials. You should evaluate these for appropriateness to your context and curriculum, and usability and accuracy (Reagan and Murray 2002). Consult Appendix B for more complete evaluation criteria.

Because software usually contains multimedia and is interactive, it may require a great deal of computer memory, or it may require a high computer processor speed. CD-ROM technology uses less digital memory (Hanson-Smith) or bandwidth than programs delivered via the Internet. DVDs can carry even more information than CDs, which is why full-motion movies from your local video store are on DVD. Bandwidth is the amount of digital information that can be carried through a cable or phone line and at what speed it can be carried. The advantage of CD and DVD resources are that they can provide rich and entertaining media for the learner. The disadvantage is that they are usually quite expensive to create and update.

Today, teachers and students with the required equipment can burn their own CDs and DVDs. Remember, if you want to do this, copyright restrictions apply.

Types of CALL Programs

There are several types of CALL software programs available, each with benefits and limitations. Those covered in this section are drills, simulations, tutorials, word processing programs, and authoring programs. We end this section with a discussion of how to evaluate CALL programs.

DRILL PROGRAMS

Drill programs were the first CALL software programs available and tended to be based on behaviourist principles (Warschauer 1996), allowing for mastery of language (Shrum and Glisan). Drill programs allow students to practice language over and over again. Like all drills, CALL drill programs vary in their power to develop communicative competence—the focus may be limited to linguistic competency such as grammar, phonology, and vocabulary. The communicative drills available today are becoming very sophisticated, including aspects such as person-to-person interaction and sociocultural and pragmatic competencies as well. Good CD-ROMs should tell students immediately how well they did.

Drills are based on the idea that repetition aids learning. The advantage of CALL drills is that "the computer never gets tired, distracted or bored, as many teachers do with rote work" Nunan (1996, 196). In addition, an individual student, small groups, or the entire class in a lab can work on a drill. Well-chosen drill programs can provide you and your students with excellent support, particularly to develop linguistic competency. Today some programs allow you to create and customize your own drills.

As emphasized earlier, it is important to select drills and drill programs that will augment your objectives and curriculum; are suited to the needs, age levels, and interests of your students; and are as communicative as possible. CALL drills that allow adaptation to your context are recommended over those that do not. A disadvantage of drill programs lies in the fact that drills usually promote passive learning and do not develop meaning-making or creation of the unique utterances required for independent speakers. Although drill programs should be used sparingly, their advantages should not be overlooked.

SIMULATION PROGRAMS

Many of us have used simulations in our language classrooms. Those familiar with computers may have played some of the elaborate computer simulations available such as SimCity or Sim Theme Park. If you are still unfamiliar with computer simulations, consider flight simulators used to train pilots. An increasing number of simulations for CALL are now available and often involve game simulations, which include elements of competition such as scoring and time limits. David Nunan points out that simulation programs present realistic scenarios that reinforce both the linguistic and pragmatic components of communicative competence. He states: "The common feature of all simulations is that the computer shows some of the consequences of student decisions or actions on the computer screen so that the user can follow a process through to uncertain outcome" (196).

John Higgins (1988) suggests, "In simulations, students manipulate the data, feed their manipulations into the computer, and then deal with the challenge or consequences posed by the computer. In many of these situations, the students (and also the teacher) are collaborating in a competitive effort against the computer" (63).

Nunan and Lamb (1996) add that the success of simulation programs depends on how a teacher manages the learning process through "adequate preparation, briefing students clearly on what is expected of them, establishing different roles within the small groups, if this is appropriate . . . [and] debrief[ing] the class . . . to say what they did and what they might have done" (196).

Remember, many simulations and most word processing programs (discussed later) are not specifically designed to teach language, but they offer much to students in the way of experiential language learning, particularly for pairwork. You may find many students prefer using software not created specifically for language learning. If you use software not designed for ESL or EFL students, be sure to evaluate the language used in the instructions. Are the vocabulary and syntax too difficult for your students to understand? It is probably important to evaluate even language learning software programs to ascertain if you need to make adaptations.

Simulation programs support proactive learning, self-monitoring, and communicative competence. Additional advantages of simulation software are that they present realistic scenarios and situations that demand authentic language use and that they promote constructivist and experiential student learning. In addition, simulation programs afford students greater experimentation with language than drills do.

Limitations of simulation programs are most likely related to a combination of your context, a relevant match to your teaching objectives, the simulation software you select, and your instructions to students. Remember that you may need to adapt the software or instructions in some way, especially if using software not intended for language learning.

TUTORIAL PROGRAMS

Tutorial software is designed to support the introduction of new concepts or material (Shrum and Glisan). For example, you can learn the International Phonetic Alphabet with "The Phonetics Files," a CALL program produced at The University of Saskatchewan (Anderson and Fredeen 1997). Another tutorial program helps students learn hundreds of French verbs.

The advantage of CALL tutorial programs is that they can help you teach new material as well as give students resources and reference material that they can use for review. These resources encourage student independence.

There are two disadvantages to such programs. First, there is a danger that the teacher will become too reliant on the program and neglect teaching the concepts sufficiently in class prior to assigning the tutorial for reinforcement of learning. Second, students may not have the skills, particularly the independence, to use the tutorials effectively. There is a danger that they will become overwhelmed and frustrated by the many resources available within a tutorial.

WORD PROCESSING PROGRAMS

Word processors are ideal for creating and editing written assignments (Shrum and Glisan) of many kinds, including initial brainstorming of writing ideas, sentence combining and cloze exercise, letters and faxes, stories, poems, and finished essays. They are ideal for supporting process writing because they allow for multiple drafts. Word processing programs can also be used to support listening comprehension, speaking, and reading. Some word processing tools include grammar and spell-checkers, drawing programs for graphics, and track changes features. Track changes features are particularly effective in writing development because they allow the teacher and student to interact on revisions to written work. Other programs allow for a split screen so teachers can comment in the margins. Still others allow for verbal feedback using microphone and playback features.

Here are some advantages of word processing programs:

- Most teachers and students know how to use them.
- You can create activities of many types from word to sentence to paragraph level as well as punctuation exercises.
- You can set up worksheets or templates for students to teach and guide them, for example, essay writing templates, or templates for taking notes.
- Students can read a text on the computer and then participate in a range of written activities that the teacher prepares to accompany it.

- Students can conduct oral interviews and write them up on the word processor.
- You can make the activities as low level or as advanced as needed to augment learning objectives and the curriculum.
- You can develop mechanical activities or those that are authentic and communicative.
- You can promote extensive editing without the tiring task of rewriting the entire assignment.
- Word processing programs allow for peer review as well as teacher feedback to students.
- The students' work has a professional look and feel when created on a word processor and printed. Students can use the word processor to create professional-looking documents such as autobiographies, school yearbooks, and school bulletins, especially if they supplement their work with digital photos or images that have been scanned or drawn using the drawing feature of most current word processing software.

Word processing activities should fit into your learning objectives and curricular goals; the word processor should not replace instruction and its use should be limited to enhance what has already been taught. Also, you need some facility with computers as well as time to develop activities using word processing software.

AUTHORING PROGRAMS

Authoring programs allow teachers and students to write their own materials and even to design courses using course management systems (see the next section). One strength of such programs is that you can create material that is compatible with your local context, course content, and student abilities. For example, publishers of some authoring software include options for making cloze and other activities. You could develop a cloze exercise with the advantages of immediate feedback, clues, and scoring but use a text and blanks suitable to your context and content. There are some products available, such as Hot Potatoes™ and Quandary that help you develop activities, as well as resource repositories such as Merlot that have ready-made content material that you may use as is or adapt. Check the Internet for these and other resources.

Students can work in groups with authoring or presentation programs to create professional-looking multimedia projects (Hanson-Smith). They can present their final products orally if using a presentation program such as PowerPoint or post them on the Internet. An important benefit is that students are working collaboratively on such materials. Remember that copyright restrictions also apply to students if they are publishing these products.

The main limitations of authoring programs are similar to those for developing activities using word processing software, that is, facility with the program and time to develop the activities. Also, you should consider the time it takes to learn to use the software. Cost of such programs and copyright restrictions may also be factors to consider.

COURSE MANAGEMENT SYSTEMS

Course/learning management systems such as Blackboard/WebCT and Moodle are authoring systems that allow educators to design entire online courses, modules, or lessons for their students. This allows a teaching-learning unit to be tailor-made to the course context, content, and students. Another advantage is that you can set up independent study for students and, if they have an Internet connection, they can access the unit of study at a distance from the classroom. However, as with other authoring programs, these systems generally have steep learning curves, especially for the computer novice, and the materials can take considerable development and maintenance time.

Course management systems such as Blackboard/WebCT and Moodle are primarily designed (at the time of this writing) for asynchronous communication among you and your students. Others, like Horizon Wimba®, Elluminate, Webex™, and WebTrain are designed for synchronous communication. The site license for some systems is prohibitive, but some, such as Moodle and Bazaar7, at time of writing, were open source and available free-of-charge. It is wise to have a computer technician who is extremely well versed in such systems to advise on which may work for you. An expert should be able to alert you to any serious limitations such as synchronous systems delay between image and voice. Also, whatever system is used, you must clear copyright if you would like to embed images, text, and other items regardless of source (i.e., Internet or scanned from print) within your unit of study. Also, if your unit takes too much memory or download time, it may be best to burn some or all of it on a CD or DVD.

One of the most useful aspects of such systems is the creation of quizzes online that can test student achievement on some or all of the course content. Such quizzes can be self-marking but these are usually limited to true/false, multiple choice, short answer and matching questions. Such questions may not provide the in-depth evaluation needed to determine if your students have mastered your materials. However, used in collaboration with other methods of evaluation, they can be effective at guiding students to making informed choices in what materials they may need to focus on or where to go next (Mittelholtz).

More on the Benefits and Drawbacks of CALL Programs

Some of the many benefits of software programs, based on our experience and the experience of others, are that they:

- motivate students
- provide immediate feedback
- provide hints and error correction
- facilitate language use and co-operative learning, for example, when students work in pairs to discuss and complete a computer-based task
- facilitate process writing through the capabilities of word processing programs to facilitate editing and revising
- are patient and never frustrated with the student
- encourage self-directed learning

There are some additional limitations to CALL programs. Hanson-Smith cautions that you not let the bells and whistles obscure the need to carefully evaluate the pedagogical value of computer applications. For example, some attractive vocabulary software programs do not provide an extended context for vocabulary. That is, students may be asked to complete cloze sentences, but each sentence is unrelated to the next. Also, the vocabulary may not be relevant to what you have been learning in class. The activities may be fun and appropriate for an advanced learner, but do they provide worthwhile language practice for lower level students? It is important that the software is appropriate to the age and proficiency level of learners, their needs, and the curriculum.

In spite of advances, much of CALL is still in an experimental stage and may not have been developed by language teachers but by computer experts. As credible language publishers develop more appropriate software, you may find that they eliminate irrelevant features in favor of appropriate pedagogy for language teaching and learning.

Beware also that students need extensive practice with real people, not only with computers, especially in communicating with native speakers and developing sociocultural awareness and competency. While students may be motivated to do some work with software programs, they typically come to our classes to learn to speak and understand English and English speakers, so they need real conversation partners. Also, students need some keyboarding skills when working with computers. Be sure that you do not penalize those who keyboard more slowly than others, especially in timed activities.

Some CALL programs designed as courses may not allow for sufficient variety in the curriculum (Gaer). Some such software may not be relevant to your student ages, needs, goals, and interests. However, there are some excellent products available.

Finally, CALL software may be expensive (Gaer), and educational software and licenses for using multiple copies are also costly, so it is important that you know what to look for. Appendix B will help you decide on your investment.

The Teacher's Role

Kiraki Spanou (n.d.) suggests teachers who are familiar with technology will use it more. The range of use will also vary according to the teacher's attitude toward technology for instruction, with some using it as a core part of their teaching, others using at as an add-on, and others using it rarely or not at all because they believe that the benefits do not outweigh the steep learning curve in becoming proficient in developing digital materials and activities. DeSzendeffy (2005) suggests that teachers recognize what they already know and learn to utilize computer-based activities to supplement their teaching gradually as they gain training and experience.

Spanou outlines two roles that CALL can take:

- as a tutor—CALL replaces the teacher, for example in conducting drills and giving guidance and feedback. This makes it suitable for self-access learning.

- as a tool or learning enhancement—the teacher controls and supports guidance and feedback.

We suggest that these points are also relevant to ESL teaching and learning using resources on the Internet. Your role is to use technology to enhance teaching and learning objectives. This means knowing how to select appropriate CALL and Internet materials.

Integrating CALL Material into Your Curriculum

You should not change your curriculum in order to allow the use of CALL material but rather be aware of how it can enhance existing teaching goals (McLaughlin and McCormick 2002). It is important to evaluate the software and see how it can best be used (Gaer 1998). Gaer notes that word processors are the easiest to incorporate into the curriculum because most courses require students to do some writing. She suggests that CALL materials can fit into theme units in a wide range of topics from shopping to racism and human rights. She encourages teachers to group students when working with CALL software to promote dialogue, teamwork, and develop problem-solving skills.

Gaer also suggests that at the beginning of the CALL experience, you provide students with instruction on how to use each software program. She suggests modeling the steps or even role-playing a program's use with students. Savvy students can help those less experienced in computer and software use. You should preteach vocabulary and content as required so they do not have difficulties with the materials because of lack of background knowledge. Gaer adds that it is important to plan follow-up work to give students the opportunity to use what they have learned on the computer. This can take many forms, including field trips, role plays, or projects.

Evaluating CALL Materials

Whether you are designing or evaluating CALL materials, they should be as communicative as possible, focusing on use rather than form in isolation. Experts suggest that communicative CALL programs should be fun and not used as replacements for adequate textbook activities. They should promote language acquisition more than drill practice. Grammar should be taught implicitly or embedded in the lesson, rather than explicitly and separate from it. Communicative CALL programs should be sufficiently flexible so that students can create original language. In addition, they should allow for student exploration of the content and of the communicative practice possibilities as they use the program collaboratively with other students. Finally, CALL programs should not over-correct or over-reward everything students do or include too many gimmicks such as distracting animations, flashing lights, or sounds (Shrum and Glisan; Spanou).

Gaer suggests when selecting software that you consider level of language difficulty, level of concreteness of concepts, familiarity of language content, and grammatical complexity. Also consider how well the language and content match your curriculum, usability of the software including navigability, and ease in recognizing the tasks required.

Designing CALL Materials

Here is advice from Suzanne Hoffman (1995, 26) for those itching to develop, adapt, or enhance their own software. These ideas can also help you evaluate programs.

- Make sure they are easy to start and operate.
- Don't put too much material on the screen as this can overwhelm students; likewise, don't leave the screen too bare as it may provide too little challenge.
- Omit "verbose praise" for correct responses. Rather, reinforce correct answers with supplementary information about the language.
- Make it possible for students to skip introductory information about the program so they don't have to read through it each time they start.
- Allow for individual pacing with an index to help students choose from among exercises and levels of difficulty.
- Provide an end test, where appropriate, for immediate feedback and to help students determine whether they should go to the next lesson or repeat.
- Develop exercises that employ structural and functional aspects of the language within a context.
- Provide synonyms, definitions, explanations, and examples with texts on interactive videodisks (CDs or DVDs).
- We would add that you should include a site map to support navigation in complex programs.

As previously mentioned, you can burn your own CD, but remember that copyright restrictions apply.

The Internet

The Internet includes both the World Wide Web and interactive capabilities, such as e-mail. To physically use the Internet, you need a computer with sufficient power to handle the Internet and web browser (e.g., Internet Explorer, Safari, Mozilla/Firefox® etc.). You also need an Internet Service Provider (ISP), which is usually a telephone or cable company, a satellite connection, or the fastest possible modem (if you are limited to dial-up access via a phone line). The higher the connection speed the more desirable it is, but you may be limited to dial-up access because of where you live or because the other alternatives are too expensive for your budget. Supplied with these tools, you open your classroom to a world of endless possibilities.

You really need to try out the web to experience the wealth of information available as well as understand the challenges of using it for teaching and learning. Becoming familiar with a variety of websites will help you generate ideas for its use. As a teacher you will find numerous materials and activities for language teachers. If your students do not have Internet access, you can still print out activities you find on the web for use in your classroom.

It would be of little use for us to list or discuss too many actual sites because of the dynamic nature of the web—sites are constantly moving so web addresses change or disappear altogether, or are updated and improved. You should be aware that there is much free material for language teachers, including free activities. You may want to start your exploration at Dave's ESL Cafe (at time of writing at *www.eslcafe.com/*). Dave Sperling has created a wonderful site with many internal links to support teaching and learning, professional development, and even locating employment online.

Consider taking your students, or having them take you, on a virtual field trip around the world! Students can find both current and archival information on any topic imaginable. In doing so, students may also be exposed to other English language varieties (Hanson-Smith), a double-edged sword that you may need to address. Besides being an up-to-date global resource, another feature of the web is hyper-linking. Clicking on web links allows you and the students to explore an endless array of topics or activities usually related to the original site. Of course, there are drawbacks to this such as getting lost in the maze or coming across undesirable sites. You will need to decide how much control to exert over your students as they explore.

Interactivity is also possible. As you explore, you will find activities for students that include interaction. Try the activities yourself before assigning them to students as some are better than others and some may not use the variety of English you are teaching (e.g., British versus North American English). Also be aware that some sites require special downloads. Sometimes these downloads can enhance your computer, such as downloads of streamed audio programs such as Real Audio®. Other times, they can cause problems. Be aware also that some seemingly good ideas, such as video conferencing, take up too much bandwidth or require the purchase of costly equipment. Ask someone knowledgeable, preferably someone who also knows about language education, before downloading anything onto your computer! For example, at the time of writing, voice recognition programs, which sound like they would be a good idea for language learning, were not yet sufficiently developed to be useful to most teachers.

A web search engine (e.g., Google™, Yahoo®, alltheweb, MSN Search, Lycos, Ask.com™, AOL Search, or others) will illustrate just how useful the web is in providing:

- songs sung by recording artists with accompanying lyrics
- information for web-based research for projects and presentations
- news from authentic or adapted-for-ESL web-based newspapers
- self-access activities for language learning and help sites such as Purdue University's online writing lab and various links within Dave's ESL Cafe

Consult your curriculum for other possible searches. You will find that the possibilities are endless! However, copyright restrictions and legalities may apply.

Online Interactive Technologies

In addition to using the web for activities, for reference, and as resource materials for you and your students, you should also be aware that there are some interactive sites. MUDs (Multi-User Domains) and MOOs (MUD, Object Oriented) are text-based spaces where students can interact in real time (synchronous) with local or international participants using Internet technology. MUDs and MOOs are still used in TESL, but now usually for shared gaming. They have been replaced by news groups and, more recently, by web logs, or blogs, and wikis (a server program allowing many to share or contribute online), all of which are asynchronous in nature (i.e., not in real time).

Some ESL and especially EFL teachers are using online interactive technologies successfully to help students develop their communication skills. Once students gain comfort with the technology, they focus on authentic discussions with a global audience. For example, you may be able to make e-mail contact with a class in another country, thereby taking advantage of the international contacts that are available.

The advantages of these systems are that the input is authentic and comprehensible for students and provides them with a safe venue for trying out language. Depending on tasks assigned, they can promote proactive and constructivist learning by creating online communities of students collaborating and negotiating meaning while learning from each other. In addition, this type of participation can help students develop autonomy and "metacognitive skills such as noticing, as learners develop an awareness of the role of certain linguistic forms in effective communication" (Peterson 2002, 1). However, you may lose control over your lesson objectives, the direction of the conversation, and the amount of time spent. Another limitation with global synchronous discussions is time differences. In addition, there are concerns about security and protection from Internet predators. You should ensure that students remain anonymous when participating in these sites.

While we're on the topic of criminal activities, be sure that students are aware that someone may try to take advantage of them, for example, through online marketing. Because of this, using a client-based e-mail system (described in the following section) usually allows you to set up private conference spaces that may be preferable to web-based options.

E-Mail and Live Chat

E-mail and live chat programs can be web-based, such as the popular Yahoo and MSN® Hotmail accounts that you can subscribe to for free. Alternatively, e-mail programs can be installed directly onto student computers, in which case they are called "client-based" programs. The advantage of client-based e-mail programs is that students don't need to wade through all of the advertisements on the website associated with web-based e-mail programs. Some programs are easier to use than others, and you will need to ask colleagues or computer experts which ones they prefer or experiment to find out which are most suitable for context.

The possibilities with this technology are endless, but there are some cautions to keep in mind as well. Some advantages and limitations are:

- Students can communicate one-on-one in private messages with you or another student. This allows you to give private feedback to students. Also, students can find e-pals (electronic pen pals) for extensive communication.

- Students can also form small groups and communicate in conference spaces online to complete a variety of activities, such as research and writing projects, developing websites for a school yearbook or other electronic publications, debating, preparing group presentations, or discussing controversial topics. As students work in groups, they will not only talk about their tasks and materials, but also about their learning, thus developing metacognition. Students can even work on projects with students in other countries. You can find teacher networks on the web that link you to other classrooms (at time of writing *www.teaching.com*). A sample conference task is provided at the end of this chapter.

- A major advantage of e-mail communication is that students who don't speak up in class are often more willing to send e-mail. Being able to interact with others this way in English may give these students the confidence they need to participate more actively.

  Be aware that writing is not the same as speaking. E-mail is a written technology and has developed its own particular conventions that you may need to teach. You may also want to limit students' use of instant messaging and e-mail abbreviations such as *BTW* for *by the way*, or *B4* for *before*. Also, anything students write electronically requires keyboarding skills. Be aware also that you have no control over private messages students send to each other. Students have received distressing e-mails from other students, so let them know they should tell you if this occurs. At the beginning of term, introduce proper netiquette—etiquette when interacting with others online.

- Students can send and receive e-mail attachments to and from you or each other. They can send print documents or pictures that they have drawn using a drawing program or that they have copied using an electronic scanner. This facilitates group collaboration and makes it possible for you to send and receive worksheets or other assignments. If you have made a worksheet on your computer, for example, you can send multiple copies to students by e-mail, reducing your time spent at the photocopy machine. Be aware, however, that students may print these out, so it doesn't necessarily save on paper. There are also copyright restrictions. Make students aware that they need to cite sources or get copyright clearance if they intend to make work with restricted elements available on a public website.

- Some e-mail programs allow for shared spaces and shared documents. This allows collaborative group writing. It also facilitates correction.

- E-mail programs allow you and your students to subscribe to listservs on topics of interest. Materials and activities for listservs are similar to web-based newsgroups and bulletin boards. You should be aware that listservs are in a closed, controlled environment within student e-mail programs while news groups and bulletin boards on the Internet are open to a global audience. You may be interested in subscribing to one of the popular ESL teacher listservs (e.g., TESL-L) or to a web-based bulletin board (e.g., Dave's ESL Cafe).

- Live chat is an e-mail feature that attracts many. It is useful for immediate communications in writing, and it does have an informal, chatty quality. However, students need good keyboarding skills to participate effectively. In our view, no more than five students should chat online simultaneously or the conversation becomes confusing. Also, be clear about why you are using chat. Would a phone call or asynchronous chat achieve the same goals?

- Group discussions among students develop their facilitation skills. Start by modeling good facilitation. This includes being a good listener, probing to keep the conversation going or to clarify what has been said, bringing a discussion topic to a close, and summarizing key points. Provide the students with an electronic handout describing good facilitation. Then, have them take turns facilitating an online discussion.

INSTANT MESSAGING

Recently, instant messaging (IM) has become a popular form of communication on the Internet and via cell phone. Because it is synchronous, IM is similar to live chat. However, as it is currently set up (technology changes so quickly these days!), those using IM have a list of "friends" who they can invite or prevent from inviting to a chat as they so choose. To date, ESL/EFL teachers are not routinely using this technology, although some are undoubtedly experimenting with its potential and it may yet prove to be another way to promote student interaction. In fact, in many instances you will serve your students well by introducing them to technology, which they will use at some time.

However, there are some cautions with IM, the greatest of which is the fact that IM commonly uses non-standard abbreviations that are only acceptable in this mode of communication. For example, abbreviations such as l8r or L8R (all lower case is most common) for *later* as in *see/talk to you later.* IM also commonly uses acronyms such as *lol* for *laughing out loud* indicating that humor has just been used in the message. Also, punctuation is minimized in IM. So, if you have students communicating via IM, at the very least you should let them know that these acronyms, abbreviations, and minimal punctuation are not acceptable in places other than IM and may not even be accepted in e-mails. After all, you wouldn't want to see your students using non-standard forms with their employers or professors. Keep up-to-date on the literature, and you may yet see some appropriate uses for IM.

PDAs

Handheld devices, known as personal digital assistants (PDAs) such as iPAQ, Clie®, Palm® and Blackberry™, have become extremely popular and educators are beginning to explore their educational value. This is especially true as the operating systems of PDAs become more sophisticated. The main limitations are:

- PDAs require wireless connections, which may be slower and less stable than wired connections (at the time of this writing).

- PDAs are limited by their very small screen or monitor size, which means instruction designed for a full-sized computer monitor must be adapted for the smaller interface to ensure full functionality of what you are trying to teach.
- There is currently a steep learning curve for teachers to effectively develop and maintain teaching materials for these devices.
- As with IM, PDA screen size means that there is a temptation to use abbreviations and acronyms rather than standard English.

Currently the advice is that these devices be used in conjunction with classroom or wired online instruction. For example, when students are away from the classroom, they can use these devices to download course materials and do simple activities (personal communication with Ivy Tan 2006; Hsu and Chuang 2005).

NOTEPADS AND OTHER PRODUCTS

Notepad devices such as Tablet PC, which operate almost like paper-based notepads, are beginning to be used in some institutions but require a wireless connection and a good local area network (LAN) for full functionality. There are and doubtless will continue to be new digitally based products on the market that may be useful in language education. However, before you commit to them, be sure that you do your homework regarding advantages and limitations and consult with knowledgeable technical experts.

Internet Tips

Following are some tips related to Internet use. Ensure when using the Internet (or CALL programs) that the activities relate to your curriculum and objectives and that you have concrete goals for using these activities (e.g., to develop writing skills, to teach computer skills). Use existing appropriate Internet activities. You should also determine how ELLs will demonstrate they have learned from these activities and that they are effective in supporting student learning. You may want to elicit feedback from students in this regard. At the same time, what works for one group of ELLs may work differently for another group. So, don't overplan online sessions; be open and leave time for students to experiment so that they can make their own discoveries. You should also be prepared for unintended outcomes. Explore the websites that you intend to use and try out the activities to ensure you are familiar with them yourself. Be sure to have the assistance of a technician available for computer sessions, should you need it, particularly when you first start using the Internet to support your teaching. Ensure ELLs' computer skills ahead of time, including keyboarding skills, mouse use, comfort with Internet navigation, and familiarity with Internet terminology. Allow them to help each other. This has the added advantage of promoting student interaction and problem-solving. While initially Internet-based activities may result in some confusion in the classroom, with patience and flexibility on your part, students will learn and gain skill over time.

Tips to Get Students Started on the Internet

Flannery Silc (1998) suggests you do the following when using the Internet:

- Teach students how to use the mouse.
- Introduce them to their web browser and other desktop icons.
- Teach them how to do web searches and be critical in their selection of information and what to do with undesirable information.

She suggests the following steps for web assignments:

1. Prepare students for an Internet-based assignment.
2. Have students define a task or problem.
3. Have students brainstorm keywords that may be useful in doing a search, to do the task, or solve the problem.
4. Have students record results of their search, including writing down the URL.
5. Do the activity (solve the problem or do the task).
6. Have students compile the information and make a report.

At the end of the activity, solicit student feedback on what they learned and how they liked the activity so that you can revise the materials or activity for future use. You may find that students are so enthused about using the Internet and learn so much language that it is worth pursuing further. In fact, some courses actually have students develop their own interactive website. Most web browsers have features that facilitate website production.

Following are three sample activities that will help you start working with some of the technology covered in this chapter.

Sample Computer-Based Activities

If you want to introduce students without a lot of experience to the Internet with homework or independent assignments, a worksheet such as the one that follows may be useful.

Visit Dave's ESL Cafe Photo Gallery

Visit Dave's ESL Cafe and Graffiti Wall.

- Double click the browser icon on your computer (Safari, Mozilla, Explorer, etc.).
- Bring your cursor to the top of the screen type in *www.eslcafe.com/*.
- Hit the return key.
- Scroll down to "Stuff for Everyone," and click once on "Photo Gallery."
  You have arrived!
- Click once on "Pictures of Interest" to read about pictures from all over
  the world.
- Describe two pictures and descriptions you find most interesting.
- Click the [← BACK] at the top of the screen to return to the beginning of Dave's ESL Cafe.
- Try another topic by clicking on the word that interests you from the "Stuff for Students"
  (Help Center, Hint-of-the-Day, Student Forums) or "Stuff for Everyone."

SAMPLE WEB QUESTS

You can involve students in collecting information from the Internet in a web quest. The goal of this inquiry-based activity is to spend time using information rather than looking for it. Web quests develop students' abilities to think critically, synthesize, and evaluate information. We have provided the process of creating this activity so that you can adapt it for your needs.

1. The teacher creates a written scenario, task, or problem, for example, finding out in which country their teacher last taught. You can send the task to students as an e-mail attachment or post it on a class website.

2. Students form small groups, similar to those in jigsaws (Chapter 3). Each group is assigned a country, for example, Mexico, and each person in the group has a specialty, for example, historian, anthropologist, geographer, and economist. The teacher writes a note to each student with clues that will help their group solve the problem. These notes need not be long and may be as simple as a list of a few websites and one or two clues. Again, you can deliver the notes to groups electronically by setting up an e-mail group conference.

3. Give student groups a time limit for the quest. For example, finding clues that will help solve the problem of where their teacher last taught. Once they have finished the quest, they should share the information with the group and develop an oral and written response for the rest of the class to convince them of the answer. They can post their response on a website set up for this purpose or prepare it as an attachment to be sent to the rest of the class.

   For example, if the teacher last taught in Mexico, the group that had that country may say something like: "We know the teacher went to Mexico because she heard mariachi music every day on her radio. Her students' first language was Spanish. She would often go to a foodstall outside the school with her students where they served tacos." The group that had Thailand can say something like: "We know that the teacher did not go to Thailand because people there speak Thai, not Spanish. She ate tacos, which is not a common food in Thailand."

4. Get student feedback on the value of the activity and what they learned from it both in terms of content and learning English through the web quest.

Sample Online Conference Activity

You can give students e-mail instructions or provide them with instructions orally in this sample activity for an online conference.

1. Select a topic related to what you are teaching, for example, a theme on the environment and the function of persuasion. Tell them that each group will prepare a convincing argument for the rest of the class about why their environmental concern is the most important issue for government to address.

2. Divide the class into groups of three to five students. Each group discusses an area of environmental concern. Supply each group with an article about

an environmental disaster to provide them with comprehensible input. They may also do a web quest, library search, or conduct an opinion poll on their topic to feed into the online discussion. Online discussion topics might include, for example, oil spills, over-fishing, traffic-related pollution, deforestation, industrial waste, and ozone depletion.

3. As with web quests, students should be instructed to share the information with their online group and develop an oral or written argument for their case to present to the rest of the class.

4. Get student feedback on the value of the activity and what they learned, both in terms of content about pollution and learning English through online discussion.

Computer-Based and Internet-Based Testing

ADVANTAGES AND LIMITATIONS OF CBTs AND WBTs

Computer-based and web-based testing (CBT and WBT) have come a long way since these technologies began to be used for testing (including placement testing, standard high-stakes testing, lower stakes and teacher made tests). For example, the International English Language Testing Service (IELTS) offers the option of either a print-based or a CBT. Now that the Test of English as a Foreign Language (TOEFL®) has become fully web based, we may expect other standardized testing services, particularly the large ones, to soon follow suit.

Carsten Roever (2001), Sanae Ko (2005), and others have identified advantages and limitations in the use of CBTs and WBTs. The main advantages are:

- They are flexible.
- They can be given independently of the instructor.
- They can be cost effective in the sense that small tests can be delivered on free servers (available on the Internet, through your institution or through your ISP).
- They can be offered any time and any place as long as there is a computer with appropriate programs or Internet connection and speed.
- Unless there is a browser compatibility issue, WBTs require no special programs or applications for delivery.
- They can provide immediate feedback to the instructor, and if desired, to the student. (Of course, this is not the case for standardized tests, such as TOEFL®, nevertheless, feedback should be faster even with standardized tests.) The feedback can be on the entire test or on each test item, making it especially useful for drill and practice.
- They can allow the inclusion of multimedia, speech recording, and interactivity for greater authenticity.
- They can be set up for quick and easy storage of student scores over time.
- They allow more easy selection of test items at a student's level, allowing for adaptive testing.

Disadvantages that you may need to consider or solve with CBTs and WBTs are:

- Availability of or access to a computer lab or sufficient number of computer stations for students to take the test, or cost of renting or setting up these facilities.
- Students may lack familiarity with computers, working online, keyboarding, and using a mouse.
- There may be a possible need for test security such as passwords and live test supervisors.
- There may be technical difficulties (difficult to solve if students are at a distance) such as breakdowns.
- Processor speed and connection speed may slow test downloading, depending on the size and complexity of test files (e.g., audiovisual components may be problematic).
- Compatibility of the test with installed computer programs may be an issue, or in the case of WBTs, there may be plug-in requirements and browser compatibility issues.
- They may be expensive to purchase.
- Teachers may not have the skills to develop them, especially if complex tests are required.
- Test validity and reliability may be a concern, although this is also a concern for paper and pencil tests.

Standard and Published CBTs and WBTs

Standard tests are usually high-stake tests, such as the TOEFL®, that have an effect on students' lives, such as gaining entry to an English-medium university. These tests are developed by teams of experts and do not demand anything extra of teachers other than appropriate language instruction (of course), perhaps finding a location and appropriate equipment (with all necessary plug-ins, software, etc.) to administer the test, and providing students with tutorials in computer use. Standardized tests have websites and published digital material available to support you as you prepare your students for taking them.

Test validity and reliability should already be in place for standardized and published tests. In the case of the TOEFL®, web-based testing allows for more authentic testing through skills integration (there is no longer a separate grammar component), inclusion of a required online speaking component that can be graded by markers anywhere in the world, and inclusion of an increasing amount of multimedia over time.

As mentioned in Chapter 2, some published products have CD-ROMs with tests or test banks. Depending on the product, this might allow you to easily develop a test on a specific linguistic item at a specific level. If you plan to use these tests, be sure that they are user friendly and not too difficult for you as a teacher to use. In some cases and depending on your teaching context and testing goals, you could use the placement tests provided with some published programs for assessment and evaluation as well as placement purposes.

TEACHER-MADE CBTs AND WBTs

Today, teacher-made tests are easier than ever to compose and an increasing number of educational institutions are investing in supporting teachers in digital test development and the purchase of programs to do so. Depending on your own computer literacy, you may need to work with computer specialists to help you develop appropriate testing instruments. Or, with just a little training you can use specialized programs available for purchase or free of charge to develop CBTs or WBTs. Half-Baked Software, for example, allows for six types of question—multiple-choice, short-answer, jumbled-sentence, crossword, matching, and gap-fill—and is available free of charge as long as you are willing to share the test. This product is also compatible with some course management systems such as Blackboard/WebCT. Most course management systems have test or quiz features built in, often with immediate feedback, that are quite easy to use. With ingenuity and creativity, you can also develop tests complete with images using word processing programs. It is possible to save word processing documents as HTML documents or to use programs such as Dreamweaver to develop web pages. If you don't have access to computer labs or stations to deliver the tests you have created, you can still compose the test on a computer and print it out. Printing out commercial tests is also possible in some cases if your students lack computer access. Roever (2001) cautions, however, that "just because it is easy to write WBTs [or CBTs] does not mean that it is easy to write good WBTs [or CBTs]."

CHAPTER 7

Project and Community Contact Materials

TANYA'S LANGUAGE LEARNING HIGHLIGHTS

Tanya, a former ESL student of ours, recently sent an e-mail reminiscing about her language learning experiences. Highlights of her learning included visits and interviews at a senior citizen's home, a community organization, and a farm—all rich projects involving real community contact.

As teachers, we need to ask ourselves how we can keep our students engaged, motivated, and learning five hours a day, five days a week. How can we promote learner autonomy? How can we ensure we are attending to their real language goals, needs, and interests? How can we best link the classroom and the real world? We concur with Fried-Booth (1986) that projects and community contact tasks can help to address these important considerations because they focus on gathering, exchanging, and producing information in English in real contexts and in an integrated way, rather than focusing only on discrete language points within a classroom setting.

This chapter includes:

- the benefits of project materials and materials that take students beyond the classroom
- materials and procedures involved in developing a project
- possible final products of projects
- project types and field task materials
- how to develop your own project materials
- how to involve your students in developing materials that facilitate language use outside the classroom

Some Challenging Questions

Before you begin, answer these questions:

- Have you ever participated in projects as part of learning, and, specifically, as part of language learning?
- Have you considered projects and community contacts for your students?
- What are the benefits and limitations in assigning class projects and community contacts?

Projects

How is a project different from other language learning activities? Fried-Booth (1986) describes projects as tasks that are typically more involved than other practice activities, although short practice activities can be part of a project. There are usually several stages to the project, culminating in a product such as a booklet, newsletter, wall display, video, or presentation. Students are often involved in developing materials for their projects such as questionnaires. Because they incorporate independent work as well as group work, projects and community contact tasks can be assigned as the final activities in themes or units of study. In an EFL context, for example, a food or restaurant theme for low-intermediate students culminates with a project that has students designing a flyer or plan for a new restaurant in their community, including its name, operating hours, decor, and an international menu, complete with prices (Rooks 1997). The Internet is a good place to find menus.

The Benefits of Project and Community Contacts

Fried-Booth, Moss and Van Duzer (1998), and our own experience point to these benefits of projects and community contacts for language development:

- The language students practice in class in preparation for the project or field task is language they really need. In other words, projects help to provide a reason for learning as well as speaking the target language.
- The materials and associated tasks are, as much as possible, based on students' interests and concerns. This makes them encouraging for intermediate or advanced students whose progress may seem slower than in early stages of language learning.
- Projects are student-centered activities. They engage students in authentic tasks that require authentic language; that is, learners communicate for a definite purpose.
- They often provide an opportunity for students to interact with native speakers.
- Students gain a sense of accomplishment in completing tasks and concrete projects outside the sheltered classroom environment. This, in turn, increases their self-esteem.

- They provide opportunities for sustained language practice.
- They often build on previous work.
- They promote greater independence in language learning.
- They enhance student-student relationships, cooperative learning, and development of social skills.
- They add variety and a change of pace to regular classroom learning activities.
- They integrate work in the skill areas and communicative competencies in a natural way.
- Assessment and evaluation of student learning can be done by the teacher, by individual student reflection, and by peers assessing each other.
- The products can become materials for other students' use.
- Projects can be motivational.

Stages in Project Development

In her book *Project Work*, Diana L. Fried-Booth outlines the stages of a full-fledged project for ESL learners. We use her headings and combine her suggestions with the ideas of others in this section. Fried-Booth's eight stages are: stimulus; definition of the project objective; practice of language skills; design of written materials; individual, pair or group activities (discussed under Project Ideas); gathering and collating information; organization of materials; and final presentation. Not every project will adhere rigorously to these stages, and if the project is the culmination of a theme unit, you will already have practiced many of the language skills within the theme unit.

STAGE 1: THE STIMULUS

The impetus for a project can come from a teacher, a reading, an individual student, or from the group in general, such as a group brainstorming session. As you develop rapport with your students, you will discover their interests and concerns. Appropriate ideas should be based on program objectives and student goals and needs. For example, one teacher assigned a project to secondary students entitled "Design the Ideal High School System" (Sangwine 1988). This idea grew out of students' interest in discussing and writing about different educational systems and according to Sangwine was appropriate to their age group and proficiency level. A similar topic would not be of interest to tradespeople in an EFL setting or to young children at a beginning level of proficiency.

After you have identified project ideas, work with those that can be explored in depth and will lead to extensive language practice. To help you select appropriate projects from the identified project ideas, it is important that you select age-appropriate projects of interest to your students. For example, a project that involves speaking to a number of people about a topic such as dating, research on dating, and reading teen magazines will allow for more depth than a classroom discussion alone on the topic. It is also important that you know your students' proficiency levels and abilities so that you select projects that will challenge them linguistically to extend language but not be too difficult. Select projects that fit into your timeframe for instruction and student homework. This may limit the number and type of activities you do for your selected project. Finally, projects should be selected based on how well they fit with and enhance your curriculum. Select projects that allow for extensive practice of the language focus of your syllabus.

In the planning stages, it is helpful to show or describe a previous project to the students so they know what you expect of them. As a teacher, you also need to communicate your enthusiasm and confidence in your students' ability to carry out the project. As in most stages of project development, you should encourage students to lead the discussion and make suggestions. To be truly student-centered, you need to make your opinions secondary to those of the students, but realize when you do need to step in and provide some direction.

STAGE 2: DEFINING THE PROJECT OBJECTIVE

If you have not developed a project objective, you will need to involve students in discussion, suggestion, and argument about it. In a project assigned by Sangwine, the students participated in defining the following project objectives: learning about 20th-century history, creating links between newcomers and older members of the community, providing information to students preparing for citizenship interviews or planning to take a history course, and developing writing and oral information-gathering skills.

Sangwine states that when defining project objectives, it is important to think ahead to the final product, if you intend to have one, and to the audience for which that product will be designed. There is a wide array of ideas from brochures, booklets, and posters to audiovisual recordings and websites. Products ideas are discussed more later.

STAGE 3: PRACTICE OF LANGUAGE SKILLS

You will need to provide students with opportunities to practice the language they feel they need for the early part of the project. For interview tasks, this includes asking for information, note taking, and starting and ending the interview. For a project in which students design a flyer for a new restaurant, students need language for group decision-making such as offering suggestions, agreeing and disagreeing, in addition to food vocabulary.

In "Project Homeland," students researched their cultures and made informative posters for others in their school (Ortmeier 2000, 12). To accomplish this large project, Ortmeier listed more than 30 language skills that students would need to complete the project. She also created a chart identifying the major tasks, associated language skills and sources of content.

Developing a chart of tasks, associated language skills, and activities is a good strategy to help you organize and keep track of the project. For example, for researching a topic, students need these skills: skimming, scanning, reading for detail, note taking, and journal writing. Students can also suggest what they need to know to carry out the tasks. Encourage them to do so. Students will find the information for a research project, for example, in libraries, on the Internet, and in databases. As the project develops, it is your task to design activities that will help students to develop these skills and subskills, as well as help them find access to the content when they need assistance. All of these skills and subskills, information, resources, and activities can be entered onto the project chart that you can use for your own purposes or share with your students.

STAGE 4: THE DESIGN OF WRITTEN MATERIALS

Involve students as much as possible in designing projects that result in written products. However, sometimes it may be more reasonable for you to design the project materials yourself because of constraints on classroom time, your teaching objectives, and the abilities of your particular student group. In such cases, it's helpful to provide students with a handout outlining the parameters of the project. For example, a restaurant project task sheet would provide a line for writing in the restaurant name and sections for listing a specified number of appetizers, main dishes, desserts, and beverages. Such worksheets give students direction and security while still allowing them to explore the topic independently. Worksheets also ensure that your expectations for the scope of the project are met.

For a project that includes surveys or interviews, handouts can specify the number and types of questions you want students to include, as in these examples.

Work Interview

Instructions: Interview an English speaker about his or her work (about 20 to 30 minutes). The following suggestions may help you in developing your questions. However, write your own questions to fit the person you are interviewing, the type of work the person does, and the type of questions you are interested in and comfortable asking. Write a minimum of 12 questions and include the following:

1. Two questions using present perfect tense.
2. The person's greatest accomplishment in his or her job.

Other possible question topics include:

- number of jobs the person has had
- the worst or strangest job
- how he or she decided on his or her current career
- kinds of things the person does in his or her job
- any special projects he or she is currently working on in the job
- kind of training or preparation the person had for the job
- how important to his or her work formal academic education has been
- advantages and challenges of the job
- what he or she likes most and least about the job
- level of stress on the job
- how work affects his or her family life
- amount of free time the job allows and what he or she does during free time

A trip-planning project for lower-level students can include the worksheets on pages 172–75.

b Surname _____

Given names _____

Street address _____

SUMMER

ACTIVITY 5

Travel Plans

Answer in complete sentences
Use *going to*.

Example: *We are going to go to Whistler.*

1. Where are you going to go?

_____

_____

2. What five activities are you going to do there?

a. _____

_____

b. _____

_____

c. _____

_____

e. _____

_____

3. When are you going?

_____

_____

4. How long are you going to stay?

_____

_____

5. Are you going to stay in a hotel or at a campground?

_____

_____

6. What are you going to take with you? Choose 5 things from this list:

- sunglasses
- camera
- mosquito repellent
- winter jacket
- bilingual dictionary

- warm sweater
- umbrella
- radio
- credit card
- first aid kit

- bathing suit
- skis
- sun screen
- hair dryer
- stamps

1. _____

2. _____

3. _____

4. _____

5. _____

Source: M. Ormiston, R. DeCoursey, and S. Fredeen, *The ESL Toolbox: Ready-to-Use Enrichment Activities for LINC Classes* (Saskatoon, SK: University Extension Press, 1994). Reproduced by permission of the University of Saskatchewan Language Centre.

b
and
i

Name: _____

Female   Male   (circle one)

Summer Holiday

ACTIVITY 8

Phoning Around

A. Do you want to travel by plane, by car, by train or by bus?
   Which is cheapest? Which is fastest?

Use a phone book. Find the phone number for:

1. A travel agent: __ __ __ - __ __ __ __

2. A airline: __ __ __ - __ __ __ __

3. A bus company: __ __ __ - __ __ __ __

4. Via Rail: __ __ __ - __ __ __ __

5. A car rental agency: __ __ __ - __ __ __ __

B. Call three of the places in A.
   Ask about the cost of your trip. Make notes.

Example:

Place: _____Calgary_____

Dates: _____June 28 to July 3_____

Plan 1:

   Type of transportation: __bus_____

   Cost: __$145 return_____

Place: _____

Dates: _____

Plan 1:

Type of transportation: _____

Cost: _____

Plan 2:

Type of transportation: _____

Cost: _____

Plan 3:

Type of transportation: _____

Cost: _____

C. Choose 1 of the plans.
   Write about it.

We are going to go to _____.

We are going to go by _____.

The cost is $ _____.

Source: Ormiston, De Coursey, and Fredeen, 1994.

STAGE 5: INFORMATION GATHERING

After practicing the language skills they will need for a project, such as an interview, students (with your assistance as appropriate) design their questionnaires and other written materials. It is best if they work in pairs or small groups when gathering information. Sangwine suggests pairing a weak student with a strong one for the interviews. One student can ask questions, and the other take notes. Alternatively, each student can interview independently. Students may record the interview (using a tape recorder or other recording device) with permission in order to have a comprehensive record of it.

Conducting interviews, surveys, and making observations are examples of typical authentic information-gathering group tasks (Crawford 2000, 34). Students may also gather information by collecting pamphlets and brochures from various agencies or by researching topics at the library or on the Internet.

In EFL contexts, interviews and surveys may involve other students and school staff more often than people outside the school, but you may be able to access some other English speakers in your community or you may be able to establish contacts with a class in an English-speaking country via the Internet. Resources for English speakers and English resources in EFL contexts are discussed later in the chapter. Smaller-scale projects such as the design of the restaurant or ideal school system would work well for EFL situations where information-gathering outside the classroom is not essential.

You or your students may need to do some preliminary work such as contacting libraries or offices that your students would like to visit to collect information. Make sure that the students will be able to gain access to various places. Fried-Booth suggests issuing cards or letters signed by your school principal or program coordinator to help students should they be questioned about their activities.

The type and amount of data collection that you and your students complete will influence the length of the project. If you need to order materials and resources for the project, be sure to do so early to ensure they arrive on time for information-gathering.

STAGE 6: COLLATING INFORMATION

Your students may want to read their interview or research notes or results aloud, or explain visuals to their classmates. Sometimes group members will use each other's information, so you may want to arrange a display or file system for organizing and storing the information that students bring in. You can also pin collected data on a wall or bulletin board. You may need to simplify some materials, such as pamphlets, that students have picked up so that the language is not overwhelming. A more advanced student in a multilevel class can do this. Or you might do it yourself if you have been involved in materials selection for the project (Fried-Booth).

STAGE 7: ORGANIZATION OF MATERIALS

The organization of project materials will usually lead to the development of the final product. In most cases you will have identified this product at the beginning stages of the project, considering the audience for which the product is being designed. The final product may be a brochure, booklet, class magazine, e-zine or newspaper, a handbook, a video, a wall display such as a collage or poster, individual diaries, group reports, audio or video recordings, a web page, or an oral presentation to another class. It can be as elaborate as you and your students like. In a book project described by Sangwine, the students used computer graphics for a cover design, laminated pages, and created a table of contents. You and your students can probably imagine other ways to organize material.

The final product usually involves a great deal of writing, and produces something tangible, but this need not always be the case. Fried-Booth describes the culminating project as "merely a vehicle for more related language work" (34). Therefore, it should be part of the process but not completely dominate it. For example, a group of foreign students who have studied English in an academic setting and met the university English entry requirements may benefit more from the oral and aural components of a project.

STAGE 8: FINAL PRESENTATION

The final presentation of the project will depend on the format of the final product, but is likely to involve speaking skills. For example, it can involve the delivery of a copy of the book produced to a library, another class, or to an organization.

This final step is important because it incorporates an element of ceremony and completion that many students enjoy. It also acknowledges and celebrates the students' accomplishments.

Do not be disappointed if the final product is different from what you had originally envisaged. Students ultimately decide what the final product will look like, and like the rest of the project, the final product will be somewhat different from what you expected. If your instructions are clear to students, balancing guidance and clear instructions and allowing for students to take responsibility for their research and learning, the final product will still have contributed to language development.

Evaluation Tools for Project Work

In projects, you work with students as a consultant, facilitator, and sometimes a coordinator. These roles leave you with greater freedom to monitor and evaluate student learning and to provide crucial feedback to students.

You may want to develop tools to help you monitor and evaluate. Sangwine suggests a marking scheme for student writing that students use to correct each other's written work. For long-term projects that will take more than a week to develop, Fried-Booth suggests weekly review and error monitor handouts (photocopiable from her text *Project Work*). The weekly review is a tool to help students become aware of their own learning as well as a way for you to gauge student progress. You can fill out the error monitor sheet discreetly while you are circulating among groups. If you like this method of receiving and giving feedback, you will probably want to design your own sheets to suit your students and the project on which they are working.

Moss and Van Duzer suggest the teacher should not be the exclusive evaluator of project work but should also involve students. This encourages them to:

> reflect on their own work and that of their peers, how well the team works, how they feel about their work and progress, and what skills and knowledge they are gaining. Reflection on work, checking progress, and identifying areas of strength and weakness are part of the learning process. Assessment can also be done through small-group discussion with guided questions. (1)

Materials and Equipment for Projects

Fried-Booth suggests this basic equipment list for projects: clipboards or spiral notepads with stiff covers, for interviews; file folders; art supplies; cameras and audiovisual recording equipment and playback units; gifts after a visit or guest speaker; postage; and magazines for images. She also suggests a budget for incidentals such as bus fares (32).

Project Ideas

This is a compilation of eight project ideas from a variety of sources, including our own experiences with projects.

WALL DISPLAYS

A wall display of affordable community entertainment or recreation is a great way to engage your students. It gives them opportunities to work with maps, compare costs of events, read entertainment columns in newspapers, collect brochures, visit tourist sites, phone for information, check local websites, and conduct a survey with on-the-street interviews.

"Project Homeland," described in detail by Ortmeier, provides "students with opportunities to learn about other cultures, validate their homeland experiences, and demonstrate to the mainstream school community that they have much to teach us" (17). In this project, students conduct research on their own or another culture and create informative posters for the entire school to view.

EXPEDITIONS

In expedition tasks, students divide into pairs or groups to research and present various aspects of a new community: entertainment, educational facilities, services, stores, restaurants, history, an interesting factory or business, environmental concerns, social problems, etc. Their presentations may be in the form of wall displays, role plays and sketches, photo stories, or even video or web-based presentations. One EFL class in Japan, for example, developed a detailed map on the Internet of their community, complete with links on how to get from place to place, services offered at various places in the city, etc.

ELEMENTARY SCHOOL TEACHING

This project involves older students in teaching small groups of elementary school children. Students decide on teaching objectives and the research necessary for the project. They then develop teaching materials, buy items, and organize the children in class to carry out the project. This might be a good project choice for adult or high school ESL students who can teach something about their culture or language to school children. Advanced EFL students might also enjoy delivering a basic English lesson to younger EFL students.

SCHOOL EXCHANGES

For this project, an ESL or EFL class pairs up with a class of native English speakers from another school or via the Internet. Students in the two classes may exchange pen-and-paper letters or e-mail, or they may decide to make a video about their class and aspects of their school to exchange with each other. If the schools are in the same community, one class can plan a joint activity for the two classes such as a dance, carnival, or field trip. Invitations can be sent; masters of ceremony chosen; and games, music, and other activities planned.

ENGLISH SURVIVAL HANDBOOK

This is a valuable product for immigrants or for EFL students hoping to visit an English-speaking country. Students compile a book of expressions, questions, and vital cultural information that other ESL or EFL students can use (Rooks).

LANGUAGE-LITERACY SURVIVAL HANDBOOK

Moss and Van Duzer describe a language-literacy project in which parents and their children developed "a coloring and activity book of community information for families living in their neighbourhood." Everyone participated, with intermediate-level parents doing the research and managing the project. Adult literacy students also participated, locating contact numbers and addresses for service agencies as well as listings for selected local stores, while children developed activities in the book for children.

BUSINESS DAY

We once had our beginning students plan a garage sale in the classroom using donated items from teachers and students. Other classes were invited as customers. Students were motivated to practice and use common expressions related to buying, selling, and bartering, and had fun in the process.

The listening and speaking textbook and video series, *Amazing 2! News, Interviews and Conversations* (Bates 1999) expands on the business day concept. After listening to interviews with small business owners and discussing the advantages and disadvantages of having a small business, secrets to success in business and preferred kinds of businesses, students are asked to plan a business day themselves. As a class, they choose a business idea such as a garage sale, a bake sale, a foreign language lesson, or production and sale of greetings cards. The project culminates with another class participating as customers.

Adapting Projects to EFL Contexts

Conducting projects and community contact activities requires extra creativity and ingenuity in EFL contexts, but it is still possible. As in the business day project examples, consider using English-speaking staff from your educational institution and other English classes for projects that involve interviewing outside the classroom. A little research may help you discover other sources of English speakers, such as embassies; clubs; or American, British, or Canadian companies that employ a large number of English speakers. If you've ever taught in an EFL context, you will probably also be aware of places that English speakers tend to gather, such as favorite restaurants or nightclubs. Consider English bookstores or tourist sites as other places to conduct projects in EFL situations.

The Internet offers wonderful resources for connecting EFL students by connecting them to native speakers and by providing information in English. If you plan ahead of time, you can arrange with colleagues in English-speaking countries to send video and audio recordings such as newscasts, interviews, biographies, and other documentaries related to your projects.

Where no native speaker or print material in English is available for information-gathering, students may have to gather information in their first language and translate it into English when presenting final products.

Service Learning: Another Kind of Project

At many language centers in the United States and Canada students are often encouraged and provided with opportunities to volunteer at community events and with community organizations. The students often attend a volunteer orientation session and sign up for several shifts to sell tickets, do face painting, usher, and participate in other jobs. A volunteer appreciation event is sometimes an added bonus of the experience. Volunteering has proven to be a valuable and rewarding way for students to develop linguistic and cultural skills and to participate in community life.

Related to but distinct from volunteering is Service Learning. Eric Kendrick (2000) defines service learning for ESL students in higher education as "experiential learning which integrates course theory with practice through volunteering and community service." It is distinct from volunteerism, he explains, because it is "connected with academic content," "involves reflection (before and after)," and "involves assessment (what students learned and how to document it)."

Recognizing the value of service learning, some high school and university programs for mainstream students as well as some teachers of ESL courses for international and immigrant students are including service learning components to their programs. These experiences can be added to student portfolios, which will be useful to them when seeking employment.

Benefits of Service Learning

The Centre for Advancement of Service Learning (CASL), Kendrick, and others point to these benefits of service learning:

- It is experiential, integrating the communicative skills in real contexts and bridging linguistic theory into practice.

- It develops fluency and interpersonal communication.
- It synthesizes student learning and can result in higher academic achievement.
- Because it makes learning relevant, it is motivational, resulting in reduced absenteeism and higher retention.
- It increases student self confidence and satisfaction in their learning.
- It improves classroom discussion and communication skills.
- It enhances active learning, problem solving, and analytical/critical thinking.
- It develops learner independence, initiative, leadership skills, and accountability to oneself, one's peers, and to the community (civic responsibility).
- It enriches awareness of the community and involvement in volunteerism.
- It develops sociocultural awareness.
- It provides opportunities for students to explore career interests, may provide work experience and can contribute to a student's resume and portfolio.
- It can raise the profile and image of an ESL program in the community, which may be valuable for funding, work placements, or other purposes.

In addition, service learning benefits the community recipients of the volunteers' service and dispels possible resistance to and stereotyping of foreign students and immigrants in the community.

General Structure of a Service Learning Project

Service learning projects involve:

- **preparation**—or developing students' content knowledge and skills about the community and specific service placement in the community as well as developing common understanding between the students and community partners regarding the goals of the project and services that will be provided by the students (best documented in writing for both partners).
- **activity**—participating in the community service placement on a long- or short-term basis. This often requires teacher monitoring with the student and community partner during the project to ensure things go smoothly.
- **debriefing or reflection**—conducted through student journals (paper-based or recorded), letter to community partner, or teacher explaining what they learned.
- **celebration**—recognizing their contribution and learning, ideally with the participation of the community partner.
- **evaluation**—ideally conducted as a discussion with the teacher to provide feedback on the value of the project and assess improvement in the skills and communicative competencies.

Examples of Service Learning

SHELTERED CONTENT SOCIOLOGY COURSE—VOLUNTEERING UNIT

A colleague developed this activity for upper-intermediate and advanced students in an English for Academic Purposes program for a university Sociology course that provides some support for ESL students. The instructor prepares students for the service learning aspect of this course by brainstorming what they most want to learn about North American society (for example, guns and crime, love and romance, poverty and homelessness). The ESL class explores why North Americans volunteer by reading articles and brochures on volunteerism. Students develop relevant questions for a volunteer panel of non-ESL community members. An ESL component of this preparation includes focusing in on difficult language and concepts raised in the readings and discussion. The action stage of this project involves students in volunteering at an organization such as a Boys' and Girls' Club, Street Kids' Club, Girl Scouts, or Food Bank. It can be arranged so that pairs of students volunteer for two hours weekly, or so that the entire class including teachers do half-days of volunteering on alternate weekends. For reflection, students debate this question: Does volunteering do more harm than good, that is, does it perpetuate a social problem? They also write a reflective journal or essay.

CHARITY FUNDRAISING

Kathyrn Bell (Penner and Bell 2003) describes a service learning project suitable for intermediate and advanced ESL learners. In the process of assisting a non-profit organization with fundraising, students develop skills in research, interviewing, writing business plans and reflection papers, and presenting their project. They also enhance their skills in group collaboration, business and management, advertising, problem solving, and community activism. The project is set up as a competition between student groups to see who can raise the most money for their charity. In the planning stage, each group researches a charity, plans and promotes the fundraising activity for that charity, and carries out the event. Fundraising ideas (action stage) included making and selling personalized fortune cookies, selling baked goods or raffle tickets, and providing a cleaning service. As debriefing and reflection, student groups submitted business plans, presented a written summary of their project for evaluation by the teacher, and gave an oral presentation on their chosen charity. Individuals also submitted reflection papers.

FUNDRAISING FOR A CHRISTMAS PARTY FOR REFUGEE CHILDREN

In this community service project described by Penner (Penner and Bell), intermediate level students spent eight weeks on a project to raise funds to support a Christmas party for refugee children in an immigrant services society. At the planning stage, students found out about the society and learned about fundraising and types of fundraising activities through guest speakers, taped lectures, field trips, and readings. They also researched how to carry out the various stages of fundraising. In the activity stage, the class selected fundraising activities, and planned and implemented all of the logistics involved in doing the fundraising, including advertising. Advertising included visiting other classes and speaking about the project to other small groups of ESL students, designing and displaying posters, and a "dollars raised tree." The actual fundraising activities included bake sales, raffle ticket sales (students gathered free prizes from their institution's bookstore and from community businesses), and a fundraising party at their institution, complete with student-developed party games and sales of refreshments. These promotional and fundraising activities also led to several unsolicited donations. Ten students assisted with decorating and cleanup at the Christmas party for refugee children, combining both the activity and celebration stages of service learning. The teacher facilitated by inviting in the guest speakers and developing worksheets for the class to support successful completion of all stages of the project.

Resources for Service Learning

Teachers using service learning in their courses are understandably enthusiastic about its value as a teaching and learning tool and are usually eager to share their experiences and projects. The number of online resources for service learning is growing. Following are three such sites (at time of writing):

- the National Service-Learning Clearinghouse at *www.servicelearning.org/*
- the Centre for the Advancement of Service Learning (CASL) at *www.howard.edu/ CenterUrbanProgress/CASL.html*
- the Service-Learning Internet Community at *www.slic.calstate.edu.*

Next we look in detail at materials and tasks for small-scale community contact materials and tasks.

Small-Scale Community Contact Materials and Tasks

Some projects may seem unsuitable for your particular teaching situation for any of the following reasons: limited teaching time and resources, limited literacy and language abilities of your students, and the limitations of teaching in an EFL context. However, you can still involve students with tasks and materials that involve authentic language use and take them outside the classroom to interact with native speakers.

You will still need to practice specific language skills in the classroom for tasks that go beyond the classroom. However, the degree of preparation will probably be less than it is for project work. A final product may also be less important and less complex, depending on the task you assign to students.

Your community contact tasks may be more teacher directed than they are in a project. They will often, but not always, be part of a theme unit you have developed. However, the field tasks don't have to be related to a particular theme. Rather, you can use such tasks simply to provide a change of pace and to expose students to a real language experience, as in the school-wide scavenger hunt described later.

The section that follows describes eleven ideas for field tasks and materials. Many of the tasks described require you to develop materials such as worksheets, maps, and questionnaires for your students.

Scavenger and Information Hunts and Materials

For a scavenger or information hunt, create a list of objects or information that students can find and have access to in the community or in a particular location. Restrict your list to items that are free of charge. Students usually work in pairs or small groups. A time limit is placed on the activity. The first pair of students to return with all the items or information required can receive a prize.

GROCERY OR DEPARTMENT STORE INFORMATION HUNT

Develop a sheet of questions or items that you require students to find in a grocery or department store. Your goal may be to familiarize students with products that are new to them, or it may be to familiarize them with consumer issues, such as buying in bulk, comparison shopping, and being aware of product ingredients. Include questions on items that students have asked about in class. Here are some sample questions for a grocery store information hunt.

Grocery Store Information Hunt

Instructions: *Find answers to the following questions in your local grocery store.*

1. What does the packaging date on ground pork tell you?

2. What does the "best before" date on whole milk indicate?

3. What kinds of foods can you buy in bulk?

4. How much is bulk rice? Is it cheaper or more expensive than packaged rice?

5. Where is the generic brand of toilet tissue in the store packaged?

6. Where are the other brands packaged?

7. Where is the breakfast cereal located in the store?

8. What are the first two ingredients in Frosted Flakes®?

9. Find two items on special today. What is another word or phrase for a *special*?

Source: M. Ormiston, *TESL 32: Materials Selection and Development* (Saskatoon, SK: Extension Division, University of Saskatchewan, 1998).

MUSEUM OR ART GALLERY INFORMATION HUNT

Museum and art gallery information hunts are similar to grocery store hunts. You will need to visit the museum first in order to make up your questions. Some museums will prepare scavenger hunts for you.

SAMPLE COMMUNITY-WIDE SCAVENGER HUNT

This activity from *Action Plans* (Macdonald and Rogers-Gordon 1984) suggests listing five to ten items for pairs of students to find, such as a map from City Hall or the Chamber of Commerce, a store catalog, and a blank bill from a restaurant.

Variation 1: During one half-day scavenger hunt, approximately 200 students were divided into groups of about 15. In order to keep the students involved in the task for at least two hours, the teachers developed a fairly long handout of information. The activity took place in a bilingual English-French setting and items on the hunt list included such things as the names of theatres that were playing English movies, the names of the movies and times, the names of five provincial parks in other provinces, the name of the mayor in a neighboring English community, and the identity of the historical figure depicted on a famous statue in the city. Students were creative in their solutions to finding answers, for example, visiting a tourist information center and calling the toll-free number of a neighboring province or state to get responses.

Variation 2: You can cooperate with another teacher in your institution to have an advanced group make up a scavenger hunt for another class using this worksheet of a well-known speaking activity.

Instructions: *Find someone who*

1. speaks more than three languages
2. plays a musical instrument
3. has a degree in literature
4. studied psychology
5. has a birthday in April.

During a break, students socialize with students in another class and ask questions in order to find names to match with each description.

The Community and School as Resources

INTERVIEWS

The interview is an excellent task for the community of the school. You will need to locate a sufficient number of English speakers in the school community for pairs of students to interview. Prior to the interview, it is helpful to students if you can give them some information about the interviewees, such as their interests and what they would be interested in talking about with other students. Pairs of students choose who they would like to interview, prepare questions, and meet the interviewee outside the class, in a coffee shop or student lounge, for example. Possible follow-up activities can include oral or written reports.

Macdonald and Rogers-Gordon suggest that beginning students should conduct a series of interviews with the same person. The content of the interviews can progress from gathering simple factual information to more complex topics. For example, in workplace preparation programs, students can ask a visitor straightforward questions about office procedures or more complex questions such as office culture and politics.

If there are a limited number of native speakers available as interviewees, invite them all for the same class period. Have groups of four students interview one person. Then switch with another group of four students and interview a second person. The interviewees will be interviewed by several groups of four, but usually they are happy to oblige. With a class of 16 students, you would only need four native speakers to keep everyone involved.

EFL teachers might want to try this teacher's technique for encouraging English use outside the classroom: Students who stopped to chat with him in his office or in the corridor were awarded tokens. The longer they talked in English, the more tokens they received. The tokens were then credited toward their course grade. To his delight, the teacher was deluged with students (Savignon 1997, 201).

COMMUNITY SERVICES

You can assign students tasks that involve using the services offered in a community. This helps them integrate successfully into the community as well as use the target language. An example of tasks that are part of a unit on the post office for a high-beginner class of immigrants is shown.

At the Post Office

Instructions: *Do each of the tasks below.*

- Buy a stamp for mailing a letter in Canada or the United States.
- Buy a stamp for a letter you are sending overseas.
- Ask for airmail stickers.
- Find out how much it costs to send a one-kilogram parcel to your home country.
- Find out the cost of sending a one-kilogram parcel to Calgary or Las Vegas.
- Find out where the postal code or zip code books are.
- Find out how long it takes to send a parcel to Australia by surface mail.
- Ask for a change-of-address card.

Source: Ormiston, 1998.

Ask the students to carry out these tasks immediately following a post office tour so they become familiar with the building with you present to support and encourage them to complete their tasks. In order to avoid making excessive demands on the post office or other service staff, and on your students, assign no more than one to three tasks to each student. It's advisable to discuss the assignment with post office personnel so that they're willing to cooperate. Don't forget to do a follow-up activity, even a class discussion to get feedback on the activity and on the learning that has taken place.

SURVEYS AS MATERIAL FOR COMMUNITY CONTACTS

Surveys are a common information-gathering tool used in project work, but they can be developed and used as activities outside the context of a project. You or your students develop questions on a chosen topic. Then students carry out their surveys in the school, interviewing other students and staff, on the street, or in another public place. Topics for surveys in secondary school may include fashion trends or favorite local eateries or entertainment spots, preferred music, opinions on a current issue, and study habits.

Maps and Map-Related Tasks as Material for Community Contacts

LABELING MAPS

Have students familiarize themselves with a community or locale and at the same time provide them with a community-based group task. Macdonald and Rogers-Gordon suggest this community-based activity: Draw a map of an area of your community, but label only a few buildings or other features on the map. You can also leave out some of the street names. On a corner of the map, provide a list of other buildings, street names, or other features for students to locate. Students go into the community and ask for directions to help them locate the buildings. They then label the buildings and unmarked streets on their map.

For variation, make a floor plan of the school, a library, grocery store, or other place of interest. Provide a list of areas or rooms related to those floor plans for students to label. Students will probably have to ask staff and other students for directions in order to complete the plan, for example, "Excuse me, where is Ms. Johnson's room?" or "Where are the ESL books?" or "Where are the computer stations?"

USING MAPS

Provide students with a map that includes the location of the building where the classroom is found and of a field trip destination. After locating the two places, students discuss the best route for reaching the destination—for example, "We can go down 4th Avenue to 23rd Street, cross 23rd street, then turn left." Armed with their maps, the students, not the teacher, then lead the way to the destination, stopping to ask for directions, if necessary. If the destination involves using the bus, provide a map with transit routes.

COMMUNITY EXPLORATION

One teacher suggests a community exploration task using a map of an interesting business district in your community or of a locale you plan to visit with your students. Distribute copies of the map to pairs of students. Each pair of students chooses a business or service designated on the map to investigate. Alternatively, the business and services can be listed separately with their addresses. A third alternative is to list only the names of places and have students find the addresses in the phone book. Develop a handout for each pair that requires them to find further information about their chosen destination. The kind of information they look for should encourage them to interact with people in the community or locale. A sample worksheet for a pair of students investigating a music store follows.

Destination: MUSICMANIA, Somewhereville

Group: _____

Part A

Instructions: *Find out the following information:*

1. The most popular compact disc and single this week

2. The most popular kind of music

3. How they classify music

4. How they decide on the number of tapes and compact discs to order

5. If they have any music in other languages

6. The average age of customers

7. If they have any recordings on special this week and how much they cost

---

Part B

8.   The people we spoke to were:

    a.   polite?   yes _____   no _____

    b.   friendly?   yes _____   no _____

    c.   helpful?   yes _____   no _____

9.   The most interesting thing we discovered was:

Source: Ormiston, 1998.

Note that this worksheet is designed so that students must formulate the questions themselves. You will probably want to spend some time practicing question formation in class before this activity. You can also ask students to make a map of the store or business. Follow-up in class can involve an information exchange in the form of oral presentations or an informal discussion.

The worksheet that follows provides students with practice in asking questions. It followed visits by pairs of students to various facilities and government agencies in the community. Students can also generate their own lists of what they would like to find out about each business.

Instructions: *Find out the following information from other students. Mark the location of the place they visited on your map.*

1. a. the location of the library

    b. the cost of renting a DVD from a library or other distribution center

2. a. the location of the Millwood Recreation Centre

    b. an interesting activity that is happening at Millwood Recreation Centre this week

3. a. the location of the Legal Aid Office

    b. how the Legal Aid Office can help you

4. a. the location of the Better Business Bureau

    b. the Better Business Bureau's office hours

5. a. the location of the municipal tourist bureau

    b. the services the municipal tourist bureau has to offer

---

Source: M. Ormiston and R. Epstein, *English Language Teaching Materials: A Practical Guide* (Saskatoon, SK: University Extension Press, 2005), 302.

Pictures and Realia as Material for Community Contacts

As discussed in Chapter 4, visual material such as pictures and drawings as well as realia are tremendous supports to language teaching and learning. You can use them effectively in small-scale community or school contact tasks. Bring a variety of objects to school, or cut pictures of objects out of magazines, such as kitchen utensils, tools, beauty care products, or toys. You will probably want to choose a category of objects related to a particular topic or theme you are working on, or objects that are of particular interest to your students. However, you also need to include unfamiliar objects. After practicing questions such as, "What's this?" or "How do you use this?" or "What's this part for?" or "Why is this part bent?" Jerald & Clark (1980) suggest you have students find other people in the school to provide them with answers to their questions about the objects and follow up with informal class or small group presentations, or with a writing assignment.

If you have chosen a high-quality textbook, there should be many possibilities for supplementary tasks outside the classroom where students can use language covered in their text. This can be as simple as sending them outside to ask three different people, "What time is it?" or "Where is the Internet cafe?" To make this language-use activity less threatening for beginners, choose questions to which they already know the answers.

A friend visiting Japan once described a bus ride in which a local girl sitting beside her said, "Excuse me, this may sound like an odd question, but does your mother go to the YWCA?" The local girl proceeded to describe how she had met a woman at the YWCA recently who had told her that her daughter taught English at the university. She ended up in a nice conversation with the local girl, even though her mother did not work at the Y. You may have used textbooks dealing with ways of asking for information, one of them being, "This may sound like an odd question, but. . . . " It could be that the local girl had been practicing her lines, and very smoothly, too!

Radio and Television as Material for Community Contacts

You can use the radio and TV as resources for community and school contact tasks in a number of ways. As homework, have students listen to a particular TV program, the news, or the sports. Prerecorded or international newscasts may be used in EFL settings. Provide students with worksheets to help to focus their listening or viewing. Follow-up in class can involve a discussion or a personal response in each student's journal. Radio and TV can also help to bridge the gap between classroom and community, especially if you find channels with local programming.

Telephone as Material for Community Contacts

The phone is a good tool for providing authentic language practice outside the classroom, although its use is mostly applicable in ESL contexts. Students can phone staff at an English language school, hotel, or other business providing services in English. To avoid overloading any one employee, students are assigned different people to call from the task sheet. Let staff know that a student might be calling them. A task sheet, such as the one on page191, facilitates the assignment.

You can also be a telephone resource for students if you don't mind spending an evening responding to student phone calls. This works in both ESL and EFL contexts.

Telephone Tasks Worksheet

Instructions: *Phone one of the following staff at your language institute. Ask for information on two topics. Take notes.*

A. Staff person: Monica (8:30–4:30 Monday–Friday; Phone 382-2222)

Topics:
- how and when to register for the next placement test
- deadline to register for the next term
- information about taking French or Spanish classes (dates and times for next term's courses, cost, content, amount of homework required)
- if the office can send an information package to your friend who wants to study here

B. Staff person: Chris (9:00–5:00 Monday–Friday; Phone 382-5555)

Topics:
- which countries students are coming from next term
- the deadline to register for English courses next term
- if the office can send an information package to your friend who wants to study here
- information about changing to a different homestay family.

C. Staff person: Rose (9:00–5:00 Monday–Friday; Phone 382-1111), or Andrea (8:00—12:00 Monday–Friday; Phone 382-1111)

Topics:
- information about new and interesting materials the library has for English students
- new computer programs that the library will soon have
- library hours during between terms
- overdue materials you may have.

Source: Ormiston, 1998.

Guest Speakers as Resources for Community Contacts

Guest speakers are always a great stimulus for students and can enhance their learning. Have students prepare questions to ask speakers or assign selective listening tasks, based on your English language study in class. Sample tasks include:

- recording hesitation devices the speaker uses, such as *ummm, well, errr, so*
- listening for examples of reduced speech, that is, contractions, dropped words or dropped word endings (e.g., singin' instead of singing), elliptical answers (e.g., in reduced speech, the answer to the question, *Where are you going?* in its reduced or elliptical form is *(to) the store* rather than *I am going to the store.*)
- taking notes of the main points of the talk in order to write a written summary

Listening tasks will help students to focus and will give them something to listen for even if they cannot understand everything. Consider preparing worksheets on which students record their observations.

Other Possibilities

Special events such as trade shows, exhibitions, and conferences may be a good place for students to gather print information and interview people working at display booths for small community contact activities. Another possibility is involving students in finding and consulting books on a topic of interest at a bookstore or in the school or public library. A final product such as an essay or oral report might follow.

Resources Index

Fried-Booth suggests creating a resource index or chart of sources of English speakers and materials. This index will be important for you to develop if you are teaching in an EFL context. It provides you with a ready reference to helpful people and places for project work, field tasks, and guest speakers. Headings for your resource list might look like this:

Place	Contact Person	Address/Phone

Some of the entries Fried-Booth suggests are advertising agencies, airports, English language radio or TV stations, embassies, and churches.

Appendix A:
Major Publishers and
Distributors of ELT Materials

ALTA ESL Book Center Publishers
Cambridge University Press
Delta Systems Co. Inc.
Hampton Brown Publishers
Heinemann Publishers
Heinle & Heinle (International Thomson)
Kagan Publishing
McGraw-Hill, Inc.
Multilingual Matters
Oxford University Press
Pearson Longman
Pippin Publishing Corporation
ProLingua Associates
University of Michigan Press

APPENDIX B:
CHOOSING SOFTWARE

(Compiled based on these sources: Gaer 1998; Rachar 1989; Reagan and Murray 2002; Software Evaluation Guide n.d.; Shrum and Glisan 1994; Spanou n.d.)

Use these questions to determine the suitability of computer software for your classroom. You may want to write comments on an additional sheet of paper. You can also use this questionnaire to assess web-based programs.

Purchasing Information

1. Program name:

   _____

2. Publisher:

3. Platform: MS-DOS   Macintosh   Windows   Windows   UNIX

   Other:

4. Cost:

General Information

5. What are the objectives of the computer program?

   _____

6. Do the objectives match your curriculum and context?   _____ Yes _____ No

7. Does the teaching approach and methods match those you use? _____ Yes _____ No

8. What activities are included?

   _____ Drill & Practice   _____ Tutorial   _____ Simulation   _____ Authoring

   Other_____

9. How does the program facilitate teaching and learning?

   _____ Supplementary exercises

   _____ Provides new or additional information

   _____ Provides self-access activities

   _____ Other _____

10. List three different situations (i.e., units of study, course types, classroom situations, etc.) in which this program might be useful for you. How might you implement its use (e.g., workstations, competitions, student preparation of materials, etc.)?

Program Mechanics

11. Is the program easy to use and navigate? _____ Yes _____ No

12. Does the program include appropriate prompts? _____ Yes _____ No

13. Does the program evaluate or provide feedback to students? _____ Yes _____ No

14. Can you easily modify the program to make it suitable to your curriculum and context? _____ Yes _____ No

15. Does the program or website download quickly? _____ Yes _____ No

16. Does the program allow for record keeping? _____ Yes _____ No

17. Is feedback provided to students? _____ Yes _____ No

18. Does the program avoid distracting elements such as unnecessary sounds, animations, and product promotions? _____ Yes _____ No

Pedagogical Considerations

19. What aspects of communicative competence do the activities promote?

_____ Linguistic competence   _____ Pragmatic competence

_____ Discourse competence   _____ Sociolinguistic competence

20. Does the program promote language acquisition? _____ Yes _____ No

21. Does the program allow for student autonomy? _____ Yes _____ No

22. Does the student have sufficient control over program content? _____ Yes _____ No

23. Does the program allow for novel or original responses? _____ Yes _____ No

24. Does the program allow for meaning making? _____ Yes _____ No

25. Is there the opportunity for proactive learning? _____ Yes _____ No

26. Is there the opportunity to develop metacognition? _____ Yes _____ No

27. Is the program interactive? _____ Yes _____ No

28. Does the program allow for group collaboration? _____ Yes _____ No

29. Does the program allow for individual work and self access? _____ Yes _____ No

30. Does the program allow for a variety of student learning styles? _____ Yes _____ No

31. Are there opportunities for unintended learning? _____ Yes _____ No

32. Does the program include appropriate authentic material? _____ Yes _____ No

33. What are the program's strongest points?

_____

_____

34. What are the program's weakest points?

_____

_____

_____

35. Other comments:

_____

_____

APPENDIX C: COMPUTER APPLICATIONS FOR LANGUAGE TEACHING AND LEARNING

Here is a sampling of current computer applications that are being utilized, explored, or may be on the horizon to support language teaching and learning:

- **E-communication and e-collaboration programs:** e-mail, class mail lists, asynchronous electronic and Web-based discussion forums, instant message (one-to-one), chat, integrated messaging (voicemail and e-mail), videoconferencing, weblogs, wikis, shared documents (e.g., for peer editing, projects, etc.); personal and shared web pages and home pages
- **Administration:** file storage (e.g., allowing teachers to store digital images in electronic files), electronic registration, electronic student databases
- **E-publishing and distribution of content:** word processing, PowerPoint, Excel, Adobe Acrobat, notepad computers, course/learning management systems (e.g., Blackboard/WebCT and Moodle), learning objects repositories, electronic library catalogues, electronic books and journals, online course paks (from book publishers), online reference materials, weblogs, wikis, podcasts, streaming audio and video, live two-way interactive video, e-portfolios
- **Assessment:** online surveys; "clicker" technology; online drills, activities, quizzes, and exams; electronic assignment and exam submission; electronic databases of exam questions; electronic feedback; plaigiarism detection

REFERENCES

Allwright, R. L. "What Do We Want Teaching Materials For?" In *Currents in Language Teaching*, eds. R. Rossner and R. Bolitho. New York: Oxford University Press, 1990.

Altano, B. *Teaching Academic Reading Processes: A Reproducible Resource for Reading Courses*. Ann Arbor: University of Michigan Press, 2005.

Anderson, L., and S. Fredeen. *The Phonetics Files*. Saskatoon, SK: Extension Press, 1997.

Ashworth, M. *The First Step on the Longer Path: Becoming an ESL Teacher*. Markham, ON: Pippin Publishing, 1992.

Auerbach, E. R., and N. Wallerstein. *ESL for Action: Problem-Posing at Work*. Reading, MA: Addison-Wesley, 1987.

Barndt, D., F. Cristall, and D. Marino. *Getting There: Producing Photo Stories with Immigrant Women*. Toronto: Between the Lines, 1982.

Bates, A. W. *Technology, Open Learning and Distance Education*. London: Routledge, 1995.

Bates, S. *Amazing 2! News Interviews & Conversations*. Vancouver, BC: Vancouver Community College, 1999.

Beaumont, M. "Reading in a Foreign Language at an Elementary Level." In *At the Chalkface: Practical Techniques in Language Teaching*, eds. A. Matthews, M. Spratt, and L. Dangerfield. Walton-on-Thames, UK: Thomas Nelson, 1991.

Bell, J., and B. Burnaby. *A Handbook for ESL Literacy*. Toronto: OISE Press, 1984.

Bell, J., and M. Holt. "It's Your Right! Race, Colour and Ethnic Origin." In *It's Your Right! Student Manual*. Ottawa, ON: Minister of Supply and Services Canada, 1988.

Bikowski, D., and G. Kessler. "Making the Most of Discussion Boards in the ESL Classroom." *TESOL Journal* 11, no. 3 (Autumn 2002): 27–30.

Brims, J. "Little Johnny's Accident." In *Recipes for Tired Teachers*. Reading, MA: Addison-Wesley, 1985.

Brown, J. D. *The Elements of Language Curriculum: A Systematic Approach to Program Development*. Boston: Heinle & Heinle, 1995.

Buckby, M., and A. Wright. *Flashcards for Language Learning*. Loughborough, UK: Modern English Publications, 1981.

Burnaby, B. "Materials for ESL Literacy Teaching." *TESL Talk* 20, no. 1 (1990).

Burt, M. "Using Videos with Adult English Language Learners." Eric Digest. Washington, DC: Center for Applied Linguistics, 1999. (ERIC Document Rreproduction Service No. ED 434 539).

Butcher, I. "Model Drawings." In *Recipes for Tired Teachers*. Reading, MA: Addison-Wesley, 1985.

Byrne, D. "Writing in Class." In *At the Chalkface: Practical Techniques in Language Teaching,* eds. A. Matthews, M. Spratt, and L. Dangerfield. Walton-on-Thames, UK: Thomas Nelson, 1991.

Campbell, J. *TESL 36—Literacy in TESL/TESD.* Saskatoon, SK: Extension Credit Studies, University of Saskatchewan, 2006.

Canale, M., and M. Swain. "Theoretical Bases of Communicative Approaches to Second Language Teaching and Testing." *Applied Linguistics* 1 (1980): 1–47.

Cassar, T. "Teaching Ideas for Upper Elementary Learners." *TESL Talk* 20, no. 1 (1990): 267–71.

Celce-Murcia, M., and D. Larsen-Freeman. *The Grammar Book: An ESL/EFL Teacher's Course.* Cambridge, MA: Newbury House, 1983.

The Centre for Advancement of Service Learning, "Benefits of Service Learning," June 12, 2002. *www.howard.edu/CenterUrbanProgress/casl/benefits.html*

Clark, R. *Language Teaching Techniques.* Brattleboro, VT: Pro Lingua Associates, 1987.

Coelho, E. "Multicultural Literature Circles in Your Classroom." Paper presented at The TESL Canada Conference, Regina, SK, 2002.

Crawford, M. J. "Developing Automatization with In-Class Surveys." *TESOL Journal* 9, no. 4 (Winter 2000): 20.

Cunningsworth, A. *Choosing Your Coursebook.* Oxford: Heinemann, 1995.

Curtain, H., and C. A. Dahlberg. *Languages and Children—Making the Match: New Language for Young Learners. 3d ed.* Boston: Pearson/Allyn and Bacon, 2004.

Curtain, H. A., and C. A. Pesola. *Languages and Children—Making the Match.* Reading, MA: Addison-Wesley, 1988.

Dahlman, A., and S. Rilling. "Integrating Technologies and Tasks in an EFL Distance Learning Course in Finland." *TESOL Journal,* 10, no. 1 (2001): 4–8.

De Szendeffy, J. *A Practical Guide to Using Computers in Language Teaching.* Ann Arbor: University of Michigan Press, 2005.

Doff, A. *Teach English: A Training Course for Teachers.* New York: Cambridge University Press in association with the British Council, 1990.

Dubin, F., and E. Olshtain. *Course Design: Developing Programs and Materials for Language Learning.* New York: Cambridge University Press, 1986.

Duncan, J. *Technology Assisted Teaching Techniques.* Brattleboro, VT: Prolingua Associates, 1987.

Dupuy, B., L. Tse, and T. Cook. "Bringing Books into the Classroom: First Steps in Turning College-Level ESL Students into Readers." *TESOL Journal* 5, no. 4 (1996): 10–15.

Edge, J. "Materials." In *Essentials of English Language Teaching.* Harlow, UK: Longman, 1993.

English, L. M. *Business across Cultures: Effective Communication Strategies—English for Business Success.* Reading, MA: Longman, 1995.

Epstein, R. I. "EDCUR 391.3/TESL 31: TESL Theory and Skills Development: Course Notes." Saskatoon, SK: Extension Division, University of Saskatchewan, 2001a.

———. "TEFL 12: Teaching English as a Foreign Language Communicatively, Part II." Saskatoon, SK: Extension Division, University of Saskatchewan, 2001b.

Flannery Silc, K. "Using the World Wide Web with Adult ESL Learners." ERIC Digest. Washington, DC: Center for Applied Linguistics, 1998. (ERIC Document Reproduction Service No. ED 427 555)

Folse, K. *Talk a Lot: Communication Activities for Speaking Fluency.* Ann Arbor: University of Michigan Press, 1993.

Folse, K. S. *The Art of Teaching Speaking: Research and Pedagogy for the ESL/EFL Classroom.* Ann Arbor: University of Michigan Press, 2006.

_____. *Discussion Starters: Speaking Fluency Activities for Advanced ESL/EFL Students.* Ann Arbor: University of Michigan Press, 1996.

_____. *Vocabulary Myths: Applying Second Language Research to the Classroom.* Ann Arbor: University of Michigan Press, 2004.

Folse, K., J. Ivone, and S. Pollgreen. *101 Clear Grammar Tests: Reproducible Grammar Tests for ESL/EFL Classes.* Ann Arbor: University of Michigan Press, 2005.

Fowler, W. S., and N. Coe. *Nelson Quickcheck Placement Tests.* Surrey, UK: Thomas Nelson, 1987.

Frankel, I., and C. Meyers. *CrossRoads 1—Student Book.* New York: Oxford University Press, 1992.

Freire, P. *Education for Critical Consciousness.* New York: The Continuum Publishing Corporation, 1981.

Fried-Booth, D. L. *Project Work.* Oxford: Oxford University Press, 1986.

Gaer, S. "Using Software in the Adult ESL Classroom." ERIC Digest. Washington, DC: Center for Applied Linguistics, 1998. (ERIC Document Reproduction Service No. ED 418 607)

Genzel, R. B., and M. G. Cummings. *Culturally Speaking: A Conversation and Culture Text for Learners of English.* New York: Harper and Row, 1986.

Gianelli, M. C. "Thematic Units: Creating an Environment for Learning." *TESOL Journal* (Autumn 1991): 13–15.

Grace, S., and C. Pigott. "Eye Witness" and "Collaborative Narration." Papers presented at the Sandanona Conference, School for International Training, Brattleboro, VT, 1991.

Grant, L. "Creating Pronunciation-Based ESL Materials for Publication." In *Material Writer's Guide.* Boston: Heinle & Heinle, 1995.

Gunderson, L. *ESL Literacy Instruction: A Guidebook to Theory and Practice.* Englewood Cliffs, NJ: Prentice Hall Regents, 1991.

Hadfield, J. *Advanced Communication Games.* Reading, MA: Addison-Wesley, 1997.

Hanson-Smith, E. *Technology in the Classroom: Practice and Promise in the 21st Century.* Alexandria, VA: TESOL, 1997.

Harris, D. P., and L. A. Palmer. *CELT (A Comprehensive English Language Test for Learners of English).* New York: McGraw-Hill, 1986.

Hart, K. (2000). Presentation at TESOL Conference, Vancouver, BC, March 2000.

Heald-Taylor, G. *Whole Language Strategies for ESL Primary Students.* Toronto: OISE Press, 1986.

Healey, D. "Are Technology-Using Students Better Learners?" Paper presented at Teacher to Teacher Conference: The Process of Language Learning, Abu Dhabi, November 6–7, 2001. *www.onid.orst.edu/~healeyd/t2t.html*

Healey, D., and S. J. Klinghammer. "Constructing Meaning with Computers." *TESOL Journal* 11, no. 3 (Autumn 2002): 3.

Higgins, J. *Language, Learners and Computers.* White Plains, NY: Longman, 1988.

Hoffman, S. "Computers and Instructional Design in Foreign Language/ESL Instruction." *TESOL Journal* 5, no. 2 (1995): 24–29.

Holmes, T., A. Kingwell, J. Pettis, and M. Pidlaski. *Canadian Language Benchmarks 2000: A Guide to Implementation.* Alberta Learning and Manitoba Department of Labour and Immigration, 2001.

Hsu, M., and Y. Chuang. "A Mobile Learning System for ESL Learners." In *Proceedings of the Third International Conference on Education and Information Systems: Technologies and Applications.* Vol II. Orlando, FL: International Institute of Informatics and Sytemics, 2005.

Isserliss, J. "Student-Generated Class News." *TESL Talk* 20, no. 1 (1990): 272–74.

Jerald, M., and R. C. Clark. *Experiential Language Teaching Techniques.* Brattleboro, VT: Pro Lingua Associates, 1989.

———. *Experiential Language Teaching Techniques: Out-of-Class Language Acquisition and Cultural Awareness Activities.* Brattleboro, VT: Pro Lingua Associates, 1980.

Jones, L., and C. von Baeyer. *Functions of American English: Communication Activities for the Classroom.* New York: Cambridge University Press, 1986.

Kendrick, E. "Service Learning for ESL in Higher Education." Paper presented at TESOL 2000, Vancouver, BC.

King, K. *Taking Sides: A Speaking Text for Advanced and Intermediate Students.* Ann Arbor: University of Michigan Press, 1997.

Knowles, P. L., and R. A. Sasaki. *Story Squares: Fluency in English as a Second Language.* Toronto: Little, Brown, 1980.

Ko, S. Personal communication, 2005.

Krashen, S. *Principles and Practice in Second Language Acquisition.* New York: Prentice Hall, 1982.

———. *The Power of Reading.* Englewood, CO: Libraries Unlimited, 1993.

Lam, C., and A. Henriques. *Incorporating an Intercultural Perspective into the ESL Curriculum.* Toronto: Board of Education for the City of Toronto, Continuing Education Department, 1991.

Larsen-Freeman, D. "Getting the Whole Picture." Audiotaped address presented at the School for International Training, Brattleboro, VT, 1993.

———. *Techniques and Principles in Language Teaching.* 2d ed. New York: Oxford University Press, 2000.

Lesley, T. *Interchange Passages Placement Evaluation Package.* 3d ed. New York: Cambridge University Press, 2005.

Lewis, M. *Implementing the Lexical Approach: Putting Theory into Practice.* Hove, UK: Language Teaching Publications, 1993.

Ligon, F., and E. Tannenbaum. *Picture Stories: Language and Literacy Activities for Beginners.* White Plains, NY: Longman, 1990.

Lonergan, J. *Video in Language Teaching.* Cambridge: Cambridge University Press, 1984.

Lotherington-Woloszyn, H. "On Simplified and Simplifying Materials for ESL Reading." *TESL Talk* 18, no. 1 (1988): 112–22.

Macdonald, M., and S. Rogers-Gordon. *Action Plans: 80 Student-Centred Language Activities.* Cambridge, MA: Newbury House, 1984.

MacLean, M. "Literature and Second Language Learning." *TESL Talk* 20, no. 1 (1990): 244–50.

Madden, C. G., and T. N. Rohlck. *Discussion & Interaction in the Academic Community.* Ann Arbor: University of Michigan Press, 1997.

Maley, A., and A. Duff. *Literature.* Oxford: Oxford University Press, 1990.

Martinez, R. *Conversation Lessons: The Natural Language of Conversation.* Hove, UK: Language Teaching Publications, 1997.

Matthews, A., M. Spratt, and L. Dangerfield, eds. *At the Chalkface: Practical Techniques in Language Teaching.* Walton-on-Thames, Surrey: Thomas Nelson, 1991.

Mayer, R. E. *Multimedia Learning.* New York: Cambridge University Press, 2005.

McAlpin, J. *The Magazine Picture Library.* London: George Allen and Unwin, 1983.

McDonough, J., and C. Shaw. *Materials and Methods in ELT: A Teacher's Guide.* Cambridge, MA: Blackwell, 1993.

McLaughlin, S., and D. E. McCormick. "Integrating CALL into Existing IEP Curricula." *CALL-IS Newsletter: Computer-Assisted Language Learning Interest Section* 20, no. 1 (2002): 5.

Mittelholtz, D. Personal communication, 2006.

Moran, P. R. *LexiCarry: An Illustrated Vocabulary Builder for Second Languages.* Brattleboro, VT: Pro Lingua Associates, 2002.

Moss, D., and C. Van Duzer. "Project-Based Learning for Adult English Language Learners." ERIC Digest. Washington, DC: Center for Applied Linguistics, 1998. (ERIC Document Reproduction Service No. ED 427 556)

Mowat, R. (1990). "Should Literacy Students Be Asked to Copy?" *TESL Talk* 20, no. 1 (1990): 275–77.

Mugglestone, P. *Planning and Using the Blackboard.* London: Heinemann Educational Books, 1983.

Naiman, N. "Teaching Pronunciation Communicatively." *TESL Talk: The Teaching of Pronunciation* 17, no. 1 (1987): 141–47.

Nunan. D., and C. Lamb. *The Self-Directed Teacher.* Cambridge: Cambridge University Press, 1996.

Omaggio, A. C. *Teaching Language in Context: Proficiency-Oriented Instruction.* Boston: Heinle & Heinle, 1986.

O'Neill, R. "Why Use Textbooks?" In *Currents of Change in Language Teaching,* eds. R. Rossner and R. Bolitho. New York: Oxford University Press, 1990.

Opp-Beckman, L. "Africa Online: A Web- and Content-Based English Language Teaching Course." *TESOL Journal* 11, no. 3 (Autumn 2002): 4–8.

Ormiston, M. *TESL 32: Materials Selection and Development.* Saskatoon, SK: Extension Division, University of Saskatchewan, 1998.

Ormiston, M., R. DeCoursey, and S. Fredeen. *The ESL Toolbox: Ready-to-Use Enrichment Activities for LINC Classes.* Saskatoon, SK: University Extension Press, 1994.

Ormiston, M., and R. Epstein. *English Language Teaching Materials: A Practical Guide.* Saskatoon, SK: University Extension Press, 2005.

Ortmeier, C. M. "Project Homeland: Crossing Cultural Boundaries in the ESL Classroom." In *TESOL Journal* 9, no. 1 (Spring 2000): 10–17.

Patrie, J. "Comprehensible Text: The Daily Newspaper at the Beginning Level." *TESL Talk* 18, no. 1 (1988): 244–50.

Pawlikowska-Smith, G. *Canadian Language Benchmarks 2000: English as a Second Language for Adults.* Ottawa, ON: Minister of Public Works and Government Services Canada, 2002.

Penner, J., and K. Bell. "Putting Integrated Language Skills into Meaningful Community Action." Paper presented at the TESL Canada Conference, Vancouver, BC, 2003.

Peterson, M. "Emergent Network Technologies in CALL: MOOs and Learning Theory." *CALL-IS Newsletter: Computer-Assisted Language Learning Interest Section* 20, no. 1 (2002): 1–2.

Reagan, N., and O. Murray. "Under Construction: ESL/EFL Textbook Companion Sites. *TESOL Journal* 11, no. 3 (2002): 49–52.

Richard-Amato, P. *Making It Happen: Interaction in the Second Language Classroom, from Practice to Theory.* White Plains, NY: Addison-Wesley, 1996.

Richards, J. C., J. Hull, and S. Proctor. *The New Interchange General English.* Cambridge: Cambridge University Press, 2002.

Richards, J. D., and T. Rodgers. *Approaches and Methods in Language Teaching.* 2^d ed. Cambridge: Cambridge University Press, 2001.

Roever, C. "Web-Based Language Testing." *Language Learning and Technology* 5, no. 2 (May 2001): 84–94.

Rooks, G. *Can't Stop Talking: Discussion Problems for Advanced Beginners and Low Intermediates.* New York: Newbury House, 1997.

Royce, T. "Multimodality in the TESOL Classroom: Exploring Visual-Verbal Synergy." *TESOL Quarterly* 36, no. 2 (2002): 191–205.

Sangwine, J. "The ESL Classroom as Publishing House." *TESL Talk: Canadian ESL Materials* 18, no. 1 (1988): 170–78.

Sauvé, V. "Life Text: A Rationale for the Place of Story in Second Language Learning." *TESL Talk* 18, no. 1 (1988): 179–89.

Savignon, S. *Communicative Competence: Theory and Classroom Practice—Texts and Contexts in Second Language Teaching.* New York: McGraw-Hill, 1997.

Shih, M. "More than Practicing Language: Communicative Reading and Writing for Asian Settings." *TESOL Journal* 8, no. 4 (Winter 1999): 20–25.

Shrum, J. L., and E. W. Glisan. "Using Technology to Support Contextualized Language Instruction." In *Teacher's Handbook: Contextualized Language Instruction.* Boston: Heinle & Heinle, 1994.

Shulman, M. *Selected Readings in Business, Millennium Edition.* Ann Arbor: University of Michigan Press, 2003.

Silberstein, S. "Outtakes from Reader's Choice: Issues in Materials Development." *TESL Canada Journal* 4, no. 2 (1987): 82–95.

Silverman, A. "Children's Literature for ESL Adults." *TESL Talk* 20, no. 1 (1990): 205–7.

Software Evaluation Guide, *www.owlnet.rice.edu/~ling417/guide.html*

Spanou, K. "Computer-Assisted Language Learning: A Story that Goes Long Back." *www.tesolgreece.com/nl/71/7103.html*

Spratt, M. "The Practice Stage: Discourse Chains." In *At the Chalkface: Practical Techniques in Language Teaching*, eds. A. Matthews, M. Spratt, and L. Dangerfield. Walton-on-Thames, UK: Thomas Nelson, 1991.

Stempleski, S., and P. Arcario, eds. *Video in Second Language Teaching: Using, Selecting and Producing Video for the Classroom.* Alexandria, VA: TESOL, 1993.

Stoller, F. L. "Using Video in Theme-Based Curricula." In *Video in Second Language Teaching: Using, Selecting and Producing Video for the Classroom*, eds. S. Stempleski and P. Aracario. Alexandria, VA: TESOL, 1993.

Tan, I. Personal communication, 2006.

Teemant, A., E. Bernhardt, and M. Rodriguez-Munoz. "Collaborating with Content Area Teachers: What We Need to Share." *TESOL Journal* 5, no. 4 (1996): 17.

Thompson, J. "Communicative Second Language Learning: A Thematic Integrated Approach." *TESL Talk* 13, no. 3 (1982): 128–36.

Tillyer, A. "The InfiNET Possibilities: English Teachers on the Internet." *English Teaching Forum* (1997): 21–22. *http://exchanges.state.gov/forum/vols/vol35/no1/p16.htm*

Tomalin, Barry. "Teaching Young Children with Video." In *Video in Second Language Teaching: Using, Selecting and Producing Video for the Classroom*, eds. S. Stempleski and P. Aracario. Alexandria, VA: TESOL Inc., 1990.

Ur, P. *A Course in Language Teaching.* Cambridge: Cambridge University Press, 1996.

Wallerstein, N. *Language and Culture in Conflict.* Reading, MA: Addison-Wesley, 1982.

Warschauer, M. "Computer-Assisted Language Learning: An Introduction." In *Multimedia Language Teaching*, ed. S. Fotos. Tokyo: Logos International, 1996.

Watson, B. M. *Drawing in the Classroom: A Handbook for Teachers of English as a Second Language.* Vancouver, BC: Vancouver Community College, 1983.

Werner, P., J. Nelson, and M. Spaventa. *Interactions Mosaic Academic Instructor's Manual, 4th ed.* New York: McGraw Hill-Ryerson, 2002.

Winn-Bell Olsen, J. *Communication Starters and Other Activities for the ESL Classroom.* San Francisco: Almeny Press, 1977.

Wong, A. "Checklist to Evaluate Reading Materials for Adult Literacy Programs." In *EDCCV 461.3: Teaching Literacy Skills to Adults.* Saskatoon, SK: University of Saskatchewan, Independent Studies Program, 1993.

Wood, D. "Formulaic Language in Acquisition and Production: Implications for Teaching." *TESL Canada Journal* 20, no. 1 (Winter 2002): 1–15.

Wright, A. *1000 Pictures for Teachers to Copy.* New York: Addison-Wesley, 1984.

———. *Visual Materials for the Language Teacher.* Burnt Mill, Harlow, Essex: Longman Group, 1981.